An Introduction to Tourism

An Introduction to Tourism

Leonard J.

Former Direc

Carson L. J

Professor of I
University of

BUTTERWORTH
HEINEMANN

OXFORD AUCKLAND BOSTON JOHANNESBURG MELBOURNE NEW DELHI

Butterworth-Heinemann
Linacre House, Jordan Hill, Oxford OX2 8DP
225 Wildwood Avenue, Woburn, MA 01801-2041
A division of Reed Educational and Professional Publishing Ltd

A member of the Reed Elsevier plc group

First published 1997
Reprinted 1997 (twice), 1999, 2000, 2002

British Library Cataloguing in Publication Data
Lickorish, Leonard J.
    An introduction to tourism
    1. Tourist trade
    I. Title   II. Jenkins, Carson L.
    338.4′791

ISBN 0 7506 1956 2

For more information on all Butterworth-Heinemann
publications please visit our website at www.bh.com

Composition by Genesis Typesetting, Laser Quay, Rochester, Kent
Printed in Great Britain by Scotprint

Contents

Preface

Tourism is now recognized as being an economic activity of global significance. As the importance of the activity has increased, so too has the attention given to it by governments, organizations in both the public and private sectors, and academics. This book is an introduction to a complex and multi-faceted industry. It is written for two main audiences: for students of tourism and for those employed in the industry who want to know more about the structure, component activities, and environment within which they work. The book aims to provide a comprehensive introduction to the tourism industry to encourage further study and to stimulate interest in the subject area. To advance these aims, the recommended 'Further reading' at the end of each chapter is selective rather than comprehensive.

In writing this book the authors have tried wherever possible to relate theoretical concepts to empirical examples, many based on their extensive international experience in the industry.

Mr Bill Richards prepared Chapter 8. His assistance is gratefully acknowledged and much appreciated.

Miss Sandra J. Miller typed the many drafts and the final manuscript. Her humour, patience, tolerance and support made the final outcome possible.

Leonard J. Lickorish

Carson L. Jenkins

Figures

Tables

1 The nature and characteristics of the tourism industry

Introduction

Tourism is an activity which cuts across conventional sectors in the economy. It requires inputs of an economic, social, cultural and environmental nature. In this sense it is often described as being multi-faceted. The problem in describing tourism as an 'industry' is that it does not have the usual formal production function, nor does it have an output which can physically be measured, unlike agriculture (tonnes of wheat) or beverages (litres of whisky). There is no common structure which is representative of the industry in every country. In France and Italy, for example, restaurants and shopping facilities are major attractions for tourists; in Russia they are not. Even the core components of the tourism industry, such as accommodation and transport, can vary between countries. In the UK many tourists use bed and breakfast accommodation in private houses; in Thailand such facilities are not available. In the transport sector, levels of car ownership and developed road networks cause many tourists to use their cars or buses in Western Europe and the USA. In India and Indonesia, most tourists travel by air. It is some of these problems of definition which have caused many writers to refer to the tourist sector rather than the tourist industry. Sometimes the terms are used interchangeably, as they are in this book.

Problems of definition

The problem of definition is a serious and continuing difficulty for analysts of tourism. In particular the amorphous nature of the tourism industry has made it difficult to evaluate its impact on the economy relative to other sectors in the economy. Techniques have been developed to facilitate measurement of impact (Chapter 5) but there is no universally accepted definition of what constitutes the tourism industry. The World Tourism Organization (WTO) has attempted to address this problem in its publication *A Standard Industrial Classification of Tourism Activities* (SICTA) which is evaluated in Chapter 3. Most academic writers tend to craft their definitions to suit their specific purposes. For purposes of this book the definition given by Burkart and Medlik (1981) is accepted:

the phenomenon arising from temporary visits (or stays away from home) outside the normal place of residence for any reason other than furthering an occupation remunerated from within the place visited

However, there are a number of features associated with tourism which are quite explicit. For example, tourism implies that a person undertakes a journey: the journey may be for less than a day (day tripper/visitor); or it may be a journey within a national boundary, therefore constituting a domestic tourist trip; or it might be a journey which crosses an international boundary, therefore being classified as an international tourism trip. These particular definitions are dealt with in Chapter 3. However, it is not only the nature of the journey which constitutes tourism, but is also the purpose of the journey which very broadly should be for leisure or business. In looking at the development of tourism historically, most attention has been given to the concept of international tourism, i.e. journeys across international boundaries.

Although the components of the tourism industry will differ between countries, there are certain subsectors which are clearly identified as being components of tourism activity, such as the accommodation sector which would include not only formal accommodation, hotels, guest houses, etc., but also camping sites, rooms in private houses and bed and breakfast type arrangements. Travel agents and tour operators are recognized as comprising another distinct subsector. Transport – airlines, shipping, rail and car hire, cars and coaches – will also be seen as being important inputs to the tourism sector. In some countries, shopping and production of handicrafts is another associated activity of tourism. In all these examples we have one major problem, which is to measure the extent to which the output of the various sectors input to the tourism industry. This gives rise to many difficulties in attempting to define the economic value of tourism; for example, in a country like Singapore a very high proportion of a tourist's discretionary expenditure is spent on shopping. In other cases we may find that shopping is almost exclusively confined to duty free purchases, such as in Barbados. These are problems in trying to measure the magnitude and importance of tourism and are referred to in Chapters 3 and 5.

Changes within the industry

If we use 1945 as being the year when the development of the major growth in the tourism industry began, we can make some general observations relating to the changes which one can discern in the tourism industry.

Before the 1950s, tourism was very much an industry which was fragmented; hotels, transport operators, travel agents, tour operators all tended to work independently of each other. Hotels were largely in the business of selling bed nights. Airlines and railways were in the business of selling seats. Travel agents of course, were selling travel and holidays but in each case they tended to operate very much as individual businesses. From the mid-1950s onwards, particularly in the UK, the growth of tour operators began to change the nature of the industry from essentially individual business activities to more integrated activities. Hotels, for example, were beginning to see customers as wanting a range of services rather than simply buying accommodation. So hotels began to develop shopping arcades and later to offer secretarial centres to try to increase the spend of guests within the hotel complex. Transport operators, particularly in the airline business, saw the sale of transport services as being integral to a much wider need. Airlines offered insurance and accommodation booking for travellers. By the 1980s many airlines were offering complete travel services including holiday arrangements, medical services, car hire, etc.

What we have seen since the 1950s is the emergence of a holiday and travel industry which is offering more integrated services. This is particularly noticeable with the forward and backward integration of some of the very large tour operators. To some extent this was determined by the nature of demand which is discussed in Chapter 4. In other cases it was a business opportunity to integrate demand and provide a service at a much more competitive price and to maintain and increase market share. By 1990 the structure of the tourism industry, certainly in the UK and Europe, was influenced by the growth of some very large companies. In the USA, American anti-trust laws discouraged, if not prohibited, the development of large integrated companies. The American experience in tour operation has been very different from that within Europe, particularly compared with the UK.

As the structure of service provision changed so did the nature of holiday taking. Up until 1946, i.e. the period between the world wars, much of international travel was for the privileged, wealthy and elite groups in society. From 1950 onwards a combination of factors, for example, increase in leisure time availability, increase in paid holidays, development of package tours, development in air transport – all combined to provide a much wider potential holiday-taking market. This market was different in terms of socioeconomic groups from the pre-1950 era.

The 1950s was the time when international travel for holiday purposes was democratized, the changing nature of demand being one of the factors which changed the structure of the tourism industry. This phenomenon of democratization is sometimes referred to as 'the development of mass tourism'. However, the volume of tourism differs greatly between countries and to use 'mass' in an isolated rather than a relative sense can be very misleading.

The changing nature of holidays was reflected in the social groups taking holidays, and in the distances which people were prepared to travel to holiday destinations. One of the major demand changes was the increased availability of leisure for a wider group in society. Rising real incomes, paid holidays and growing propensity to demand foreign holidays, or a combination of these, were important and continuing factors stimulating international tourism demand. These factors were not simply economic determinants but also social. As the world recovered from the Second World War there was growing evidence to indicate that people were spending more time on leisure activities and on travel. These tendencies were reflected in the protection that many people gave to holiday expenditures, these expenditures being the last to be surrendered in the face of income changes. These factors are discussed in more detail in Chapter 4.

An analysis of international tourism travel trends reveals a number of features. First is the continuing but declining concentration of international

Table 1.1 International tourist arrivals and receipts

	1995 Results*							
	Tourist arrivals (thousands)		% Change		Tourism receipts (US $ million)		% Change	
	1994	*1995*	*95/94*	*94/93*	*1994*	*1995*	*95/94*	*94/93*
World	546 269	567 033	3.8	5.4	346 703	371 682	7.2	10.4
Africa	18 477	18 800	1.7	0.7	6 530	6 915	5.9	8.5
Americas	107 176	111 944	4.4	3.0	95 084	95 239	0.2	4.8
East Asia/Pacfic	76 973	83 624	8.6	10.6	61 990	69 349	11.9	18.7
Europe	329 819	337 240	2.3	5.1	174 811	189 820	8.6	11.0
Middle East	9 875	11 041	11.8	10.0	5 129	6 653	29.7	6.8
South Asia	3 949	4 384	11.0	11.0	3 159	3 706	17.3	13.1

* Subject to revision.

Source: *World Tourism Organization*, 1995.

tourist movements within Europe and between Europe and North America. Inter-country tourist movements between the USA, Canada and Mexico generate very large numbers. The traditional tourist-generating countries in Western Europe and the USA are seeing more travel to long-haul destinations in the Caribbean, the Pacific, Asia and Africa. Tourism is becoming a more global activity, and as real per capita incomes and discretionary leisure time availability increases, some of the traditional tourist-receiving countries such as Japan, Hong Kong, Singapore and within certain social groups in India, are now generating increasing numbers of outbound tourists. Many of these 'new tourists' are travelling for leisure rather than business purposes. Table 1.1 indicates the volume, value and distribution of international tourism movements.

The table should be interpreted with caution as it is compiled by the WTO from data supplied by member countries which do not always have reliable or definition-consistent statistics. Furthermore, the international receipts figures do not include air fares generated by tourist movements which constitute a substantial input to the airlines' receipts in many countries.

This development of long-haul travel could not have taken place without the increasing specialization of the travel trade. The emergence of tour operators in particular tended to concentrate activities either in the short-haul or the long-haul market. Within Europe, for example, the growth and consolidation of very large tour operators like Thomson Holidays in the UK, Neckermann and TUI in Germany and Tjerborg in Denmark was indicative of the demand for international travel. Within this trend there was also an increasing supply of specialist tour operators normally looking to meet the demand for a lower volume but a higher per capita spend tourist who wanted to travel to distant countries or enjoy a special interest experience. Specialism within the travel field has been one of the features which has helped change the structure and the nature of the travel industry.

The role of government

In addition to the structural changes within the industry, it is relevant to note the role of government (Chapter 11). Government, particularly in developed countries, has often played a supportive but essentially background role in the development of tourism. In the UK, for example, in 1969 the government through its Development of Tourism Act not only supported through funding the development of new hotels within the UK, but also set up the various National Tourist Boards in Wales, England and Scotland and also the British Tourist Authority. Government has tended in most developed countries to take a 'hidden' hand role, i e it provided the infrastructure and intervened as necessary to direct and to encourage the growth of tourism. However, in the developing countries we find that governments have had to take a much more active and pro-interventionist role (Chapter 12).

There is considerable debate about the role of government in the tourism industry. One proposition is that in most developed countries government has tended to play the role of supporting tourism development, as mentioned above, by providing infrastructure and a representative national tourism authority. Many governments offer investment incentives to encourage development of the tourism industry. In developing countries such as India, the government through the Indian Tourism Development Corporation has invested in tourism facilities, such as ski resorts and hotels, and also in tourism services such as travel agencies, buses, car hire and airlines. There is no definite pattern which reflects the role of government in the development of the tourism industry. For example, in the USA the Regan government abolished the United States Travel Services which was to later re-emerge in a smaller form as the United States Travel and Tourism Agency. The Clinton government has now abolished it.

In the early 1990s, institutional pressure from international bodies such as the World Bank and the International Monetary Fund encouraged, if not coerced, many governments in the developing world to relinquish their commercial activities to the private sector. The Structural Adjustment Programmes agreed with many governments insist on a progressive privatization of governments' commercial assets and activities in return for financial support as part of the economies' restructuring process. In tourism, this means that more governments in the developing world are now providing support for tourism rather than taking an entrepreneurial role. These changes are discussed in Chapter 12.

Global tourism

Mention has been made of the globalization of tourism. This term is frequently used, but has ambiguous interpretations. It should be used to refer not only to the scale of tourism activity, but also to include the distribution of tourism activity. Tourists are not only travelling to the traditional destination countries, but also new tourism destinations and generating countries are represented on the global tourism maps. Within Asia, intraregional tourism is particularly important, and 'new' destination countries such as Vietnam, Laos and Cambodia are emerging. Within Africa, the political changes in South Africa have stimulated tourist arrivals within the Southern African region; with the cessation of the civil wars, countries such as Mozambique and Angola can become significant tourist destinations in the future.

The globalization trend does not simply replicate past trends. There are different groups of people travelling and travelling longer distances. As people become more sophisticated travellers, the travel trade has adapted to meet their needs. Safety, comfort and reassurance are still travel pre-requisites. In Europe, the European Union's Package Tour Directive attempted to improve conditions on travel and holiday contracts which aimed to ensure the provision of quality standard promised in the tourist receiving countries. The worldwide concern for environmental quality and protection is beginning to influence the travel trade in the way it selects its partners, and also in the conditions which tourists expect to find at the destination. Destination management is becoming an increasingly important issue in the tourism industry.

In Europe, the ageing population has provided a reservoir of mature tourists with both the leisure time and disposable income to travel. This so-called third age tourist has become an important, and will remain an important, segment of international tourism demand. As many of these tourists are retired and therefore have the choice of when to travel, they can help to overcome seasonality problems in some destinations.

Although there is a trend towards more independent travel, the inclusive tour has not lost its vitality or importance. The inclusive tour, which is a package of travel, accommodation and service arrangements sold at a single price, has become more flexible. No longer is it necessary for all the tour group members to stay at the same hotel, or even at the same resort; standards of accommodation can vary for different prices. So an inclusive tour may still depart by chartered flight, but at the destination might offer a range of serviced accommodation choices, or self-catering operations, rooms in private houses or self-drive arrangements. The choice permutations are varied, but the volume of tourists attracted by these arrangements still generate the economies of scale which keep prices low and permit more people to become international tourists.

The inclusive tour has not only encouraged travel through price reductions, but has diminished much of the risk and uncertainty associated with foreign travel. This has been particularly important in the development of long-haul tourism to developing countries. Long-haul tourism was principally the business of a group of specialist companies catering for small-volume but high per trip spend tourists. In the UK, Kuoni, Bales Tours and Cox and Kings are three examples. On the international market, American Express is another example. However, as more experienced tourists are seeking 'faraway places', many of the very large tour operators such as Thomson Holidays and Airtours, are now offering long-haul destinations in the Caribbean, Africa, New Zealand and Australia. Although not a large part of their total turnover, the economies of scale enjoyed by such companies do enable them to provide relatively cheap holidays in long-haul destinations, thereby widening the market.

The growing interest in the long-haul market by the large tour operators is further evidence of the changes taking place in the tourist industry. The large tour operators are diversifying into market segments formerly the preserve of small, specialist tour operators, and also airlines have developed their own holiday businesses.

Many of the larger, international airlines have developed relationships with tour operators using their aircraft on a full- and part-charter basis. The development and increasing sophistication of information technology, perhaps best seen in massive computer reservation systems (CRSs), has given airlines the opportunity to compile databases with important customer profile information. More airlines are using these databases not only for scheduling and operational purposes, but also for marketing. Many airlines now can both facilitate travel arrangements and also offer a complete holiday package. The options for the potential tourist are ever increasing.

Supply-side factors

Although many of the changes described so far can be categorized as demand-side factors, i.e. factors which influence the volume of demand, supply-side factors are also important. It is possible to identify a number of supply-side characteristics which have been of importance to the development of the tourism industry in many countries.

Perhaps the most obvious, but sometimes the most ignored factor is the development in tourism receiving countries of a tourism culture. As visitor arrivals increase and are sustained over time, the host community or resident population becomes familiar with the needs and demands of the tourists. Facilities and services are developed either directly or indirectly to support the tourism industry. As the industry grows, so usually do the economic, financial and other benefits which tourism creates. A certain tourism dependency is created to the extent where it can substantially underpin the local or national economies. Examples of this phenomenon can be seen in the Lake District in England, Benidorm in Spain, Agra in India, and the Maldives. The development of a tourism culture is not always wholly beneficial, as Chapters 6 and 12 demonstrate. However, tourism development often provides an economic and social catalyst for change.

As tourism develops, so does the related need for more and appropriate levels of accommodation. The range and types of accommodation needed for tourists will reflect not only the level of tourism development, but also the type of tourist targeted. As tourism develops and diversifies it is often possible to bring more accommodation modes into the market; for example, self-catering, camping and caravanning, bed and breakfast in private houses are options. In Scotland, for example, it is estimated that approximately 75 per cent of tourist hotel accommodation is available in small hotels and guest houses. Tourism is a highly segmented business, with a high propensity to provide opportunities for small-scale operators. At the other extreme is the larger, standard hotel which depends, often extensively, on package tourists sent by the large tour operators.

To support the development of the tourism industry further, there is a plethora of services, such as banking, car hire, shopping and cultural attractions (see Chapter 8). As previously noted, the component activities of tourism will vary between countries, but all contribute to the overall attractiveness of the destination to the tourist.

In destination areas, governments often provide supportive and direct services for the tourism industry. Infrastructure, the basis for tourism development, is still mainly provided by governments, as is much of the transport and police services. Governments usually fund National Tourism Administrations and advertise their country abroad. Despite the changing role of governments in tourism development, they still have a vital contribution to make in ensuring standards and tourists' personal safety.

Increasingly, these diverse supply-side factors are being integrated into some sort of destination management plan. In the same way that a country or region may formulate a tourism development strategy and plan to determine priorities for development and to allocate resources, increasingly it is being recognized that an *ad hoc* approach to destination development has its dangers. The main danger is that certain substandard components can damage a good overall image and reputation. Poor and unhygienic hotels may deter tourists and tour operators, despite outstanding scenic attractions. A reputation for high prices and poor service may have the same effect. For these and other reasons, destination management planning is becoming a more accepted concept. It also reflects another aspect of the globalization of the tourism industry – that standards are important wherever tourists may be.

Summary

We can conclude that, especially since 1945, tourism has developed into a significant international industry. As it has developed it has also become more specialized, with vertical and horizontal company amalgamations creating different scales of operation in various market segments. The growth in international airlines, advances in information technology and the growing flexibility in inclusive tour arrangements have all contributed to the present structure and characteristics of the tourism industry. Among the most significant characteristics are the following:

1 The growing volume of international tourism.
2 The democratization of holiday taking, with a wider range of socio-economic groups participating.
3 The continuing importance of air transport in the globalization of tourism.
4 The increasing flexibility of the inclusive tour to sustain tourism demand and to facilitate long-haul travel.
5 The emergence of specialist travel services, e.g. tour operators and travel agencies, to facilitate choice and provide information.
6 The continuing development of information technology to manage the 'information explosion' relevant to the tourism industry.
7 The growing recognition by many governments of the potential significance of tourism in national and sub-national economies.

One final point to note is that most attention is given to inbound, i.e. international, tourism. This attention obscures the fact that in many countries it is domestic tourism which is by far the largest activity. Because much of domestic tourism is self-organized and difficult to measure, it is often overlooked in preference to the more high profile international tourism.

References

Burkart, A. J. and Medlik, S. (1981) *Tourism: Past, Present and Future*, Heinemann, London

Further reading

Cooper, C., Fletcher, J., Gilbert, D. and Wanhill, S. (1993) *Tourism: Principles and Practice*, Pitman, London

Holloway, J. C. (1994) *The Business of Tourism*, 4th edn, Pitman, London

Lundberg, D. E. and Lundberg, L. B. (1993) *International Travel and Tourism*, John Wiley, Chichester, UK

McIntosh, R. W., Goeldner, C. R. and Ritchie, J. B. (1990) *Tourism: Principles, Practices and Philosophies*, 7th edn, John Wiley, Chichester, UK

Medlik, S. (1996) *Dictionary of Travel, Tourism and Hospitality*, 2nd edn, Butterworth-Heinemann, Oxford, UK

Morrison, A. and Christie-Mill, R. (1985) *The Tourism System: An Introductory Text*, Prentice-Hall International, Englewood Cliffs, N.J.

Sinclair, M. T. and Stabler, M. J. (1991) *The Tourism Industry: An International Analysis*, CAB, Wallingford, UK

2 How tourism developed – the history

Introduction

History is instructive in a study of tourism, not simply because there may be lessons to learn, but rather because the seeds of future growth are to be found in the past. Many historic inventions and innovations are effective in the contemporary scene. There is a vast legacy of infra- and superstructure from earlier development. Indeed much of the heritage, especially in landscaping and resort architecture, is highly prized. The city of Bath is one of the treasures of Britain and Europe, built principally in the eighteenth century as a tourism centre. It is hardly an exaggeration to say that Beau Nash was the country's first professional tourist 'director' and so successful that he created a magnificent town. He was, in fact, employed by the proprietors of the Assembly Rooms, a unique and successful tourism enterprise, not by the municipality.

Tourism is, however, a recent invention. The word was unknown in the English language until the last century, and increasingly came to have a somewhat suspect meaning, describing group travel of the cheaper kind, with an element of an insular dislike of strangers and foreigners. In contrast, the words travel and traveller were respected, reflecting the quality of the earlier travellers who were associated with the rich, educated, or aristocratic and society leaders. Thus travel for recreation and as an enjoyable activity was a relatively new concept.

In medieval times and almost up to the end of the sixteenth century the population living in agricultural communities was static, rarely moving from the village or local area. Even with the beginning of the industrial revolution, which was making a slow start in the eighteenth century in urban and factory development, a richer 'elite' class alone enjoyed leisure and travel, while the workers worked *in situ*. Indeed as industrialization got under way, according to Pimlott (1947), leisure time or holidays where they existed tended to decrease. The Bank of England closed on 47 days in 1761, but on only 4 days by 1834.

While there had always been some travel due to wars or on pilgrimages, by government officials, landowners, clerics, university students and teachers, the volume was very small and entirely purposeful or specialist.

The expansion of tourism with the growth in population and wealth in the eighteenth century was stimulated by the classic determinants of demand – leisure time, money and interest – or what is now termed consumer preference. Development can be followed in four distinct stages (discussed below), greatly influenced by transport changes, since transport is the key service in the business of going away from home to a new destination. The introduction with industrial technology of cheap and safe travel, with a major reduction in journey time, had a dramatic effect on the lives of the population in Britain and other European countries, and in the new colonized lands of North America and other continents transport influenced travel to a greater extent than perhaps any of the other forces released by the revolution in wealth-creating industry.

However, the improvements in transport did not create tourism. The latent interest or demand was already there. Wealth in the form of disposable income was an essential requirement, and lifestyles or fashion proved to be as important in the early days as they are today, even if the concept of marketing had not been invented. As we shall see, although the pioneers in the trade had never heard the word they were in fact very good in practice. In the early stages each improvement in transport created quickly more traffic than was expected, and more traffic than the new resources could bear, a phenomenon known to this day.

The beginnings of tourism – the four stages

Prehistory tourism

The first of the four stages covers the long period of what might be called prehistory tourism: the medieval times and into the early seventeenth century when the first signs of industrial growth began to affect the way of life which had been established over the centuries. Gradual increase in wealth, the extension of the merchant and professional classes, the effects of the Reformation and the secularization of education stimulated interest in other countries, and the acceptance of travel itself as an educational force.

Transport

The railway age represented the second stage when steam trains and steamships transformed travel opportunities. Rapid growth of population and wealth created an enormous new market in a short period of time. Mass travel was invented and with it resort development and the introduction of the travel trade of agents and tour operators with new marketing methods such as organized tours, travel packages and posters and brochures. These remain as key marketing tools today.

Although transport was a major factor in growth, there were other essential elements and also some problems because, as today, the coordination of transport plans and tourism policies or projects was limited or inadequate. They are distinct but evidently related areas of mutually dependent activity. Development of accommodation and resort infrastructure generally followed expansion of transport capacity and traffic movement with some delay and uncertainty.

The interwar period

The third stage, almost an interregnum, is represented by the interwar period between 1918 and 1939. The full flowering of the age of railways and steam was halted abruptly by the First World War in 1914. As has happened before and since, the war gave a great impetus to some forms of technical development very helpful in the longer term, notably the expansion of road transport and considerable investment in aviation.

However, it was above all the age of the motor car. New fashions were introduced; in what might be called social tourism, through the extension of holidays with pay; an extension in a variety of recreational and specialist leisure activities; camping and caravanning; the spread of youth hostels; cheap transport and tours by motor coach. A substantial growth in foreign travel occurred. Many of the organizing interests were run by non-commercial or voluntary bodies. Once again expansion and experimentation was hindered by the great depression of 1930 and finally brought to a halt by the Second World War in 1939–45.

Tourism take-off

The period from 1945, through the postwar years up to the present time, represents the fourth or 'take-off' stage. It has been an era of revolution in technology, massive industrial development and change, which resulted in related acceleration in wealth creation and escalation of disposable incomes. Far-reaching changes in individual lifestyle and in personal and group communication have proved to be new factors in moulding society. Furthermore, the speed and scale of change has greatly increased.

Determinants of demand have never been more favourable for spending on travel and leisure. A continuous increase in gross domestic product (GDP), of 3 per cent or more per annum in the prosperous years, for Organization for Economic Cooperation and Development (OECD) countries, stimulated travel growth of 6 per cent or more each year. Tourism has proved to be highly income elastic. After a certain income threshold, when all necessities in life have been met, discretionary income in the richer countries tends to be spent on what were formerly regarded as luxuries and services. In these countries, travel spending has increased at almost double, or even more, than the rate of growth in national income (or GDP). Of course, this is not a law of nature, because demand trends and fashions can change dramatically and quickly, but in the tourism take-off period, with few exceptions, the rule seemed to apply.

However, massive growth was concentrated in the industrialized countries (the member countries of the OECD), some 25 in number, principally in Europe. According to the WTO, world tourism flows increased by an average annual rate of 7.32 per cent from 1950 to 1991. These countries, with less than one-quarter of the world population, accounted for nearly 85 per cent of world tourist arrivals and over 80 per cent of world expenditures in 1991. Technical advances in transport and other forms of communication strongly reinforced the economic factors favouring tourism expansion. Television in particular provided continuous reminders of the interest and variety of foreign countries' attractions. As the old saying goes: farther away the grass is greener. Gradually the appeal of foreign destinations overtook the interest in the domestic product or staying at home. The richer world was on the move.

During this period, in the industrialized countries the population became mobile through mass car ownership which changed lifestyles fundamentally. Trains and buses, the mainstay of public transport, lost their prime importance although remaining important carriers. In the USA, however, rail passenger travel was reduced to a minor position. The most revolutionary transport development took place in air travel. Before the war, airlines provided minimal services. Transatlantic airlines were no more than a dream. After 1945, greatly helped by engineering advances spurred on by wartime pressures, aviation embarked on rapid massive expansion, providing fast and safe longer distant transport, at increasingly cheaper prices in real terms. New tourism destinations were created, taking over from the railway age resorts. Long-distance travel gradually became a popular attraction and towards the later years of the period the fastest growing travel 'segment'. A business travel network between principal cities in Europe, North America, and linking continents, transformed business travel. Indeed it created new forms of such travel in the widespread expansion of conferences, trade shows and incentive trips. Cheap holiday transport in Europe, through charter traffic controlled to a substantial extent by tour operators, stimulated mass movement from Northern Europe to the Mediterranean. Private car travel by the newly mobile urban dwellers supported the revolution in holiday taking and related tourism investment.

The rapid rise in tourism movement continued over the period year by year, with few interruptions, but the reappearance of cyclical factors or recessions, and towards the end of the period structural changes and some political instability, began to cast a shadow over expectations of never ending growth.

Tourism had never enjoyed the status of a senior industry deserving national priorities. Indeed much of this massive growth was left to market forces, with modest and at times decreasing government intervention in regulation or encouragement. Towards the end of the period signs of change, of uncertainties and criticism, and doubts about economic and social cost benefits, began to emerge. One might almost sense a turning of the tide by 1990, since when the Gulf crisis, recession and structural change has led to reviews of tourism's place, a marked decline in some major traffic flows, limitations in investment and changes in commercial organization.

Each of these four periods deserves more detailed examination.

Early days

Roman roads provided an effective network for travel and communication in Europe. Following the destruction of the Roman Empire, inland transport improved little throughout the medieval period. Indeed, in some parts, including Britain, communication deteriorated. Horse transport was limited to individual travel or vehicles with very small capacity. Unreliable and seasonal, such movement was very slow, with speed little more than 3–4 miles per hour. There was in fact little progress until the eighteenth century when engineers like Telford, MacAdam and Metcalf greatly improved the road system in Britain.

In medieval days, wars and pilgrimages created substantial movement from time to time. Chaucer describes the Wife of Bath in the Canterbury Tales as highly esteemed because she had made the pilgrimage to the famous shrine of St James of Compostello in Spain. Pilgrims were distinguished by the scallop shell badge of achievement, perhaps the earliest travel award. Merchants and officials were on the move. Universities encouraged visits by teachers and students, and travelling friars roamed the land.

Reformation and the secularization of learning stimulated movement. By the seventeenth century, travel was becoming accepted as part of a gentleman's education. John Milton travelled extensively in Europe as a young man with his servant. Young men of good family, hoping for careers as administrators, lawyers or soldiers, were encouraged to go abroad, on an early version of the grand tour, sometimes returning rather the worse for wear. Arguments for and against the value of such 'tourism' were by no means uncommon. Thus the debate about the cost benefits of tourism had very early beginnings.

Kershaw and Lickorish (1958, p. 22) noted that by the eighteenth century the grand tour was well established. Lord Shaftesbury is quoted as saying:

By the knowledge of the world I mean that which results from the observation of men and things from an acquaintance with the customs and usages of other nations; for some insight into their policies, government, religion; in a word, for the study and contemplation of men; as they present themselves in the greater stage of the world in various forms and under different appearances. This is the master science which a gentleman should comprehend and which our schools and colleges never hear of.

Lord Shaftesbury anticipated that the young gentlemen would return to enrich their own country from the benefits of their travels:

Where would be the harm if Britain were the seat of Arts and Letters as well as Trade and Liberty. Then might we be travelled to, in our turn, as our neighbours are at present; and our country amidst its other acquisitions, be enriched by a new species of commerce.

Perhaps this is the first recognition of tourism as potentially an important trade for Britain.

Travel by the elite in this way was followed by a wider interest in travel for health with the development of the spas. Although Buxton and Bath had been mentioned in the Poor Law Act of 1572 as 'places of resort for poor and diseased people' (Pimlott, 1947), growth was modest and numbers small until the end of the seventeenth century when provision for entertainment as well as the cure proved to be an important innovation. However, movement was very limited. The population of Bath, the most famous of the spas, did not exceed 2000 in 1700. Spa development began in a substantial way in the eighteenth century: first the inland 'watering places' as they were known, and then competition from the seaside followed after Dr Russell's 'Dissertation on the use of seawater' in 1752 which led to the rapid growth of Brighton from a small fishing village to a famous resort enjoying royal patronage. The marine spas, as they were known, created a fashion for cold seawater bathing. The first grand hotels in these resorts were known in Britain as the hydros, short for hydropathic establishments.

These, at first patronized by royalty and the upper classes, soon attracted a middle and professional class clientele, as wealth and population increased, and as towns grew and industrial expansion speeded up. The trend for fashion in resort appeal to be dictated from the top society leaders and the wealthy continued for a time, with the elite moving on to new destinations as the lower orders took over. Later in the twentieth century the creative initiative was to change so that innovation came from lower in the social scale. Camping and sporting holidays became popular linked to hobbies and interests at home, and specialized institutions developed in the tourism and leisure field. As examples, the National Trust was founded in 1895 to safeguard the heritage, and the Trust House hotel group was founded in Victorian times by philanthropists, to ensure accommodation suitable for gentlefolk and especially ladies. Social tourism in fact began to spread throughout Europe, with many of the tourism clubs and societies developing holidays and foreign travel for the working classes. The Workers Travel Association (WTA) was established in Britain as an offshoot of the Workers Educational Association (WEA). In this way, 'social tourism' played a role alongside market forces in catering for a special clientele, an early form of responding to what is now called market segmentation.

Road and canal improvement helped traffic growth. Turnpikes in Britain and other countries, now strangely returning to favour, were constructed rapidly. There were 22 000 miles of turnpike roads eventually in Britain. The mail coach system established better and more reliable services, so that by the beginning of the nineteenth century all major cities and towns in Britain were connected by stagecoach, with up to 30 services each day. Journeys of up to 200 miles were completed in one day, but the number of passengers carried by modern standards was very low and the cost was high. Even as late as 1831 there were little more than 200 seats per day available on services between London and Portsmouth, then with a population of 30 000 (Burkart and Medlik, 1981, p. 8). Records were broken in travel to Brighton, when 480 passengers were carried in one day. Coach travellers for the whole year were estimated at 50 000 (Pimlott, 1947). Bath, the most important British resort at the end of the eighteenth century, was receiving some 1200 visitors in the season, but most others reported very modest figures, Cheltenham, for example, no more than 1000.

According to Pimlott (1947):

in 1840 it cost as much to travel post from St Leonards to Tunbridge Wells, a distance of less than 30 miles, but involving the payments of three postmasters and post boys and twelve turnpike men, as to stay a fortnight at the former.

Travel for pleasure can be said to have its beginnings in the last years of the eighteenth century and the early years of the nineteenth century. Major changes in society, in lifestyles, in industry and technology were altering the shape of the community. There are times in history of exceptional change and material expansion. The nineteenth century witnessed such an economic expansion, to be followed by an even greater industrial and scientific revolution in the second half of the twentieth century. Tourism was a major beneficiary, to become towards the end of the century the world's largest industry.

At the end of the seventeenth century the population of Britain was little more than 5 million, but by 1801 there were more than 15 million people and by the mid-nineteenth century 25 million. Industry and commerce took over from agriculture as the main source of wealth and economic power. Landowners no longer had a monopoly of authority. These changes led to a large expansion in the 'leisured' class. A wider distribution of wealth, and improvements in literacy and thus communication, proved to be powerful factors in unlocking the latent potential demand for travel, to meet other people and to see foreign countries. One can just imagine the extent of interest in simple sightseeing in foreign lands when the large majority of the population had never had the opportunity of travelling away from home.

By 1837 the number of visitors to Brighton by horsedrawn road transport had reached 50 000 in the year, a level believed to be unsurpassable. The well-known sailing ships, the 'Hoys' from the Thames to Margate, carried increasing holiday traffic, rising from 18 000 passengers in 1800 to 98 000 in 1830 (Kershaw and Lickorish, 1958, p. 27). These were small volumes by later standards, but an indication of change. Tourism was becoming visible as a movement and a trade in its own right. In addition to the new economic forces, perhaps the most important new factor was the change in demand or fashion, deriving from alteration in lifestyles and preferences. The Romantic movement in art and literature stimulated interest in nature, scenery and mountains for example in addition to the earlier interest in architecture, art and places of historic fame. Horace Walpole was reported to say of the Alps in 1737: 'I hope I shall never see them again.' Goethe declared: 'Switzerland at first made so deep an impression on me that I was bewildered and restless.'

Nature had been seen as unkempt and fit to be tamed by development. The enclosures of common land and landscaping by famous architects such as Capability Brown and Humphrey Repton created the English country-side, with Georgian buildings and furnishings to match. So much of this excellence in heritage was destroyed quite recently in an age of planning and control, when the controllers had no talent to sense that the result was a catastrophe.

As Burkart and Medlik observed (1981, p. 10), when the railways first appeared the 'new' approach saw them as enhancing the landscape. They were largely welcomed and indeed the subject of paintings by Turner and the Impressionists. The idea of conflict between development and the conservation of natural resources had not arrived. It was much later in Victorian times that concerns about the ravages of uncontrolled industrial expansion began to emerge.

The railway age

The railway age witnessed the first great explosion in demand for travel, with major effects on the country, the economy and social habits. The first passenger railway (Liverpool and Manchester) opened in 1830. Expansion first in Britain and then in the rest of Europe and North America was rapid: 2 million passengers were carried in Britain annually by 1841, 79 million by 1851, 160 million by 1860, 817 million by 1980 and 1455 million by 1914 (Kershaw and Lickorish, p. 32). Table 2.1 gives an indication of the revolutionary railway expansion in Europe.

Table 2.1   Miles of railway track built, 1835–85

	1835	1845	1855	1865	1875	1885
Great Britain and Ireland	471	3277	13 411	21 382	26 803	30 843
France	176	883	5 535	13 562	21 547	32 491
Germany	6	2315	8 352	14 762	28 087	37 572
Austria-Hungary	-	728	2 145	5 858	16 860	22 789
Russia and Finland	-	144	1 048	3 940	19 584	26 847
Italy	-	157	1 211	4 347	7 709	10 484
Belgium	20	576	1 349	2 254	3 499	4 409
Holland and Luxembourg	-	153	314	865	1 407	2 804
Switzerland	-	2	210	1 322	1 948	2 850
Europe, including Great Britain and Ireland	673	8235	35 185	75 882	142 494	195 835

Source: Table quoted by A. J. Norval in *The Tourist Industry*, published by Sir Isaac Pitman and Sons Ltd, London, 1936.

Thomas Cook introduced the first package tour in 1841, but in fact by that time the railways themselves were offering excursion trips, for a traffic which they had not originally expected to carry. The first objective had been carriage of freight, and secondly the provision of faster transport for the current stagecoach travellers at far from cheap prices. The popularity of cheap excursion fares for special events was not expected. Kemball Cook (1947) noted in his book that on Derby Day in 1838, eight trains were advertised to run from the Nine Elms terminus. The authorities were confounded by 5000 excursionists coming to the station.

In 1851, 774 910 passengers to and from London were carried by excursion trains of the London and North Western railway. In the second half of 1844, 360 000 passengers travelled from London to Brighton, a more than tenfold increase in just seven years due to the railway.

However, Thomas Cook's unique contribution was the organization of the whole trip – transport, accommodation and activity or 'satisfaction' at a desired new destination – the true tourist product. As an agent for the principal suppliers of transport and accommodation, he was able to meet a specific market demand. He invented an essential service – a package or an individual tour. His innovation was followed throughout the world. He did more than any other single entrepreneur through this invention to change the attitudes to travel from a necessary and far from enjoyable activity, an education and a hard task, to a pleasure, an entertainment and a new concept – a 'holiday'.

He started out and indeed continued, even when his travel activities had grown, as a printer and publisher. Guidebooks and timetables were highly regarded. It was said of Baedeker that his guidebook was not a publication but a way of life. In these early years of tourism invention and development, many of the entrepreneurs and leaders came into tourism for purposes other than making a successful business. Education inspired, for example, the establishment of the Workers Travel Association which was an offshoot of the Workers Educational Association, as mentioned earlier. The Cooperative Travel Organization developed the Cooperative Travel Service as a major company, and some trades unions operated holiday camps and services for social objectives. Organizations related to the churches were very active.

Thomas Cook and his company expanded rapidly. He brought 165 000 excursionists from Yorkshire alone to the Great Exhibition in 1851 and organized his first tour to the Continent in 1856, and to the USA in 1865 (Kershaw and Lickorish, 1958, p. 32).

Encouraged and in some cases created by the railway companies, large hotels were established in cities, especially at or near railway termini, and in the fast-growing resorts. Some of these new towns such as Bournemouth were built up quickly from little more than fishing villages in a few years. They were very much a British invention. However, growing demand stimulated the German spas, which were favoured until later in the century when the move to the seaside led to the expansion of Mediterranean centres, notably Nice and Cannes in France. The railway hotels were concentrated at their termini in large cities and large resorts. The coaching inns lost traffic, but they had never serviced mass movement, and continued to cater for road travellers in rural areas and small towns.

Hotel companies were developing modern practices by the turn of the century – the beginning of hotel chains, the extension of catering services in tearooms and restaurants. Entertainment and marketing activity contributed to the attractions of city and resorts. The hoteliers of Monte Carlo started the Monte Carlo rally to attract off-season trade before 1914. Similarly a hotel company played an important part in creating the London to Brighton vintage car event.

Transatlantic travel for pleasure started in the 1860s, and the grand tour concept was followed. Improved transport and increasing wealth found a strong latent demand, motivated by curiosity and the appeal of education values and new experience. Health and recreation were not powerful motives, as America itself could satisfy such needs. Heritage, cultural interests, personal and business links, together with curiosity were the appeal.

Even after the war it was said of American visitors that they entered England as though visiting a cathedral. One of David Ogilvie's most popular advertisements for the British Travel Association, the predecessor of the British Tourist Authority, showed a full-page colour photograph of Westminster Abbey with the caption 'Tread softly past the long long sleep of kings' (see *British Travel Association*, 1975).

The five-month voyage of the *Quaker City* to the Mediterranean and the Holy Land in 1867 with 60 passengers (including Mark Twain), who recorded the journey in *The Innocents Abroad* was probably the first ocean cruise conceived and advertised for tourists. The cost of the passage was $1200 for each adult passenger and it was estimated that $5 in gold a day would cover shore expenses. The cost by modern standards was enormous. (Kershaw and Lickorish, 1958, 35.)

The number of Americans travelling abroad was estimated at no more than 26 000 in 1860, but rose rapidly to 50 000 annually until the 1880s when another expansion in movement occurred. American citizens returning were estimated at more than 120 000 in 1900 and over 286 000 in 1913. Passenger movement from the UK and Europe to North America increased largely due to the migrant movement and in the years 1910–13 exceeded 1 million annually, reaching a peak (1 689 000 in 1914) in sea traffic, never to be surpassed. Britain enjoyed by far the largest share of the movement, reporting outward traffic in excess of 1 million passengers in the boom years of 1910–13 (Kershaw and Lickorish, 1958, p. 38).

The growth of travel in the USA saw the establishment of the Wells Fargo company, the predecessor of American Express, first as a carrier of bullion and coach passengers and then into travel. In Britain also companies already established moved into travel, sometimes as a sideline or ancillary service. Cox and Kings, for example, were bankers and merchants in India and the East with a big trade catering for the Indian Army and Civil Service, so arranging passages as well as overdrafts was a sensible extension of their trade. Pickfords and Dean and Dawson in London dealt in freight and traded as forwarding agents which led them into travel, the former expanding substantially in travel in recent years after privatization from the nationalized railways. In fact, through the British Transport Commission set up after the last war the state owned all the large travel companies, including Thomas Cook, but made little progress with them, nor with their hotel chain which was the largest in the country.

Statistics published by the Board of Trade (Table 2.2) indicate the growth in passenger travel from Britain to the Continent. There would have been little migration in the figures, and although British residents predominate, there was by then an increasing flow of European travel to Britain as well.

Thomas Cook was soon offering a range of tours in Europe, America, Egypt and further away. Social events were a feature for some early 'package' tours. Cook's took 75 000 visitors to the Paris Exhibition in 1861. Sir Henry Lunn's British visitors were the principal influence in creating the winter sports trade in Switzerland, which later spread to other areas, involving massive investment in mountain resorts.

Table 2.2   Passengers – Britain to Europe, 1891–1900

1891	418 003	1886	479 913
1892	405 998	1897	569 150
1893	395 362	1898	590 226
1894	477 318	1899	609 570
1895	493 946	1900	669 292

Source: UK Board of Trade.

The extension of travel from its specialist base of serious purpose, business, professional or for health and education was not to everyone's liking. Some of the criticism of pleasure tourists or excursionist behaviour in the early days would be familiar today. A writer in *Blackwood's Magazine* in 1869 refers to tribes of unlettered British over the cities of Europe'. A more objective article in Charles Dickens's magazine *All the Year Round* in 1864 (Burkart and Medlik, 1981, p. 15) reports:

the trip to Edinburgh and the short excursions in England attract tradesmen and their wives, merchants, clerks away for a week's holiday. In the return trip from Scotland to England come many students of the schools and universities. As for the Swiss excursions the company is of a very different order; the Whitsuntide trip has a good deal of the cockney element in it and is mostly composed of high spirited people. From these roysterers the July and August excursionists differ greatly; ushers and governesses, practical people from the provinces, and representatives of the better style of the London mercantile company, many of them carry books of reference and nearly all take notes.

However, Gladstone, the famous British statesman, writing at the time took a favourable view:

Among the humanising contrivances of the age I think notice is due to the system founded by Mr Cook and now largely in use under which numbers of persons and indeed whole classes have for the first time found easy access to foreign countries and have acquired some of the familiarity with them which breeds not contempt but kindness.

Many modern marketing practices were in fact invented by the Victorians. They practised market segmentation. Resorts were designed for the appropriate clientele. Cheerful, popular gregarious Blackpool and Brighton, and quiet 'select' smaller resorts such as Frinton, catered for very different markets. Entertainments, theatre shows and special events were created for a new trade. The pioneers knew instinctively that tourism was a theatrical business. Early parties to Switzerland got up at dawn to see the sun rise over the Alps.

The change from travel for serious purposes to travel for pleasure was gradual, in addition to resort development there was a marked expansion in specialist leisure travel, for sports and hobbies, which in turn led to the growth of specialist agencies and voluntary bodies able to offer their members sporting or cultural activities at reasonable prices. This new trend in travel and holidays occurred not only in Britain but in other European countries. Touring Club de France was established in 1890 and the Alliance Internationale de Tourisme in 1898.

Posters, brochures and guidebooks developed, many to a high standard. These marketing tools are still the main media to sell and inform today. Strangely the guidebook in recent years lost its status, and too often came to be regarded simply as an advertising medium. Travel writers had an important role in the early days, as they do today. Mr Clement Scott, a journalist on the *Daily Telegraph*, made the North Norfolk coast a popular area by describing it as Poppyland in the late nineteenth century.

In fact, modern tourism had established itself, with the main elements in place, by the outbreak of the First World War in 1914. There was by then a substantial infrastructure of resorts served by the railways throughout Europe. Attractions, organizations and marketing practices were well developed. Transatlantic traffic, served by large and relatively fast steamships, had grown substantially. The traffic was so great that it took some time to re-establish the movement on the same scale after the war ended. The motor-car and the bus had appeared, but travel was still largely rail dominated.

Between the wars

The relatively short time between the two world wars, 1918 to 1939 – a brief 21 years – was greatly affected by the major world recessions, beginning in 1930. Travel recovered relatively quickly after the First World War, when prosperity returned. The war had brought a change in attitudes, greater expectations, a rise in living standards, an interest in peace and mutual understanding, and a less rigid social order, with a more active role for women in society. Another important factor was the technical advances speeded up by wartime needs and state spending. Cars and buses had not only improved in efficiency, but there was a large stock of buses used by the armed forces and now redundant. A number of important tour operators were able to provide cheap transport for tourism purposes. The British firm, Frames Tours, started by taking large numbers of visitors to the war graves in France and Belgium. Their fleet of coaches provided the basis for a successful tour operation. Aviation became a practical means of transport. It was the beginning of an age of mobility and communication, completing the cycle of moving from the static to the mobile community, with far-reaching effect on communities and countries.

Table 2.3 shows the expansion of car ownership in Britain and the importance of bus and coach travel. From this it will be seen that the process of creating the mobile 'man' had still some way to go when the Second World War started. Travel was still largely public transport carried. Air traffic was growing fast, but from a minute base rising to a peak in 1938 of 220 000 passengers on Imperial Airways Empire routes, and a total of 95 000 passengers from UK to Europe.

One-third of British holidaymakers now travelled by coach. The prewar trend to new forms of holiday taking continued. In Britain, holiday camps became popular and youth hostels expanded. Camping increased and caravanning started as the motor-car began to change holiday habits. There was a continuing interest in social aspects of tourism and holidays, with government intervention. Voluntary bodies, some in Europe with state help including Germany and Italy, continued to expand, but holidays were still limited to at best one or two weeks a year; certainly an improvement on the one-day August Bank holiday introduced by legislation in 1871. In 1937 the Ministry of Labour in Britain estimated that there were only 1.75 million workers covered by holidays with pay agreements. However, with government action the numbers enjoying holidays with pay increased rapidly. By 1939, 11 million out of the total workforce of 18 million enjoyed this benefit.

Table 2.3   Vehicles in use in Great Britain, 1926–39

	Private cars*	*Buses and coaches*
1926	683 913(2)	40 118
1927	786 610	42 458
1928	884 645	46 298
1929	980 886	49 889
1930	1 056 214	52 648
1931	1 083 457	49 134
1932	1 127 681	47 656
1933	1 203 245	45 656
1934	1 308 425	45 689
1935	1 477 378	47 215
1936	1 642 850	49 116
1937	1 798 105	50 979
1938	1 944 394	53 005
1939	2 034 400	Not available

* In comparison: 1978, 14 million in the UK; 1987, 156 million in Europe.

Sources: Board of Trade journals to 1939; later figures from *Annual Abstract of Statistics* and British Road Federation.

The greatest change was the development of foreign travel in Europe following the rise in living standards, especially for the middle classes in Europe and America. All the factors for growth which were to create mass movements after 1945 were present, but to a minor extent. The inter-war years were almost a rehearsal for tourism take-off after the Second World War. Tour operators, now grouped in an aptly termed British Creative Travel Agents Conference, offered remarkable value for money, with transatlantic package tours from Scotland to Canada for example available for £50. A week's holiday in Ostend, a popular resort for British visitors at the time, cost £5 all in. Germany and Italy, suffering major economic difficulty, offered remarkably low prices. In spite of such attractions the 1930s recession had a major effect in limiting the development of travel movements. For many of the traffic flows, across the Atlantic for example, a rapid rise to a peak in 1930–31 was followed by recession. Recovery was beginning when the Second World War started.

British visits to Europe were only 7 per cent higher in 1924 than in 1913, but increased to a level 47 per cent higher by 1930. Visitors to Austria rose to 1.8 million in 1928, and 1 million to Switzerland in 1929. Traffic dropped sharply after the recession, in some case by 50 per cent or more (Kershaw and Lickorish, 1958, p. 43).

Transatlantic travel increased up to 1930 when a new peak of 477 000 returning American citizens was recorded, a figure not to be reached again until after the Second World War. Thus in this inter-war period development was halted cruelly, first by severe economic recession and then by war, but the way ahead for revolutionary change was already clear. Holidays and travel had become more an accepted part of life, rather than a luxury. In Britain holiday taking was no longer an elite practice but a national habit. By the late 1930s some 15 million people took an annual holiday and the trend was similar in other countries.

Mass travel

The fourth stage in modern tourism, the postwar years from 1945 until the present time, has been a period of technological revolution; in fact, a second industrial revolution. This resulted in a massive increase in wealth and disposable income, together with equally far-reaching changes in lifestyles and behaviour. The speed as well as the scale of change has been greater than never before.

Accordingly, it has been a period of massive growth in travel in the industrialized and richer countries of the world. Transport and other forms of communication, notably television, strongly reinforced the economic factors favouring tourism expansion, with constant reminders of the interest and variety of foreign countries' attractions. Gradually the appeal of foreign places overtook the interest in the domestic product or staying at home. In the richer countries the population became mobile. Car ownership expanded dramatically. Car registrations worldwide grew from 100 million in 1970 to 394 million 1987. In Europe alone car registrations more than doubled in this period from 68 million to 159 million or by 135 per cent.

The OECD reported that private cars are responsible for 80 per cent of inland transport (passenger-kilometres). The European Community's Survey 'Europeans on Holiday' estimated that the private car was by far the most important means of holiday transport, 58 per cent of the total. Over the period, trains and public road transport (buses and coaches) lost their prime importance; indeed, in some countries such as the USA railways became minor passenger transport providers. Table 2.4, from the OECD Report of 1995, shows the position in Europe.

Air travel increased at an even faster rate, as the table of scheduled air travel (Table 2.5) indicates. However, this is only part of the story, as non-scheduled traffic (charter services) also increased substantially, making up an estimated 18 per cent of total movement by the 1980s and 50 per cent or more on European routes, where the charter traffic took over the greater part of the holiday movement, as tour operators developed their own services.

Aviation was a minor force in passenger transport before the Second World War. Transatlantic travel was exclusively by sea. The rapid and large-scale development of air passenger transport after the war was greatly assisted by the revolutionary introduction of wide-bodied jet aircraft, and greater efficiency in equipment, which led to a substantial reduction in travel time and a continuing reduction in real price. Charter services used extensively by tour operators, especially in Europe, expanded to meet the enormous growth in demand.

The world was on the move, at least in the richer industrialized countries. The scale of expansion was unparalleled. According to the WTO, total world tourist arrivals grew from 69 million in 1960 continuously with rare interruptions, to 537.4 million in 1994, an increase of nearly 800 per cent.

Table 2.4 Foreign tourism by mode of transport

	1992 Breakdown of arrivals (%)				Total volume (thousands)	1993 Breakdown of arrivals (%)				Total volume (thousands)
	Air	Sea	Rail	Road		Air	Sea	Rail	Road	
Australia[1]	99.5	0.5			2 603.3	99.6	0.4			2 996.2
Japan[2]	97.3	2.7			3 926.3	97.7	2.3			3 747.2
New Zealand[3]	99.0	1.0			1 055.7	99.2	0.8			1 157.0
Belgium[4]	6.0	2.1	92.0		157 659.0					
Iceland	95.0	5.0			142.6	95.2	4.8			157.3
Ireland[5]	58.6	36.2			3 300.0	61.1	38.9			3 330.0
Italy[6]	13.6	2.8	8.2	75.5	50 088.7	14.3	3.3	7.7	74.6	49 909.7
Portugal[6]	90.9	6.1	3.1		4 059.2	91.2	6.3	2.5		3 835.3
Spain[7]	32.8	3.1	4.3	59.8	55 330.7	41.9	4.3	5.0	48.9	46 263.4
Turkey[8]	42.1	10.1	1.1	46.8	7 076.1	54.2	12.0	0.6	33.1	6 500.6
United Kingdom[6]	68.5	31.5			18 179.0					

[1]Arrivals of short-term visitors (less than 1 year).
[2]Visitor arrivals, including those of returning residents and excluding crew members.
[3]Tourist arrivals.
[4]Air and sea include both arrivals and departures of foreign and domestic visitors; rail refers to international traffic only.
[5]Visitors on overseas routes (average of arrivals and departure).
[6]Visitors arrivals.
[7]Visitor arrivals, including Spaniards living abroad.
[8]Traveller arrivals.

Source: *International Tourism and Tourism Policy*, OECD, 1995.

Table 2.5 Development of world air transport, 1972–94*

	1972	1974	1976	1978	1980	1982	1984	1986	1988	1989	1990	1991	1992	1993	1994
Scheduled international and domestic passengers carried (millions)†	450	514	576	679	748	766	848	960	1082	1119	1165	1133	1152	1139	1227
Passenger load factor %	57	59	60	65	63	64	65	65	68	68	68	66	66	65	66
Scheduled international passengers carried (millions)†	88	102	118	143	163	170	185	198	243	262	280	266	302	318	344
Passenger load factor %	54	56	57	62	61	62	65	63	68	68	69	66	66	66	68
Scheduled domestic passengers carried (millions)*	362	412	458	536	585	596	663	762	839	857	885	867	850	820	883
Passenger load factor %	59	62	62	67	65	65	64	66	67	68	67	67	66	63	65

* Figures are rounded, so that the component figures may not add up to totals.
† The figure for 1993 is revised.

Source: *International Civil Aviation Organization.*

Europe: the world's leading tourism region

Europe, as the world's chief tourism region, accounted for 73 per cent of world arrivals in 1960, but this fell to just under 62 per cent in 1991. Although volume rose massively, Europe in fact lost world market share substantially. Similarly, Europe's share of world tourist receipts, which increased faster than total volume of traffic, decreased slightly from 57 per cent in 1960 to just under 52 per cent in 1991.

During this period of massive expansion in total volume, there were also some major changes in trends and traffic movement. By 1990, international arrivals in Europe reached a new peak of 337 million arrivals, but then declined in 1991 due to the recession and Gulf War crisis. But as the OECD observed, these crisis elements obscured some of the longer term structural changes in tourism movements. There were losers as well as winners, declining as well as expanding tourism areas.

As total traffic expanded, travel flows altered and changed direction. Long-haul travel increased faster than shorter distance trips, as explained in Chapter 13.

While the mass movement from cold northern industrial cities to warm sunny beaches, a fairly simple product to package, increased substantially, as years passed there was an increasing segmentation in travel. A number of quite distinct mini mass markets developed, with varying characteristics in rate of growth, potential, resilience to recession (e.g. senior citizens) and consumer preferences. Much of the movement was specialist in character. Business travel, for example, expanded in new ways, notably in the form of organized trips for conventions, trade shows and incentive tours. Cultural and educational travel expanded substantially. Travel for sports and hobbies developed, and movement to visit friends and relatives became important on some routes, including long-distance routes which had witnessed major migration flows in the years after the war.

Towards the end of the 1980s the original more simple mass flow travel from colder industrialized northern urban areas to warm sunny beaches began to show distinct signs of weakness. Packaged travel to the Mediterranean and notably to Spain decreased greatly. After reaching a peak of 12.5 million package trips out of Britain, the total in two years 1990–91 fell by nearly 20 per cent – more to some popular destinations – a volatility both dangerous and largely unexpected by the tour operators. At the same time the outward movement from Britain did not decrease, so there was a marked diversion to other types of destination resulting from demand changes. In contrast, in the same period travel outward from Southern European countries such as Spain and Italy increased to a marked extent. Much of the growth resulted in travel to the cooler Northern European countries.

Investment impacts

The new scale of growth required massive capital investment. Vast new resort areas, largely in the Mediterranean region in Europe, but also in the Caribbean and in a number of warm climate developing countries around the world, were constructed rapidly. In some cases the expansion was

uncoordinated with growth in ancillary services and environmental investment or protection. Some of these 'cities' by the sea, constructed in an urban
form with high-rise buildings, have experienced difficulties. Their appeal
came into conflict with the 'green movement', and a strong and still-growing
interest in environmental quality and freedom from pollution, as the search
for quality in general became a more important consumer preference.

The expansion of business and professional travel, including conference
and trade fair movement, represented an increased demand for high-
standard city centre hotels, stimulated by the introduction of wide-bodied
jets, making personal contact and long-distance travel relatively easy and
much cheaper. Frequent journeys and high spend per trip made this market
segment especially important to sectors of the travel industry. It is estimated
that over 50 per cent of first-class city centre hotel trade comes from this
market segment, and the percentage is even higher for some services such as
car rental. In the UK, over 25 per cent of total foreign currency earnings from
visitors comes from the business traveller.

Both access to capital and the technology for massive new developments
guaranteed the rapid expansion of infrastructure. In the UK, for example,
total national stock of international class accommodation (rooms with bath)
doubled in little more than three years between 1970 and 1974, with the help
of an open-ended subsidy from the government paid for each new hotel
bedroom built. Up to the time of the legislation providing this incentive there
had been very little hotel building of any kind since before the depression
years of the early 1930s. In 1969 there were then only 900 rooms with bath in
Edinburgh, the capital city of Scotland, less than in one of the big London
hotels. By then, with the advent of the wide-bodied jets (Jumbos), the need for
substantial investment to meet demand was recognized. But government
intervention was clumsy. Expansion of accommodation on a scale far greater
than expected was followed by the major oil crisis, the first postwar recession
and the consequent collapse of transatlantic travel to Europe. This halt in
growth threatened a heavily extended hotel industry.

Fortunately recovery was swift from this the first postwar recession after
an extended period of growth which seemed almost without end. A second
recession followed in 1981 and then a more serious economic decline in 1991
compounded by the Gulf War. Each of the three recessions has taken longer
in recovery. In the 1991–92 decline there were certain structural changes in
addition to the cyclical fluctuations. Although difficult to identify, the
structural changes are more lasting in effect. So far as Europe is concerned
they are negative in their influence on tourism growth. The decline of
manufacturing industry and reduction in the workforce at all levels,
including management, tended to increase longer term unemployment and
lower consumer confidence.

Effects of segmentation

Different market segments began to show differing characteristics, some
resilient to recession and structural change such as senior citizen movements. Demand for services favoured by the elderly, e.g. cruise traffic,
continued to expand.

The 1980s had been a decade of continuing but slower growth overall, with the exception of the new fast-expanding regions such as Japan and the Far East. New emerging trends reflecting changing lifestyles and consumer behaviour differed from those of Western society in the 1950s and 1960s. Marketing rather than greater technological improvement was becoming more important. Overall growth could no longer be taken for granted.

Holiday taking in Europe, where over 50 per cent of the population went away from home at least once a year, was reaching a more mature stage. In fact, a vast market of sophisticated travellers accustomed to journey in foreign countries could now, for the first time, enjoy individual travel. The majority of European holiday travellers were already moving in their own cars. Much of their accommodation and other services are now self-provided, such as second homes, private accommodation, rented accommodation, or camping and caravanning.

An awareness of quality and sensitivity to environmental satisfaction were new factors influencing consumer preferences. Reaction to political instability also added to the pressures, introducing a new volatility to previously more traditional and stable tourism flows.

Length of stay per trip continued to fall over the years. OECD reported average length of stay on international visits in European countries varying from two to a maximum of five nights. This trend was matched by increased frequency of travel. The European Commission holiday survey, studying 140 million holiday trips, reported that a third of all European holidaytakers took more than one holiday per year.

Seasonality continuously improved as the trend to frequent holiday taking increased and the appeal of active and specialist holidays encouraged year-round travel. A more mobile population enjoyed more flexible holiday opportunities, with the majority of the population unconstrained by fixed holiday dates. In fact, seasonality or the problems of peak movement could by the end of the 1980s be considered more a marketing challenge than an insuperable difficulty.

In the boom years of the Western industrialized economies, many of the institutions from the railway age, such as social tourism groups and non-commercial or voluntary institutional organizations, went out of business. Nevertheless, although the political climate went against them, the role of the specialist non-profit-making institutions remained important, especially in the conservation, heritage and environmental field. In the UK the National Trust, a charitable and voluntary organization formed in the railway period to conserve the heritage and landscape, decided to enter the tourist trade, not only by providing greater public access to their historic properties, but in catering, entertainment, souvenirs, holiday cottages and organized tours.

An enormous day-trip movement developed with the universal use of the car. Estimates of this market in Britain suggest traffic as high as 1 billion trips each year, including visits to friends and relatives. The UK Day Visits Survey 1993 reported a figure of nearly £17 billion expenditure on leisure day trips. The statistics are notoriously difficult to use, and comparisons internationally impossible because of differences in definitions. This is a growth area in British holiday taking and represents a level of spending greater than all British holiday spending in Britain on trips of one night or more. There are some signs that total movement has reached a peak, but there is still a good response to marketing initiatives. Recession, however, can affect some types of attraction, but may also stimulate some day-trip movement as a substitute for longer holidays.

City tourism has proved an important innovation not only as a result of the popularity of conferences, which resulted in substantial investment in large conference centres, but in the expansion of large-scale visitor traffic for special occasions. Entertainment, cultural and sporting interests add powerfully to the appeal of large city services in shopping, hotels, restaurants, and good transport and communications. Short trips, weekend packages, all the year round including winter, have radically changed seasonal patterns to the great advantage of the service industries concerned.

In this era of massive growth there have been losers, and declining destinations and services, largely the result of inaction, failure to invest, to develop products to match changing markets, and tourist demand in general. The resorts in Britain, for example, have lost much of their traditional 'seaside holiday' trade and some have not replaced this trade from new markets and modernization of accommodation and facilities. There have been exceptions such as Blackpool, Bournemouth and Torquay which have held on to much of their business. However, a number have almost abandoned tourism and left the large cities to compete successfully for short trip, conference and other specialist traffic in growing market segments.

Britain has also lost out to foreign competition. While the marketing of international traffic into Britain has been energetically pursued by the British Tourist Authority with government support, the failure of the domestic market to compete with foreign destinations and the incursion of foreign transport links serving the UK has led to a deficit on the travel account of nearly £5 billion, or a substantial part of the total national deficit in 1994. In the mid-1970s, in contrast, the travel balance of payments reached a figure of over £1 billion in surplus. Of course, the world situation is now different. But this previous success demonstrates that Britain has tourism resources and attractions that can be offered worldwide and successfully, with the right approach and appropriate national policies.

Changes in government and industry organization

Towards the end of the postwar period major changes were taking place in industry structure and organization. The introduction of the European Community's Single Market in 1993 offered greater prosperity through an increase in GDP and disposable incomes in Europe over the longer term. However, in the short term effects were limited. Indeed, borderless Europe failed to emerge and the burden of taxation, notably VAT, increased rather than diminished, with little progress in the harmonization or lowering of excise duties. In theory there were the challenges of greater competition, but the almost imperceptible effects in the short term were overshadowed by major forces for change in industry, such as the creation of larger units operating worldwide rather than nationally or on a purely European scale.

Changes in distribution, in the growth of large wholesale and retail networks and in technology (computer reservation systems) were becoming apparent. Industry sectors had for some time shown signs of globalization in America and Europe. The creation of multinational companies evident in aviation extended to hotel chains and travel trade companies. Thomas Cook is owned by a German bank with major travel interests, French companies previously largely domestically based have expanded worldwide, such as Carlson WagonLits which owns Club Mediterranée and Accor, one of the world's largest hotel companies.

More significant, and presenting some problems for the trade as a whole, is the trend for governments to reduce their role in promotion and development. At the beginning of the postwar period, tourism received a high priority in state policies and funding. The US Marshall Plan for the postwar reconstruction of Europe financed major government intervention in tourism promotion and industry investment through the Organization for European Economic Development (OEEC), the predecessor of the OECD. Tourism's potential in terms of increased dollar earnings was highly regarded by most governments. In addition to national activity, the OEEC financed marketing campaigns in the USA by the European Travel Commission (ETC) with a subvention of 300 000 US$ in the early postwar years, a larger amount in real terms than the ETC received from its government agency members in the 1990s for an enormously greater trade. It is perhaps not surprising that Europe has lost market share, as the private sector cannot on its own provide the platform for major collective action.

For some years after the war European governments intervened substantially to support tourism growth, with foreign currency earnings as the main public benefit. It was a time of socialist-inspired state planning, and subsidies for development especially in the hotel industry were common. In Britain, however, state support was largely confined to marketing action.

These policies were followed in the 1970s by attempts to channel as well as increase tourism flows, using the trade as an aid to regional policies by directing tourism to poorer or declining areas. This policy reached an unrealistic point in Britain where the government ordered the promotion of London with state funds to cease, in an attempt to increase traffic to the poorer regions. The British Tourist Authority pointed out that London was the main gateway, and that if tourists were discouraged from coming to London, the majority would not come to Britain at all. Tourism is first and foremost a market in a highly competitive world marketplace. There may be little national destination monopoly value. The first task is to attract visitors to the national destination.

Regional development was followed more recently by employment creation as a principal objective for state intervention. Social and environmental objectives, sometimes in conflict, have emerged as public interests appealing to political policymakers. Their intervention has increasingly taken a negative approach involving constraint, regulation and taxation. As the priority given to tourism has declined, so also has the necessary coordination of government policies impacting on tourism, one of the main tasks of the public sector in providing conditions for prosperous growth.

Thus in recent years consistency of effort by the state in tourism policy has been lacking. International tourism requires a longer term strategy for success. Towards the end of the 1980s, governments in the richer countries increasingly questioned the role of the state in destination marketing, seeing this as the task of the commercial or private sector.

Era of change

For most of the period the industrialized countries, notably in Western Europe, North America and Japan, have dominated the world tourism scene, but in the 1980s major changes began to affect tourism flows and economic impacts. First, Europe has become a major originating tourism market for outward travel. By 1991, for example, European visits to the USA equalled or exceeded the flow of US visits to Europe. Secondly, Japan, Asia and the Far East have become major international outward travel markets and the fastest growing region in increasing world share. Long-haul travel in general has become one of the major new growth areas and more resilient to recession than mass short-haul movement.

There is no longer a large homogeneous world traffic and the distinct markets show varying rates of growth and response to economic forces. By the 1990s in Europe and the industrialized countries, a highly segmented market was well established. Traditional demand and behaviour has been overtaken by new fashions and preferences, and new interests of a highly mobile population, experienced and sophisticated in travel and recreation. There is a growing interest in specialization in activity, travel for a purpose, for sport, learning, health or pursuing hobbies. The major reduction in the real cost of foreign travel, especially on long-distance routes, has opened up new possibilities, and greatly increased competitive forces. An expectation for higher quality, value for money and interest in environmental satisfactions are important new factors affecting overall demand. The appeal of former simple 'mass products' such as hot sun, sea and sand is no longer sufficient to ensure long-term success.

Growth for the first time in modern travel history can no longer be taken for granted in a world marketplace where barriers and constraints to free world movement have been progressively removed. In such circumstances marketing becomes a predominant factor. Marketing embraces product development as well as presentation. The last decade of the twentieth century began to show some serious weaknesses in the task of securing consistent long-term growth in harmony with human and natural resources.

References

Burkart, A. J. and Medlik, S. (1981) *Tourism Past Present and Future*, Heinemann, London
Kemball Cook, H. (1947) *Over the Hills and Far Away*, Allen and Unwin, London
Kershaw, A. and Lickorish, L. (1958) *The Travel Trade*, Practical Press, London
Pimlott, J.A .R. (1947) *The Englishman's Holiday*, Faber and Faber, London

Further reading

Bonsor, N. R. P. (1955) *North Atlantic Seaway,* J. Stephenson and Sons, Prescot, Lancashire, UK

British Tourist Authority (1975) *British Travel Association 1929–1969*, BTA, London

Countryside Recreation Network (1993) *UK Day Visits Survey,* CRN, Cardiff

European Commission (1986) *Europeans on Holiday* EC, Brussels

Fraser Rae, W. (1891) *The Business of Travel*, Thomas Cook and Son Ltd, London

Norval, A. J. (1936) *The Tourist Industry,* Pitman, London

OECD (1995) *Tourism Policy and International Tourism in Member Countries 1992–93*, OECD, Paris

Sutton, H. Y. (1980) *Travellers*, William Morrow and Co, New York

Towner, J. (1996) *A Historical Geography of Recreation and Tourism in the Western World 1540–1940*, John Wiley, Chichester, UK

World Tourism Organisation. (1992) *Tourism Trends 1950–1991*, WTO, Madrid

3 The measurement of tourism

Introduction

The measurement of tourism and related statistical practices involves (a) concept and definitions, and (b) uses and users of travel statistics, categories of statistics, methods and sources of information.

Tourism is basically a movement of people, a demand force rather than a single industry. Originally in the English language tourists were referred to as travellers, as mentioned earlier. In recent years tourism has become the all-embracing term, describing the movement of people away from their place of permanent residence for a temporary stay in a different location. This mobile population's activities and expenditure involved in this change of location, on transport, accommodation, catering, activities at the visited destination and a wide range of services required to make the trip possible, together make up the tourist trade and represent the economic impact of tourism (Chapters 5 and 8).

However, governments, local administrations and their policies are generally concerned with the interests of the resident population. For this reason, government records and statistics are based on the residential population, so that it is never easy to measure the incidence of tourism flows. This creates many problems and weaknesses in administration and burdens for the industry sectors through lack of information.

Tourism can claim to be the world's largest trade. The 1995 World Travel and Tourism Council Report (WTTC Travel and Tourism, 1995, pp. 7 and 8) indicated that tourism generates more than US$3 trillion, which is over 10 per cent of world GNP, and employs more than 200 million people worldwide, or 1 in 9 employees, and in addition contributes US$655 billion to governments in direct and indirect taxes or 11 per cent of total tax payments.

The tourist product is a combination of all the services and goods that travellers seek or buy in preparing and completing their trip away from home. There are a variety of reasons for travel within the tourism definition, usually for business or pleasure, but education, health and religion (pilgrimages) are also major travel generators.

There must be two main elements in the product which control the choice and thus the markets. These elements must be present together; first, the combination of services required to make the journey, such as transport and accommodation, and secondly a desired satisfaction at a chosen destination, such as relaxation at a seaside resort, or attending a business conference in an acceptable city. The combination of the two elements is essential, and marketing must be built around this combination, which is often achieved successfully in tourism packages.

The tourist definition covers most travellers away from home whatever the purpose of travel, excluding some categories such as migrant and commuters. There is an increasing variety in purpose of the journeys as in destinations available. The definition embraces travellers in the country of residence and abroad, although usually a distinction is made between domestic and international travel where greater social, political and economic impacts need separate study.

It is essentially an economic concept, based on the fact that the traveller, as covered by the 'tourist' definition, spends money at the destination visited, which is earned outside that locality or country. Thus tourism represents an external injection of wealth and substantial revenues for the visitor reception area.

Definitions

There are a number of definitions which all basically aim to distinguish the temporary visitor and his expenditure from the residents' economic behaviour and impact. The Swiss Professors Walter Hunziker and Kurt Krapf, quoted by Burkart and Medlik (1981, p. 4), published their general theory of tourism in 1942, defining the subject in this way:

Tourism is the sum of the phenomena and relationships arising from the travel and stay of non-residents, in so far as they do not lead to permanent residence and are not connected with any earning activity.

This concept was later approved by the International Association of Scientific Experts in Tourism (AIEST).

In 1968, the Statistical Commission of the United Nations, following the first Intergovernmental Conference on Tourism, Rome 1963, approved the following guidance:

For statistical purposes the term 'visitor' describes any person visiting a country other than that in which he has his usual place of residence for any reason other than following an occupation remunerated from within the country visited.

The International Union of Official Travel Organizations (IUOTO) later to become the World Tourism Organization (WTO) agreed with this description but recommended that the term 'visitor' should be divided into two categories: 'tourist' to cover all visitors staying at least one night in the country or place visited, and 'excursionist' or day visitor.

The early post-war work on travel statistics, a field of study often neglected by academics and the tourism industries at that time, was largely directed to measuring international travel in view of tourism's increasing importance in international trade and the balance of payments. However, domestic movement and day trips in particular increased substantially and began to contribute massively to GNP and both national and regional prosperity in the areas visited.

In 1991 more than 25 years after the first United Nations conference on tourism (and tourist statistics), the WTO organized an International Conference in Ottawa, Canada, to review tourism statistics as a basis for consideration by the United Nations Statistical Commission to bring systems up to date. The WTO rightly appreciated the massive expansion of world tourism and the need for improved information for both government and industry. Furthermore, the old systems of statistical measurement based on state controls were disintegrating in the developed countries as liberalization of travel and border crossings led to the removal of checks and records. In a sense the weak inherited the earth, as the old systems could not cope with massive traffic flows.

With the full support of governmental and industry organizations the WTO carried out an effective study of new needs and new methods, principally revision of definitions covering the whole field of travel, domestic as well as international and 'day trips' which have become a major source of trade. Originally governments had been the main producers of statistics, but as the tourism trade became larger and more complex, industry sectors and institutions added to national data by producing their own material, making up some of the deficiency in the government systems. However, problems of compatibility and access to much of the information limits its use. Nevertheless, the WTO examination of user needs followed by a similar exercise in Europe by Eurostat (EC) was a helpful initiative. One of the problems lies in the differing needs. Governments seek public benefits or data to guide public policies, whereas industry needs marketing information and guidance for investment, manpower and training. There is some common ground, but the production of data is not well coordinated and a greater uniformity in method and production would benefit both public and private sectors.

The WTO, in its recommendations to the United Nations, wisely reaffirmed the validity of much of the earlier work, but sought improvement and greater precision in definition and by extending the range of measurement. They recognized, as the earlier systems indicated, that tourism is essentially an economic force, a market rather than a single industry, although with considerable social and environmental impact. Accordingly the principal methods of measurements must relate to the demand side. Nevertheless, the WTO paid much attention to the supply side and gave guidance on the need to include tourism in systems of national accounts. This is a complex subject and in part theoretical. Supply-side economics in tourism must be studied by each main sector separately. There is, strictly speaking, no tourism 'industry'. Accommodation can be measured through night stays or occupancy rates, but not all the consumers are tourists. Industrial and institutional catering (in offices, factories, schools and hospitals) accounts for a substantial part of that sector's business. The sectors require different approaches by treating each separate trade in its own right.

It is the concept of tourism as a market and a demand force which gives it its unity and identity. There are many subdivisions or segments needing special treatment, such as travel for business (including large movements to conferences and trade fairs), travel for pleasure in an increasing variety of products, travel by senior citizens, young people, education and health.

Each segment needs careful description or labels. There is a tendency for loose or vague definition. For example, 'social tourism', an imprecise term, is used to classify poorer or subsidized movement, and also the whole phenomenon of subsidized travel and leisure. It is to some extent confined to certain European countries, notably France, Belgium and Eastern Europe.

In addition to measuring volume or traffic flows, statistics are needed to report expenditure. This is difficult and in many cases poorly carried out because of inadequate methods. Whereas official records based on police or immigration controls can provide fairly reliable measurements of flows, expenditure cannot be recorded in this way. Governments have in some cases relied on exchange records from banks. Where there is an effective system of exchange control this may help, but the results are generally unreliable. The only sound method is a system of sample surveys, including household surveys, asking travellers about their behaviour and spending. Increasingly, survey methods are being introduced to measure volume, and travel characteristics including expenditure, and to provide much additional information from time to time for administrative and industry use.

Definitions were originally devised to measure international movement, as governments' needs were greater in the international field, but they could easily be adapted to cover domestic movement. In addition the tourism definitions should be consistent with current international standards and classifications in related areas such as demography, transport, business, migration, balance of payments, and national accounts, so that useful comparisons could be made.

The principal revised definitions agreed (WTO, 1994) are as follows:

1 Tourism comprises 'the activities of persons travelling to and staying in places outside their usual environment for not more than one consecutive year for leisure, business and other purposes'.
2 The use of this broad concept makes it possible to identify tourism between countries as well as tourism within a country. 'Tourism' refers to all activities of visitors including both 'tourists (overnight visitors)' and 'same-day visitors'.

Forms of tourism

In relation to a given country, the following forms of tourism can be distinguished:

1 Domestic tourism, involving residents of a given country travelling only within this country.
2 Inbound tourism, involving non-residents travelling in the given country.
3 Outbound tourism, involving residents travelling in another country.

The same forms of tourism may be described by replacing the word 'country' with the word 'region'. In this case these forms of tourism would no longer refer to a country or to a group of countries.

The three basic forms of tourism can be combined in various ways to derive the following categories of tourism:

1 Internal tourism, which comprises domestic tourism and inbound tourism.
2 National tourism, which comprises domestic tourism and outbound tourism.
3 International tourism, which consists of inbound tourism and outbound tourism.

The term 'domestic' used in the tourism context differs from its use in the national accounts context. 'Domestic', in the tourism context, retains its original marketing connotation, that is, it refers to residents travelling within their own country. In the national accounts context it refers to the activities and expenditures of both residents and non-residents travelling within the reference country, that is, both domestic tourism and inbound tourism.

Basic tourism units

Basic tourism units refer to the individuals/households which are the subject of tourism activities and can therefore be addressed in surveys as the statistical units (notwithstanding broader or different concepts of statistical unit, e.g. 'unit of observation, enumeration, classification, analysis'). The overall concept of 'traveller' refers to 'any person on a trip between two or more countries or between two or more localities within his/her country of usual residence

An international traveller is defined as 'any person on a trip outside his or her country of residence (irrespective of the purpose of travel and means of transport used, and even though he or she may be travelling on foot)'.

A domestic traveller is defined as 'any person on a trip in his or her own country of residence (irrespective of the purpose of travel and means of transport used, and even travelling on foot)'.

These concepts do not correspond to those of 'passenger' in transport statistics, since the latter usually exclude crew members as well as non-revenue or low-revenue passengers.

A distinction is made between two broad types of travellers: 'visitors' and 'other travellers'. All types of travellers engaged in tourism are described as visitors. Therefore, the term 'visitor' represents the basic concept for the whole system of tourism statistics. The term 'visitor' is further divided into two categories: 'tourists (overnight visitors)' and 'same-day visitors'.

Visitor

For purposes of tourism statistics, the term 'visitor' describes 'any person travelling to a place other than that of his/her usual residence for less than 12 months and whose main purpose of the trip is other than the exercise of an activity remunerated from within the place visited'.

The three fundamental criteria that appear sufficient to distinguish visitors from other travellers are as follows:

(a) The trip should be to a place other than that of the usual environment, which would exclude more or less regular trips between the place in which the person carries out his or her work or study and the place in which he or she has his or her domicile.
(b) The stay in the place visited should not last more than 12 consecutive months, beyond which the visitor would become a resident of that place (from the statistical standpoint).
(c) The main purpose of the visit should be other than the exercise of an activity remunerated from within the place visited, which would exclude migratory movements for work purposes.

Usual environment of a person

The main purpose of introducing the concept 'usual environment' is to exclude from the concept of 'visitor' persons commuting every day or week between their home and place of work or study, or other places frequently visited. The definition of usual environment is therefore based on the following criteria:

(a) Minimum distance travelled to consider a person a visitor;
(b) Minimum duration of absence from usual place of residence;
(c) Minimum change between localities or administrative territories.

Usual residence

The country of usual residence is one of the key criteria for determining whether a person arriving in a country is a visitor or other traveller, and if a visitor, whether he or she is a national or overseas resident. The underlying concept in the classification of international visitors by place of origin is the country of residence, not their nationality. Foreign nationals residing in a country are assimilated with other residents for the purpose of domestic and outbound tourism statistics. Nationals of a country residing abroad who return to their home country on a temporary visit are included with non-resident visitors, though it may be desirable to distinguish them in some studies.

Resident in a country

For purposes of international tourism statistics 'a person is considered to be a resident in a country if the person:

(a) has lived for most of the year (12 months) in that country
(b) has lived in that country for a shorter period and intends to return within 12 months to live in that country'.

Resident in a place

In parallel with the definition of the previous paragraph, for purposes of statistics on domestic tourism 'a person is considered to be a resident in a place if the person:

(a) has lived for most of the past year (12 months) in that place, or
(b) has lived in that place for a shorter period and intends to return within 12 months to live in that place'.

Nationality

The nationality of a traveller is that of the 'government issuing his or her passport (or other identification document), even if he or she normally resides in another country'.

Nationality is indicated in the person's passport (or other identification document), while country of usual residence has to be determined by means of a question. Nevertheless, a traveller is considered either an international or domestic visitor on the basis of his or her residence, not his or her nationality.

Visitors according to forms of tourism

For the purpose of tourism statistics and in conformity with the basic forms of tourism, visitors should be classified as:

(a) International visitors
  (i) tourists (overnight visitors)
  (ii) same-day visitors
(b) Domestic visitors:
  (i) tourists (overnight visitors)
  (ii) same-day visitors

For statistical purposes, the term 'international visitor' describes 'any person who travels to a country other than that in which he has his or her usual residence but outside his/her usual environment for a period not exceeding 12 months and whose main purpose of visit is other than the exercise of an activity remunerated from within the country visited'.

International visitors include:

(a) Tourists (overnight visitors): 'visitors who stay at least one night in a collective or private accommodation in the country visited'.
(b) Same-day visitors: 'visitors who do not spend the night in a collective or private accommodation in the country visited'.

The following categories of travellers should not be included in international visitor arrivals and departures:

(a) Persons entering or leaving a country as migrants, including dependants accompanying or joining them.
(b) Persons, known as border workers, residing near the border in one country and working in another.
(c) Diplomats, consular officers and members of the armed forces when travelling from their country of origin to the country of their assignment or vice versa, including household servants and dependants accompanying or joining them.
(d) Persons travelling as refugees or nomads.
(e) Persons in transit who do not formally enter the country through passport control, such as air transit passengers who remain for a short period in a designated area of the air terminal or ship passengers who are not permitted to disembark. This category would include passengers transferred directly between airports or other terminals. Other passengers in transit through a country are classified as visitors.

For statistical purposes, the term 'domestic visitor' describes 'any person residing in a country, who travels to a place within the country, outside his/ her usual environment for a period not exceeding 12 months and whose main purpose of visit is other than the exercise of an activity remunerated from within the place visited'.

Domestic visitors comprise:

(a) Tourists (overnight visitors): 'visitors who stay at least one night in a collective or private accommodation in the place visited'.
(b) Same-day visitors: 'a visitor who does not spend the night in a collective or private accommodation in the place visited'.

The following categories of trips should not be included in domestic visitor arrivals and departures:

(a) Residents travelling to another place within the country with the intention of setting up their usual residence in that place.
(b) Persons who travel to another place within the country to exercise an activity remunerated from within the place visited.
(c) Persons who travel to work temporarily in institutions within the country.
(d) Persons who travel regularly or frequently between neighbouring localities to work or study.
(e) Nomads or persons with no home.

Uses and user needs

Travel statistics are generally criticized. This is partly because governments, the principal suppliers, are slow in publishing data. In recent years many have not modernized their recording systems as the old methods failed as a by-product of diminishing controls. The intention of the European Community (EC) to create a borderless Europe will in theory lead to a disintegration of the old systems and their records.

Fortunately, the introduction of sample surveys, and the greater role played by industry, institutions and market research organizations, has substantially increased the available data. There are now many producers in addition to governments. Provided that statistics are clearly described and labelled, even partial records can be useful as guides and as a basis for estimates. One of the problems, however, arising from this dispersion of data collection is the difficulty of access, partly because there are few comprehensive data or documentation centres, and access is often restricted, especially in the case of commercially produced information.

There are differences in user needs, and thus in statistics produced by the state, trade sectors or institutions. Generally, governments seek information to guide national policy, macro rather than micro studies, and indications of tourism impact on the national economic well-being. These broad-trend measures are useful for the trade, but they do not go far enough. Industry needs marketing data and guidance on productivity, competition and forecasting relating to investment.

Government records usually measure volume (traffic) and value (expenditure), indicating tourism's contribution to transport, trade and balance of payments. The provision of market information is often not a priority, and may not be covered at all, although basic market descriptions are usually needed to guide the public sector in its own tourism policy formulation and programmes.

The state is not only a regulator in tourism and a major beneficiary from tourist taxation, but also in many cases a major operator. A great part of public transport is state owned. Much of the cultural, natural and historic heritage may also be largely state owned and local and regional governments operate many tourist facilities on a commercial basis including their own sea and airports.

Unfortunately there is little coordination of statistical information among the producers, except on a voluntary basis. However, in the USA a valuable example of such cooperation is the US Travel Data Center in Washington, and the US Travel and Tourism Research Association.

Partly as a result of this lack of communication, government and industry figures are often not compatible, adding to problems of delays in publication in the public sector. Even when agreement is reached in theory, the acceptance of ideal definitions is lacking because the old systems are not capable of adaptation to meet the new standards. Eurostat, the official statistical agency of the European Union (EU), started a two-year programme in 1991 to improve tourism records. But as the EU itself is not in general a producer of basic statistics, this being the prerogative of each member government, its contribution is mainly an exercise in methodology and recommendation, with limited impact, at least in the short term.

Increasingly the principal tourism countries with large traffic flows to measure look to sampling methods. Sample surveys are capable of providing substantial information on demand and market data, valuable to industry as well as government, to report rapidly and provide up-to-date records. This becomes increasingly important as tourism generates mass movement, with a high degree of volatility, reacting quickly to economic or political change. The Gulf War crisis in 1991, for example, led to a halt in travel from the USA to Europe for some months. Traffic loss over the year exceeded 2 million visits and some 2 billion dollars in lost revenue.

One of the chief weaknesses in tourism statistics, official, and non-official is the failure to label or describe figures accurately. For example, most records of 'arrivals', as published by the WTO in its reports compiled from national sources, refer to arrivals at frontiers. With increasing frequency many of these 'arrivals' include repeat trips by one and the same individual, but markets are made up of individual clients or consumers not 'arrivals' and 'night stays'. The WTO, for example, gives a figure for US visitors to Europe, or 'arrivals' in Europe, of 15 million in 1990, whereas the official US records report a total of about 7 million US resident visitors, or about half. Since the US figure counts separate return trips, it represents an accurate tourism traffic flow, which the WTO arrivals at frontiers cannot give.

The differing systems still have their uses, provided that the statistics are carefully described and the users take care to understand the basis of measurement. A number of different sources can also be useful in providing cross-checks which help to arrive at reasonable estimates. For example, the separate European country figures of US and Canadian visitors to their country can be compared with the official US and Canadian government records of their residents' travel abroad. In a number of countries there are official or unofficial sample surveys of residents' travel abroad. When this becomes common practice, it will be possible to provide reasonable estimates of international traffic flows through a collation of outward travel reports. In contrast, the official systems in the past have nearly all been based on measuring incoming movement. Ideally, both outgoing and incoming movements should be recorded.

Both the WTO and the EU, through its statistical agency Eurostat, have devoted much time and effort in recent years to improving statistical systems. The WTO has concentrated on definitions and concepts, and Eurostat has carried out a thorough study of user needs, and a review of methodology used by member governments with a view to making recommendations to secure compatibility and a wider scope. The results of the user study have been summarized by Eurostat in Table 3.1.

Statistical methods

There are four categories of tourism statistics:

1 Demand
   (a) Records of scale or size, volume and value. Traffic movement (volume) and expenditure (value).
   (b) Market information – market research analysing demand and consumer preferences and trends.
2 Supply
   (a) Capacity – stock of tourist equipment or plant, services and facilities available for the visitor.

Table 3.1 Users' needs for demand-side statistics

Level of priority	Type of statistics	Variables
High	Holiday market	Volume of tourism, nights spent Variables on visitors' patterns Use of travel agencies and tourist organizations Expenditure of visitors by type of expenditure Non-participants Main reason for holiday Type of destination Variables on groups
	Day visitors	Home, outbound and inbound (volume and expenditure) Destination Type of activities and motives Profile of participants Duration of trip, distance travelled
	Business travel	Variables on travel patterns Volume of travel, nights spent Expenditure Profile of travellers (employment details) Use of travel agencies
Medium	Holiday market	Variables related to holiday planning Holiday habits
Low	Day visitors	Non-participants

Source: Eurostat, 1992. User Needs for Statistics on Tourism at European Level

(b) Production records, including tests of efficiency of operation by product sector (e.g. occupancy rates for accommodation, load factors for transport).

There are two principal systems; first, the traditional official control records based on police records (hotel registration) or frontier immigration controls, and secondly, sample survey systems, either of traffic flows for example, at ports of entry or transport terminals and tourist sites or centres, or traffic checks by operators. Airlines carry out extensive in-flight surveys. Hoteliers analyse guest records. Household samples are very effective in measuring domestic tourism.

These systems aim to record volume or traffic flows. Expenditure measurement is a more difficult task. Again there are two main methods; first, foreign exchange records through the banking systems, and secondly surveys of travellers, at points on the journey (including borders and ports) or at home. This latter method is relatively reliable if the sample is large enough, whereas the bank reporting method is unsatisfactory, as previously explained.

Volume and value data may satisfy governments' minimum needs, but industry requires much more detailed marketing information which is increasingly sought through trade-supported surveys.

In practice, both needs could be satisfied by survey techniques, and national systems developed for such joint purposes as in the UK have been very successful. They have also been supported substantially by private sector resources. Unfortunately progress in developing compatible systems meeting essential needs on a European basis has been inadequate and the collection of pan-European statistics on travel has suffered, while the industry grows substantially.

The basic unit of measurement is the 'visit', ideally one return trip by one visitor. However, some countries concentrate on visitor nights (one visitor spending one night), Switzerland, for example. If the average length of stay is known, visits or visitors can be estimated, otherwise visitor nights on their own do not provide a practical measure of volume and will not give necessary market information. Countries which concentrate on visitor 'arrivals', usually at frontiers, can also estimate nights stays, if length of stay is known. The 'arrival' statistics are usually more effective for marketing purposes.

Official records normally aim to provide basic information on volume and value, in the form of arrivals, or overnights (night stays), place of permanent residence, to distinguish tourists from residents returning, and expenditure. This will give governments basic information needed to report movement and economic impact, including the share of tourism in the balance of trade and payments.

Key characteristics of the travel movement include:

1 Seasonal variation, traffic by month.
2 Length of stay.
3 Purpose of visit (business, pleasure, health education); in fact the more detailed this classification can be made the better for marketing purposes as segmentation of the total market develops rapidly.
4 Country and place of residence.
5 Destination or places visited.
6 Sociodemographic information (sex, age, income, education).
7 Expenditure (including transport payments).
8 Travel behaviour (transport and accommodation choice).

In addition to these principal characteristics, surveys can provide much additional data from time to time, such as type of travel, arrangement (independent or package tour), and time of booking. Data can be analysed in detail by market segment.

Forecasting, largely a demand projection, is an important task for public sector partnership, especially as an indication of potential for marketing and development action, and to assist sectors and operators in policy formulation and target setting. But simple extrapolation of past records is no longer a reliable base for action in a fast-changing world. In addition to estimation of external factors, consultation with trade experts (Delphi surveys) is an essential ingredient in getting a reliable assessment of changing forces, especially demand trends. These are becoming more volatile as segmentation increases.

Day visits

One of the most difficult tasks is the measurement of day visits and excursions. In many tourism destinations these short visits may account for the major part of substantial movement, with high visitor expenditure. For many areas, short-stay and day visits show a long-term growth trend, whereas length of stay in total declines, especially for main holidays.

Day visits to a resort town can be estimated approximately by a series of checks such as traffic counts on roads, at car and coach parks, rail and air termini, visits to major tourist sites, e.g. cathedrals, castles, town centres, etc. In such places where visitors congregate quota sampling can provide information on satisfaction as well as origin, transport, accommodation and expenditures. Surveys at hotels, restaurants, shops and entertainments can also assist.

For reliable results household surveys are the best method, but they tend to be costly. Because details of short trips are easily forgotten, surveying must be on a continuing basis, and interviews timed within a short time after the trip, if substantial detail is required.

Definitions are a problem and vary from survey to survey. Indeed, to an extent this reflects differing habits according to country or region. A visit of 20 miles (32 km) in an urban area may involve an hour or more travel time. In open country, the USA for example, a day trip of 100 miles (160 km) may not be uncommon. Surveys should use time and distance criteria, (e.g, exceeding three hours away from home and a distance of 25 or 50 miles (40 or 80 km) according to the environment, and to conform to the UN definition of 'outside the usual environment'.

The Department of Employment in Britain published a large national survey of day visits in 1990 (DOE *Leisure Day Visits*, 1988–89). The initiative was continued in 1993 by the Countryside Recreation Network, a consortium of state agencies concerned with recreation, and supported by the Department of National Heritage.

The survey focused on leisure day visits from home made by the adult population (age 15 and over) in Great Britain; 3000 interviews were made from a random selection of households covering the period April–September (summer).

During the period April–September 1993 the adult population of Britain made over 2200 million day visits from home, including 145 million visits from holiday bases, and 52 million business trips. Expenditure (excluding business trips which were not covered) was estimated at £16 900 million an amount almost double total expenditure on all holidays of one night or more in the UK.

The WTO recommends that the concept for same-day visitors should be the same as for tourism in general 'a non routine break away from the usual environment'. The term international same-day visitors describes an international visitor who visits another country for less than 24 hours and does not stay overnight. Cruise passengers and crew members are included. The definition of same-day domestic visitor is similar. However, there are various types of domestic same-day visits which may need to be distinguished separately:

1 Round trip starting from usual place of residence.
2 Round trip starting from a place of second residence or from the place visited by the tourist.
3 During the course of a trip, whatever the purposes, a stopover by air, by sea (cruise or other trip where the passenger stays aboard ship), a stopover on a trip by land without an overnight stay.

Alternative methods

Liberalization of international travel and removal of controls is much to be desired. 'Borderless' Europe is becoming a reality. One result of the removal of frontiers and police controls, such as the hotel registration forms, is the gradual disintegration of the old systems of travel records. This official 'census' of international travel was never perfect. Survey systems tailor-made for tourism are needed and some progress is being made by Eurostat.

It would be possible to secure considerable improvement if the major countries which carry out officially or privately surveys of their domestic market or outward flows use standard systems and the WTO standard definitions. Most official systems are based on inward flows, but in practice full coverage of outward flows would also give satisfactory results, with each country dependent on their neighbours for key information.

Supply-side statistics are important, but this information usually needs to be obtained industry by industry. Operational data are required by each of the main trade sectors, but are not always available. Most countries have some record of accommodation occupancy, and public transport carriers regularly report traffic statistics and load factors. However, it is not always easy to translate these into tourist movement, and in certain cases much of the traffic may not be tourism movement, for example, cross-border commuter traffic, migration, transport staff.

Supply-side information is also useful for governments in attempting to include tourism in systems of national accounts, although much of this work is currently rather theoretical. The World Travel and Tourism Council (WTTC) commissioned the Wharton Econometric Forecasting Associates (WEFA) group in the USA to assess the size, scope and importance of the travel and tourism industries in terms of gross output, value added, capital investment, employment and tax contributions. They hope in this way to demonstrate that tourism is the world's largest industry, and to produce convincing data comparable with measures of GNP and the contribution of other main industries to national and world economies.

The WTO, in its recommendation to the United Nations Statistical Commission, advocated a restructuring of standard industrial classification systems (SICs), so that tourism as a major element in economic activity could be identified, described and reported adequately to governments. In this way it is hoped that the role of tourism will be better understood by governments in formulating public policies and initiating economic development programmes. The WTO's recommendations for the introduction of a Standard Industrial Classification of Tourism Activities (SICTA) was approved by the United Nations Statistical Commission in 1993, together with WTO recommendations for definitions and concepts in tourism measurement. The SICTA conforms to the general International Standard Industrial Classification (ISIC), accepted officially.

There are problems, since tourism measurements are largely demand based, whereas national accounts systems are based mainly on the supply side and industrial output figures.

There is much more work to be done before the results will be of general practical use. Progress towards these macroeconomic measurements is essential if tourism is to be developed adequately in the future, and to ensure that governments play their indispensable role in guiding the growth of the world's largest trade. For example, clear indications of tourism's key role in its contribution to GNP, and in the creation and maintenance of large-scale employment, are essential for the success of mainline governmental policy. Such information will become even more critical as tourism grows in relative importance compared with other economic activities which it seems likely to do.

Sources of data

In recent years there has been a great change in the source of data. Originally governments were the main if not the sole producer of statistical information on travel. With the enormous expansion of world tourism, and the participation of large commercial organizations, and the increasing interest of technical and academic institutions, there has been a substantial expansion of research. This new and major source of data, probably now in total greater in volume than the official material, which has been declining in scope and reliability, takes two forms. First, economic and social studies measure the growing importance of tourism and its impact on economies and societies, and secondly, market research helps efficient operation by large companies such as international airlines. A variety of techniques is used, including surveys and records of travellers and potential markets.

There is a problem that much of the new information is not easily accessible and indeed if commercially valuable may be kept confidential. However, much is published and available for more general use. This is the case with the increasing activity of national tourism organizations and the professional sector bodies which carry out much of their work on a cooperative basis. For example, British, American, German and a number of other major country studies on outgoing travel markets are available. Segmentation studies on American and European senior citizens' travel, or on social, cultural and business travel, are carried out from time to time by international groups and commercial organizations. An independent annual report on world and North American travel (the *Travel Industry World Year Book*) has been published for some years in the USA giving a useful overview of trends and statistics.

The OECD, representing the governments of the richer industrialized countries of the world, produces an annual report 'Tourism Policy and International Tourism in OECD Member Countries', which is a valuable account of recent developments in international tourism. This analyses tourist flows to and from member countries. International tourist receipts and expenditure are fully reported. These annual reports also examine in depth major issues from time to time, such as transport and tourism, and more recently the role of government in tourism, especially in regard to promotion and employment.

The EU began to take an interest in tourism only in recent years, and their statistical office Eurostat has so far made a limited contribution. One of the first activities was a European Holiday Survey 'Europeans on Holiday' which reported on European holiday movement in the 12 member countries in 1985. This was a useful exercise, as the information generally available on a comparative European basis was difficult to find. The weakness was, and is, that the exercise was not repeated so that there are no trend indications.

Principal official sources are, first, national governments and their national tourism offices, for source material on a national basis, and secondly, intergovernmental bodies for editing and collating national material to provide an international account. The WTO provides the most comprehensive data of edited information from the individual countries' official figures. The statistics are well presented and published regularly with some inevitable delay, covering volume, value (expenditure) and varying degrees of additional data on transport, seasonality and visitor demographics and behaviour.

In addition, the WTO publishes useful forecast information based on studies of past traffic records and expert advice on changing trends and the influence of external factors, such as economic trends, political and security impacts. The work of the WTO in the statistical field is of a high standard, but inevitably it is in the main an editing or collecting task rather than an original source. The problems of deteriorating raw material affects the results. Volume figures are shown as visitor arrivals not individual visitors or travellers, so that world regional comparisons can be unreliable. Expenditure figures can be suspect. Total movement if not broken down by market segment cannot be a sure base for future projections, when demand changes can be sudden and massive, as the dramatic short-term falls in transatlantic movement to Europe, and intra-European package travel to Spain, in recent years have shown.

Progress is slow, as the action lies mainly with national authorities where there is limited coordination in method and data. However, following the implementation of the EU Directive on Tourism Statistics (1995), governments will be required to introduce a system of minimum reporting on demand covering domestic and outward tourism, based on each country's own statistical survey. Incoming traffic likewise is to be measured according to an agreed common methodology by supply-side figures of overnight stays in commercial accommodation. This unfortunately will not provide the data needed on demand, with little or no information on expenditure.

The EC has carried out an extensive programme of studies under the Tourism Action Plan 1993–95 on economic, cultural and social aspects of tourism. Some but not all have been published or have been the subject of a seminar with trade and professional sector interests participating. The action plan recognized the importance of work to improve the knowledge of tourism and the industry in general. Most of these studies were not part of a continuing series, nor related to a follow-up programme, and so were limited in value.

Market research information can be helpful in filling in the 'gaps', but it is often restricted because of commercial competitive values. A number of institutions both in the public and private sector publish useful material from time to time. The European Travel Commission, with industry support including the European Tourism Action Group (ETAG), sponsors research, sometimes in cooperation with the EC, in such fields as forecasting and market segmentation studies (e.g. senior citizen, youth and incentive travel). The Pacific Asia Travel Association and other regional bodies have useful research programmes.

The WTTC to which reference has already been made, publishes estimates of current and forecast gross output, contribution to GDP, employment, investment, tax revenues and other tourism economic impacts, based on new research. The council publishes its information at world, region and country level.

The European Travel Monitor, a non-government initiative, carries out a continuous survey of 24 West and East European countries, including all the major states, interviewing 360 000 European residents about their travel abroad. These are covered in a comprehensive way, by volume, expenditures, residence and area visited, by time of year, length and purpose of stay, and details of services used. The data is capable of extensive analysis by segment and region, and published yearly.

National tourist offices in many countries have a long record of comprehensive market research, increasingly carried out with industry support. Britain has one of the best systems. Its island location facilitates measurement of traffic flows in and out through a relatively small number of sea and airports.

International movement is surveyed at a number of ports continuously throughout the year. This International Passenger Survey (IPS) carried out by government (the Office for National Statistics) covers foreign travel in detail, volume characteristics, expenditures, length of stay, etc. Both incoming and outgoing (residents) travel is surveyed. Results are published in the *Business Monitor* regularly.

In addition, the state tourist organizations have devoted their own extensive surveys. For example, the British Tourist Authority (BTA) and the English, Scottish and Wales Tourist Boards carry out continuing household and other surveys to report in detail on British residents' travel and expenditure at home and abroad (*United Kingdom Tourism Survey Annual*). These surveys are much used by the commercial sector because they provide essential market research data for which the businesses concerned pay.

The IPS carries questions from other agencies from time to time to provide additional information on key sectors, such as business travel (e.g. the size and make-up of visits to Britain).

The BTA and ETB publish a variety of survey and statistical reports of value, notably a *Digest of Tourist Statistics*, and a *Tourism Intelligence Quarterly*.

A number of National Tourism Offices or Government Tourism Ministries publish useful data and survey material on a regular basis. France, Germany, Netherlands and other large countries, for example, are covered by regular large-scale surveys.

Governments and their National Tourism Offices, institutions such as the WTTC, and commercial companies, notably aircraft manufacturers, airlines and their associations (the International Air Traffic Association, (IATA) and the Association of European Airlines (AEA)) prepare forecasts and publish useful statistics.

Large consultancy firms also publish studies and related statistics on hotel operations, investment and profitability. There are quite extensive statistical reports on hotel occupancy, some official and some unofficial.

Other sectors prepare and publish studies and statistics from time to time. Some are also covered by official records, especially in transport and employment. Government regulation can be the basis for supply-side data, such as the records of licensed establishments (hotels, taxis, travel agents, etc.).

Summary

Tourism is not only the world's largest trade, but a phenomenon of great social as well as economic importance. It is a mass movement of people impacting on a large number of destinations visited and many service trades, with major consequences.

Regional measurement of such impacts are important for governments and industry sectors alike. There is room for a much closer partnership to improve the knowledge and understanding of this industry. Government organizations such as WTO, OECD and the EU have recognized this and made some attempts to improve the situation. In this decade the UN guided by the WTO and the EU has invested in studies to revise definitions and methodologies to modernize existing systems. Revolutionary progress in information technology should make rapid progress possible. So far, however, implementation of agreed methodology has been slow and resources frustratingly inadequate. Collective action on an international basis, to improve both production and publication of basic and fully compatible data has been lacking.

References

Burkart, A. J. and Medlik, S. (1981) *Tourism: Past Present and Future*, Heinemann, London

Department of Employment (1991) Leisure day visits, *Employment Gazette*, London

World Tourism Organization (1994) *Tourism to the Year 2000 and Recommendations on Tourism Statistics* (a co-publication with the UN) WTO, Madrid

Further reading

British Tourist Authority Digest of Tourist Statistics (1995) No. 19 (annual), and *Tourism Intelligence Quarterly*, London

Countryside Recreation Network UK (1993) *Day Visits Survey*, CRN, Cardiff

European Commission (Eurostat) (1986) *Europeans and Their Holidays*, EC, Luxembourg

European Travel Commission (1995) *Europe's Youth Travel Market*, ETC, Paris

European Travel Monitor, (annual and regular reports), IPK, Munich

Frechtling, D. C. (1996) *Practical Tourism Forecasting*, Butterworth-Heinemann, Oxford, UK

Jefferson, A. and Lickorish, L. (1991) *Marketing Tourism*, Longman, Harlow, Essex, UK

Lickorish, L. (1975) *Reviews of United Kingdom Statistical Sources*, vol. IV, Heinemann Educational Books, London

OECD (1991) *Manual on Tourism Economic Accounts*, Paris.

OECD (1995) *Tourism Policy and International Tourism in OECD Countries*, (annual), Paris

Office for National Statistics, *International Passenger Survey (IPS)*, (annual and regular reports in Business Travel Monitor), DNH, London

Waters Somerset, K. (1995–6) *Travel Industry World Year Book*, Child and Waters Inc., New York

World Tourism Organization, *Year Book of Tourism Statistics*, (annual) WTO, Madrid

World Tourism Organization, *Tourism Market Trends by Region*, Tourism Trends Worldwide, Madrid

World Travel and Tourism Council (1995) *Travel and Tourism Progress and Priorities*, WTTC, Brussels

4 Factors influencing demand for tourism

Introduction

There is a wide range of factors which can influence the demand for tourism. These factors are normally to be found within the tourist-generating countries. However, there are also pull factors which are often based on tourism attractiveness and are determined within the tourism-receiving country. In this chapter we consider the factors which can influence and direct demand.

These factors are not necessarily discrete and for the purpose of exemplification certain arbitrary distinctions are made. For example, an increase in personal real disposable income can give rise to a number of expenditure options. However, we do know from past experience that as real disposable income increases it is likely that a proportion of this net increase will be spent on travel and tourism. Increased disposable income to be spent on travel would also be affected by the availability of leisure time and of a supporting transport infrastructure. In this sense the factors are interlinked; for the sake of exposition they are separated here.

Domestic and international tourism

As described in Chapter 3, it is usual to separate domestic from international tourism and leisure from business travel. Domestic tourism involves a person travelling away from home for recreational or business purposes and is characterized by a trip within the frontiers of a country; for example, a trip for shopping purposes travelling from Bradford to Manchester or from New York to Miami. The trip will involve an overnight stay or otherwise it is classified as an excursion. In the two examples given it will be noted that the two trips involve very different travel distances. For definitional purposes, this does not matter; what distinguishes domestic from international tourism is whether or not the trip is taken within or outside national frontiers. This situation often gives rise to considerable difficulties in analysing trends. In very large countries such as the United States, Australia and the People's Republic of China, long-distance travel (e.g. from Beijing to Gangzhou) would be classified as domestic tourism; a journey from Brussels to Luxembourg, however, would constitute an international trip.

The dichotomy between international and domestic tourism is important for a number of reasons. First, as international travel implies the crossing of a frontier, there is a foreign currency implication. Inbound foreign tourists will bring with them currency to spend in the host country and therefore contribute to the economic impact of tourism. For most countries seeking to attract foreign tourists it is the potential to earn foreign exchange which is the important objective in supporting and developing the tourism sector. For developing countries, it is usually the priority objective (see Chapter 12). Another relevant factor is that on a per capita spend basis, international visitors tend to have a higher per trip spend than domestic tourists.

With the exception of relative higher per visit expenditure and the generation of foreign exchange, domestic and international tourists cause similar general economic impacts; both groups generate employment, incomes, contribute to tax and other revenues, and through locational decisions contribute to regional development. As a global phenomenon, domestic tourism is estimated by the WTO to contribute approximately 80 per cent of all tourism trips, although with a much lower proportion of total tourism spend, but is a major force in tourism. That disproportionate emphasis is given to international tourism is based largely on its foreign exchange potential. In many developing countries the domestic tourism market is small and economically insignificant.

It is not only the expenditure of the visiting international tourist which is of importance but also the ancillary expenditure, eg. transportation costs. A French visitor to Australia travelling on Quantas airline would contribute a foreign exchange credit to the Australian economy. A ticket purchased on Air France would effectively remain within the French economy. As tables of international tourism receipts exclude air fares, these gross figures often substantially understate the total revenues generated by tourism activity. For countries with airlines that have extensive international networks, air fares can be a major source of foreign exchange as Table 4.1 shows for the UK.

In considering the determinants of demand, it is useful to separate economic from social determinants, and structural from motivational determinants. The structural determinants also give us some insight into the short-term and the long-term trends in demand.

Economic determinants of demand

Leisure travellers

The major economic determinant of demand is the availability to the potential tourists of a sufficient level of real discretionary income. Real income is a measure used to track the purchasing power of income. Real income is the purchasing power of received income after adjusting it to take into account inflation. For example, an increase in a person's annual income by 10 per cent is a nominal increase; if inflation, as measured on a cost of living index is 5 per cent per annum, the increase in the real income is only 5 per cent. Once the person has received his net income, i.e. after statutory deductions for taxes, insurances and pensions, this is termed as disposable income. From the disposable income the person will meet basic living

Table 4.1 Fares: credits and debits, 1989–94

	Sea transport £m						Civil aviation £m						Total £m					
	1989	1990	1991	1992	1993	1994	1989	1990	1991	1992	1993	1994	1989	1990	1991	1992	1993	1994
Credits: passenger revenue (visitors to the UK)	165	172	163	199	200	197	1590	1833	1630	1907	2182	2340	1755	2005	1793	2106	2382	2538
Debits: passenger revenue (visitors from the UK)	282	337	358	428	458	455	1965	2088	1934	2181	2425	2503	2247	2425	2290	2609	2883	2958

* Figures are rounded, so that component figures may not add up to totals. The credit items refer to payments made to UK carriers by passengers who were visitors to the UK; the debit items refer to payments made to foreign carriers by passengers who were visitors from the United Kingdom.

Source: Credits and Civil Aviation Debits: BTA Estimate; Sea Transport Debits; Department of Transport, London, 1994.

expenses such as mortgage or rent payments, heating, food, clothes and similar expenditure. After these necessary expenditures have been met the remaining income is termed as discretionary income, it is that proportion of his disposable income which he is free to spend (or save) as he wishes. In totality, it is the availability of discretionary income which determines demand for tourism.

Although economists have measured demand for travel and tourism at the macro level, i.e. relating changes in real income levels to overall demand (number of trips made), an important travel determinant for leisure travel is family income levels. The extension of the working family (working wives/partners) has considerably increased family per capita income levels.

From an economic perspective what is important is derived demand, i.e. a desire and ability to travel, supported by a sufficient income level to facilitate this desire. Potential demand is where the necessary conditions to facilitate travel exist, but for some reasons people choose either not to become domestic or international tourists. It is well known, for example, that over 90 per cent of the American population have not taken an international trip. There is potential to do so, but for whatever reasons this has not happened. Potential markets are important because they are areas where tourism marketing can be targeted.

Business travellers

The business travel market is very large and is international in scale, as Table 4.2 shows. Business travel is affected by economic circumstances but, for most companies, travel by their representatives is essential rather than a luxury expenditure. In times of business decline or recession, companies may switch from a higher to lower class of air fare, from expensive to less expensive hotels, or limit the duration and number of trips. Forgoing an annual holiday is not going to be life-threatening to the potential tourist; a failure to overcome recessionary conditions could be for a business. Therefore, business travel, even at lower levels, will continue when leisure travel might suffer severe disruption because of prevailing economic circumstances.

Table 4.2 European outbound trips, 1990–94

Purpose of trip	Trips (millions)	Share (%)
Holiday trips	163	76
Change 1994/93		+ 2
Visits to friends and relatives/other trips	22	10
Change 1994/93		− 13
Business trips	29	14
Change 1994/93		− 2

Source: *European Travel Monitor*, 1994/93.

Business travellers have broadly similar demand characteristics as leisure travellers – they require transport, accommodation, food and services. The main differences relate to the types of services bought and the levels of transport and accommodation. Many business travellers will buy executive class air tickets and choose hotels which in location and services provided will facilitate the conduct of their business. Expenses will be paid for by their companies and not from personal resources. Business travellers will therefore tend to be higher per visit spenders than tourists; their net value to destinations will usually be higher than leisure travellers.

Business travellers can also be an important part of tourism by utilizing their non-business time for leisure pursuits. So a business traveller in Delhi, for example, might take advantage of his location to use free time to visit the Taj Mahal. Similarly, a business visitor to Sydney might visit the Opera House. Tourism organizations in many countries have been slow to realize the potential of business travellers to become leisure travellers when they are at their destinations.

Supply factors

Although levels of real discretionary income are the main determinants of demand for tourism, there are also supply factors which 'pull' tourists to specific destinations. Some of these factors include the supply of accommodation and amenities and the ease of access to the destination. These factors combined can be regarded as a measure of the attractiveness of the destination. Relative attractiveness is an important aspect of choosing a destination, but will always be constrained by the budget available to the potential tourist. For example, if a potential tourist has a holiday budget of £1000 (including discretionary spending money at the destination) available, he or she will not consider holidays costing in excess of £1000. As most travellers calculate holiday budgets as a total, i.e. cost of holiday plus spending money, not many people will squeeze the discretionary expenditure part of their budget to a level which might jeopardize the enjoyment of their holiday. For these reasons the travel cost of the proposed holiday will constrain the range, choice and destinations and the concept of relative value will become important in the actual choice of destination. Real discretionary income levels will determine the volume of demand for tourism; relative prices will influence the choice of destination.

The price levels in the destination will be affected not only by the cost structures within the particular country, but also according to the level of exchange rate which applies. This can be demonstrated by looking at travel trends between the USA and Europe. When the dollar moves to a stronger position against European currencies, then more American travellers come to Europe because Europe becomes a cheaper destination. The reverse applies when the dollar declines in value against the European currencies. The parity of exchange rates has a role in determining where people travel, but in an era of floating exchange rates the time lags between purchasing and taking a holiday can mean that fluctuations in exchange rates no longer have the same influence that they once had. For example, if a Spaniard purchases a holiday in the USA and if the peseta should decline against the dollar, i.e. making the USA a more expensive destination, the Spaniard is unlikely to cancel that holiday, particularly if it involves a cancellation charge. The cancellation charge itself might be greater than the actual increase in his holiday expenditure budget caused by the change in the exchange rate. This is a very complicated area, but generally the volume of demand for international travel is determined by the growth in real incomes and particularly in real discretionary incomes. The direction of demand is affected in the short term by motivational and marketing factors and in the longer term will be influenced by relative changes in exchange rates and travel prices. The precise influence will depend very much on the income elasticity of demand and how that is affected by exchange rate influence on prices.

It should be noted that exchange rates reflect general economic conditions within a country. Many of the factors which affect exchange rates, such as rate of inflation, balance of payments and economic outlook, are important national economic indicators but may not be particularly relevant to the visiting tourist who is more concerned with the relative prices of tourist consumption items, e.g. accommodation, food, drinks, shopping, and so on. Some countries have tried to reflect tourism-specific items in a tourism cost of living index, attempting to disaggregate tourism from general consumption items. At the simplest level this is done by tour operators who cost items such as a 'meal for four', 'bottle of wine' or a 'packet of cigarettes'. The attempt is to provide a relative cost of purchasing these items compared to similar purchases in the home country. It further attempts to differentiate destinations on the basis of 'value-for-money'.

The value-for-money concept is very important at all levels of holiday expenditure. It is particularly significant at the lower levels of budget because it provides more purchasing power for the discretionary expenditure portion of the holiday budget. Macro evidence of this fact can be seen in Europe, where relatively rich countries such as Germany, France and Britain have significant outflows of tourists to relatively poor and therefore cheaper countries such as Greece, Portugal and Turkey.

In addition to the relative price factors, the quality of amenities and accommodation at a destination will influence demand. There has to be a sufficient critical mass of attractions, supported by accommodation and good access to stimulate market demand. In many countries where tourism is based on a limited range of attractions, e.g. beach tourism in the Caribbean area, then there can be a high degree of substitution between country destinations. Countries have to develop a range of attractions which in totality enable some form of market differentiation to take place.

Real disposable income levels facilitate travel. However, as the importance of the inclusive tour has increased, so the nature of the travel decision has changed. The packaging of travel has meant that tour operators have actually become surrogates for the individual travellers. This means that the tour operator will package destinations and offer that package to the potential tourist. In this sense the potential tourist buying a package from a travel agency or a tour operator will be choosing from a range of products which have been interpreted for him by the tour operator. The tour operator then becomes the 'interpreter and coordinator' of demand. It is the tour operators' specialist knowledge which allows them to offer particular destinations, knowing that there is a market for that destination within a particular price band.

Most tourists, except repeat visitors, do not have a good knowledge of a location. The holiday purchase decision is made within the individual's budget constraint. They have a notional idea of how much they want to spend on a holiday and their choice will take place within a range of prices available and products. Over a period of time it is the tour operator who promotes or drops destinations according to his interpretation of the relative price and value for money attractions of the area. So, in many cases, it is the tour operator who provides the major channel of demand for international tourism. However there are now large numbers of experienced foreign travellers able to make their own individual travel arrangements and enjoy the freedom and flexibility this offers.

Transport

For intercontinental travel the main mode of transport is by air (Chapter 8), whereas within Europe it is by car and coach, taking advantage of a well-developed road network and relatively short distances. Also in Europe, the growing network of high-speed rail routes has offered point-to-point journey options. There is now a wider choice of travel options for tourists, particularly since the opening of the Channel Tunnel. Rail developments have speeded travel times and have done much to bring trains back into consideration for journeys up to four hours or so.

Improvements in aircraft technology and the development of safe, reliable and punctual services have shrunk destinations in terms of time; for example Singapore and Hong Kong are now just 13 hours' non-stop flight from London. The extension of long-haul flight services, together with the ability of tour operators to reduce prices by special package deals, have created new long-haul destinations. The improved ability of airlines through development of computer reservation systems (CRSs) to offer 'seat sales' on certain routes has further stimulated independent air travel. The price effect stemming from developments in air transport has been a major catalyst channelling potential into actual demand.

Non-economic factors

There are a number of non-economic factors which influence demand for international tourism. It is useful to divide these into structural and motivational factors.

Structural factors

One of the long-term factors affecting demand is the way in which population structure changes.

Population

Population is the raw material of tourism. In analysing tourism demand, absolute population numbers have very little relevance. If we look at the population sizes in the world we find, not surprisingly, that many of the poorest countries have some of the very largest populations. It is not only the size of population which is important but also the ability to afford holidays and travel. The ratio between population and the propensity to travel is quite surprising, with some of the smallest countries of the world having some of the highest propensities to travel. In Europe which has been a traditional supplier of tourists, we find that certain trends are emerging which are beginning to slow this growth. There are three trends which are important.

First, in many European countries, particularly those which have traditionally supplied tourists to the international market, there are declining birth rates. This obviously has the effect of not only reducing new entrants to the international market, but it also means that population is stagnating or declining and is certainly ageing. Because of this ageing, it is now fashionable to describe a new 'third age' market or an area which is sometimes called 'grey' tourism. The third age market has importance in its own right because these are people who have largely discharged family responsibilities and have fairly high levels of disposable income, and also have the ability and time to travel.

Secondly, the effect of declining birth rates obviously means that average family size reduces. The reduction in family size, coupled with growing levels of disposable income means that more family income is available to buy holidays and travel. Within this trend there is the changed role of women. In Western countries, women are increasingly becoming a larger proportion of the workforce. The development of contraception suggests that birth rates in the future will continue to stagnate, possibly decline, and that most family units will see a rising discretionary expenditure possibility. These trends are supported by changes in social attitudes towards holiday taking.

Thirdly, in every developed country employees are entitled to paid holidays, an entitlement which has increased over the years. A growing number of people are now taking more than one annual holiday, with one of their holiday trips being international.

Leisure time activity

In developed countries the improvement in living standards together with the activities of trade unions have increased the average worker's entitlement to paid holidays. The increased entitlement is reflected in a number of ways. First, by the reduction in the average working week; secondly, by the reduction in the average working year; and thirdly, by the reduction in the average working life. The latter reductions are particularly important for international tourism demand. It is a common phenomenon now for most people in developed countries to take at least two holidays a year. The concept of the second holiday is well developed, particularly through activities in the travel industry with the emergence of weekend breaks and special event packages.

As people retire earlier with better health standards and pension rights, there is a growing volume of people who have the time, health, inclination and income to travel. The so-called third age tourist has become a particular feature of the international market, certainly within and from the European countries. It is an interesting phenomenon and one which may yet change in the future. As people live longer and remain healthier there is a growing view that early retirement, i.e. around the age of 55, is no longer an expectation. Many people are legally challenging the rights of government to curtail their working careers. For example, in the UK the pension age for women has recently risen to equate with that of working men, i.e. 65 years. In the USA there have been legal challenges to an early retiral age. Obviously over a period of time these trends may vary, but at present there is no doubt that the increasing availability of paid leisure time, the fitness of people to travel and the growing importance of travel and holidays as social activities will stimulate demand. It is not only the level of demand which will change, but also the nature of demand. The ageing market now characteristic of Europe will provide a more discerning, flexible and quality-conscious market; changing market structures will have a significant effect on travel patterns and motivations.

Motivational factors

There are a number of motivational factors which are important as determinants of demand for travel. The factors will vary according to countries but perhaps five are sufficiently important to be regarded as generally applicable – education, urbanization, marketing, the travel trade, and destination attractions.

Education

In most developed countries education is a compulsory requirement, at least until the age of 16. As people progress through the education system we find that growing numbers go on to secondary and tertiary levels. There is a correlation between the level of education and the income levels which are earned by groups in society. We find from American studies particularly that there is a well-developed correlation between the level of education achieved by a person and his or her propensity to travel. There is believed to be a connection between the level of education and a person's cultural curiosity. Many long-haul travellers, perhaps because of the expense of the journey, are relatively wealthy people, often with high education levels.

At the other extreme, other long-haul travellers are budget tourists sometimes associated with the ubiquitous phrase 'back-packers'. These are people, usually young, who are prepared to travel often vast distances, to seek information, knowledge and experience. The proliferation of travel guides, e.g. *Lonely Planet*, provides some testimony to the scale of this market.

Urbanization

It is noticeable that most international tourists live in urban areas. This reflects the fact that people living in urban areas tend to enjoy higher income levels than people living in rural areas. They are also more exposed to television and media information, which includes travel data. Most urban environments are well served with a network of travel agents, tour operators and transport hubs. These factors combine to influence the number of holiday trips.

Many people living in urban areas experience a higher level of pressure in terms of their living environment compared with people in non-urban areas. This tendency is often seen in the choice of holiday destinations, where the urban dweller will seek holiday destinations which give them a different environment from that in which they usually live. Environmental quality and the quality of holiday experience are both becoming very important determinants of demand.

Environmental quality will become one of the 'pull' factors which induce tourists to visit one destination rather than another. As seen in Chapter 7, environmental management is a key factor in sustaining development. A growing realization that resources are finite and therefore must be used carefully is now permeating tourism development planning.

Marketing

One of the motivational factors in tourism is the promotion which is aimed at the potential tourist. There is a plethora of publicity material, some general and some specific, which has become a relatively well-developed art form.

For most people a tourism destination is bought 'sight unseen'. This means that many tourists are first-time visitors to a destination. Because they lack personal knowledge of the destination, many tourists have bought a holiday on the recommendation of friends or through media information. In a world where many countries offer a fairly homogeneous tourism product, such as beach tourism, mountain tourism or skiing, tourist destinations have to segment their markets, with the segmentation taking place on the basis of attempting to differentiate a product. So, for example, two relatively identical beach destinations might be differentiated by the potential travellers through associated factors, perhaps that one beach is to be found on a tropical island whereas another might be found as part of a more urbanized environment, such as Antigua or Puerto Rico. Marketing is a very important factor in the development of tourist destinations. Motivation for travel is stimulated by advertising and by the provision of information.

Marketing of tourism is considered in Chapter 9. Sufficient to say here that it is one of the most influential factors determining the choice of a holiday destination. Potential tourists are influenced by publicity material, other media and by recommendations made by the travel trade.

The travel trade

The travel trade, including tour operators and travel agents collectively, exerts a considerable influence on the holiday decision. As more destinations come onto the market and holiday and travel literature proliferates, it is becoming more difficult for the independent traveller to access and understand the information available. The emergence of CRSs has made access to information quicker and booking almost instantaneous – but not for the independent traveller. As more potential travellers seek advice and information from the travel trade, they become open to persuasion. The travel trade can influence and often change initial perceptions of a proposed destination. This power of influence is reinforced by the customer's need for reassurance relating to his travel arrangements and choice of destination. It is this 'reassurance factor' which is often a powerful motivator in choosing a destination.

Destination attractions

People travel to satisfy a range of personal needs, both physical and psychological. Potential travellers can be grouped into market segments (cultural tourists, winter sports, gambling, diving, etc.), which are then targeted. The wide range of special interests has created its own markets. The individual traveller has his own motivations – the destination is developed to provide the facilities for the particular market. There are many examples: gambling facilities in Las Vegas and in the Bahamas; cultural tourism at the Edinburgh Festival; hiking in Nepal. Matching markets to facilities is the purpose of tourism promotion; it is part of the process which can influence the potential tourist to choose one destination in preference to another.

Summary

From this chapter is will be appreciated that tourism demand is influenced by many factors – financial, economic, social and cultural. Special interests are particularly powerful motivators; however, essentially demand is a function of real discretionary income levels conditioned by motivating factors.

Further reading

Bull, A. (1995) *The Economics of Travel and Tourism*, 2nd edn, Pitman, London

Cooper, C., Fletcher, J., Gilbert, D. and Wanhill, S. (1993) *Tourism: Principles and Practice*, Pitman, London

Pearce, D. (1995) *Tourism Today: A Geographic Analysis*, 2nd edn, Longman, Harrow, UK

Pearce, D. (1996) *Tourism Development*, 2nd edn, Longman, Harrow, UK

Vellas, F. and Becherel, L. (1995) *International Tourism*, Macmillan Press, Basingstoke, Hants, UK

5 Economic impacts of tourism

Introduction

The main economic impacts of tourism relate to foreign exchange earnings, contributions to government revenues, generation of employment and income, and stimulation to regional development. The first two effects take place at the macro or national level, whereas the other three impacts occur at sub-national levels. These effects are interrelated but for analytical purposes it useful to separate them.

Before examining these impacts it should be noted that with the exception of earning foreign exchange the other economic impacts can also be gained from domestic tourism activity. However, encouragement of domestic tourism may save foreign currency which would otherwise be spent on foreign travel. Obligations under the General Agreement on Trade and Tariffs (GATT) and the newer General Agreement of Trade in Services (GATS) would prevent most if not all developed countries from introducing measures to limit their citizens travelling outside their respective countries. It is still prevalent in most developing countries to have limits on the amount of foreign currency made available to citizens for travel abroad for leisure purposes, in order to conserve scarce foreign exchange reserves.

Domestic tourism therefore can still be of considerable significance in relation to the national economy. Unlike international tourism, domestic tourism represents a transfer of purchasing power within the economy.

International economic impacts

It is now generally accepted that international tourism constitutes one of the most significant of global trade flows. As a conglomerate, multi-faceted activity it is difficult to be precise about the value of international tourism. It is probably the biggest sector in the world economy. It has been a noticeably resilient activity, less prone to economic fluctuations than other sectors. There are no grounds for suggesting that future global demand will decline.

International tourism has two main impacts; first, in trade, and secondly, in its redistributive effects.

The trade effect is a characteristic of tourism demand. As tourists travel to visit countries, the act of travelling itself stimulates trade. Most long-haul travellers travel by air. Most aeroplanes are manufactured in and then exported from the USA. At the destination the tourist might use accommodation owned and managed by non-residents and consume some food and drink not supplied domestically. For example, a German tourist visiting Sri Lanka might arrive on Air Lanka using a DC10 aircraft (made in the USA), stay in a foreign owned and managed hotel (Taj Group India), drink French wine and Scotch whisky and eat Australian beef. To the tourist-receiving country these imports represent leakages. To the international economy they constitute trade opportunities and generate exports.

The redistributive effect of international tourism refers to the fact that most international tourists come from high-income developed countries and spend a part of their discretionary income in lower income countries by the purchase of holidays. In this sense some of the surplus spending power of the richer countries is through tourism redistributed to other countries, many of them being in the developing world. The relatively wealthy countries of Western Europe and North America are major generators of tourists. Those countries with high surpluses on balance of payments, such as Japan, encourage residents to travel abroad as one means of reducing and redistributing the surplus.

These redistributive effects are important as they provide for developing countries one of the very few opportunities to enter tariff-free export development. International tourism has specific impacts on the tourist-receiving countries.

Balance of payments

The balance of payments of a country reflects at a particular time a set of accounts representing the country's trade with the rest of the world. Trade flows are given in financial terms and there are three main accounts. The current account has two sections, the merchandise account, i.e. the import and export of physical commodities like rice, tea, coffee, cars; and the invisible account, which includes mainly services such as tourism, insurance, and banking remittances. It is on the current account that reference is made to deficits or surplus on balance of payments. The capital account reflects the import and export of capital by government and the private sector. In most non-oil-exporting developing countries, grants and loans represent the main inflow of capital. The reserve account shows the countries' reserves of gold and currencies.

Balance of payments accounts must balance either by a transfer to or from reserves or by external borrowing. In most non-oil-exporting developing countries there are usually deficits on current accounts, often of a long-standing and chronic nature. In those developing and developed countries with a large tourism sector, earnings from tourism help reduce and occasionally eradicate such deficits. This has long been the case in Italy and in Spain, for example. It is also true in countries such as the Bahamas, Fiji and Thailand. It is this potential to earn foreign exchange which is the major reason for governments' support for tourism in developing countries and also in many developed countries.

Balance of payments accounts are interpreted by government and international observers as reflective of the economic health of a country.

There can be factors which dislocate the accounts in the short term, e.g. concentrated import of capital goods in one particular year such as purchases abroad of oil rigs to be used in the North Sea. Another example would be imports of a number of commercial aircraft. The dislocating effect comes from the fact that the balance of payments in these examples reflects import costs, but cannot show these items as capital assets which will give rise to income flows in the future. Care has to be taken in interpreting monthly and annual accounts. However, a continuing deficit on the current account will be interpreted as a negative sign, i.e. the country is not able to cover its imports through export earnings. Inevitably, this will lead to a reduction in the par value of the national currency against other currencies. The reduction in the par value (or exchange rate) of the national currency will obviously make future imports more expensive and exports cheaper, but may eventually work through the economy to make export prices rise. A weakening currency can attract more tourists as the country destination becomes relatively cheaper. Whether increased tourist arrivals will compensate for the deficit on balance of payments will be uncertain.

Tourism and foreign exchange earnings

Foreign exchange earnings from tourism are the receipts of non-domestic currency earned by selling goods and services to foreign tourists. It is useful to classify earnings into hard, i.e. convertible currencies and soft, non-convertible currencies. Hard currencies such as the US dollar, the deutschmark, the yen and the Swiss franc are freely convertible, internationally acceptable and can be exchanged without restriction. As these currencies are issued by the most economically advanced countries they are most used in international trade. On the other hand, soft currencies are those which are not freely convertible, and have severe limitations imposed on exchange outside their country of issue, such as the Indian rupee or the Thai baht.

However, there is a discernible trend for more countries to make their currencies freely convertible. Although this trend will make more currencies available for trading, it does not mean that traders will want to use or hold these currencies. The more unstable the economic situation in a country, the greater the prospect of currency fluctuation and therefore losses on currency holdings or on trading contracts.

The value of a currency is expressed as an exchange rate, which is the value of a unit of one currency against a unit of another, e.g. pound to dollar. The determination of nominal and real exchange rates is a complex subject. A nominal exchange rate is that which is quoted for one particular currency against another at a particular date. This is the rate which a tourist receives when buying and exchanging foreign currency. A real exchange rate is the currency dealers' view of the 'true' value of any currency, i.e. what its 'true' or 'real' purchasing power is in the international market relative to other major trading currencies. The real exchange rate is important for future transactions, with many forward contracts having different rates quoted for buying specified currencies one, two and three months ahead of delivery. For tour operators who have to pay future accounts in foreign currencies, the forward exchange market is important as a means of hedging against major currency fluctuations and limiting potential losses through currency depreciation.

Most governments in developing countries encourage international tourism because such tourists usually travel from hard currency countries. Earnings of hard currency permit governments to finance, at least in part, their development efforts. Estimates of foreign exchange earnings from tourism are usually derived from sample surveys of tourist expenditures and returns from tourism-related activity such as airlines and banks. These estimates are found in the travel account of the balance of payments. Air fare payments are in the transportation account. There are some very serious problems related to the measurement of foreign exchange derived from tourism (Chapter 3). It should be noted that these estimates are usually expressed as gross estimates and in current prices.

Gross earnings mean that no attempt is made to deduct the input costs necessary to earn the receipts. For example, foreign currency earnings received from the sale of air tickets to foreign tourists are not adjusted to account for payments for operating charges overseas, or perhaps to foreign crews. In a similar example, part of the foreign tourist payment for accommodation could accrue to overseas owners of the facilities. These leakages and import content are not calculated in the balance of payments accounts. They are not unique to tourism, but apply to all items of international trade.

Earnings of foreign exchange are also usually expressed in current prices, e.g. the amount of foreign currency earned from tourism in a particular year, say 1996. Unless a deflator is used to express earnings in constant prices, earnings figures will not take into account inflation or changes in par values of currencies. Again this is a complicated area for analysis, but generally caution should be exercised in interpreting figures relating to foreign exchange earnings.

It is possible to make estimates of the net effect of tourism activity on the economy including the earnings of foreign exchange. Probably the most used technique in measuring the impacts of tourism on an economy is the multiplier. Another approach is through the use of input–output tables. Multiplier techniques are not specific to tourism, as they can be used in other sectors of the economy.

Multiplier analysis

Multiplier analysis is used to estimate the ongoing impact of tourist expenditures in the economy. It is recognized that initial tourism expenditure will give rise to import demand to service tourists' needs, and that much of the initial expenditure will percolate through the economy to stimulate further indirect expenditure and expenditure induced by the initial expenditure. These three terms reflect the fact that tourism is a multi-faceted activity. It is essentially interdependent, relying for its activity on inputs from many sectors of the economy, from agriculture, industry and general services. The initial amount of tourism expenditure will generate changes in the economy – in output, income, employment, and contribution to government revenue. The changes in the various categories may be less than, equal to, or greater than the initial (additional) change in tourist expenditure which started the economic process. Tourist multipliers refer to the ratio of changes in output, income, employment and government revenue to the original change in tourist expenditure. Tourist multipliers can be divided into five main types:

1 *Transactions or sales multipliers*. An increase in tourist expenditure will generate additional business revenue. This multiplier measures the ratio between the two changes.
2 *Output multiplier*. This relates the amount of additional output generated in the economy as a consequence of an increase in tourist expenditure. The main difference with the transactions or sales multiplier is that the output multiplier is concerned with changes in the actual levels of production and not with the volume and value of sales.
3 *Income multiplier*. This measures the additional income created in the economy as a consequence of the increased tourist expenditure.
4 *Government revenue multiplier*. This measures the impact on government revenue as a consequence of an increase in tourist expenditure.
5 *Employment multiplier*. This measures the total amount of employment created by an additional unit of tourism expenditure.

There are a number of methodological approaches to calculating multipliers and the choice of methodology will give rise to different coefficients, i.e. in measuring the relative impact of the original increase in tourist spending. An alternative approach is to use an input–output model approach.

Input–output models are constructed to provide a table to represent in matrix form, regional and/or national accounts. Each sector in the economy is shown as a column representing purchases from other sectors in the economy and in row as a sector of each of the other sectors. The purpose of input–output tables is to demonstrate the intersectoral effects caused by increased demand in the economy. The models can be refined to include a tourism column. However, input–output tables require a great deal of data and time to construct, and much of the data is often some years out of date and may not be particularly relevant to the tourism sector.

Although multiplier analysis is widely used as a convenient and readily available technique to measure aspects of the impact of tourism on an economy, its results have to be interpreted with caution. Two such considerations relate to basic data assumptions and the static nature of the multiplier. Often available data are insufficient or unreliable to use in multiplier analysis. Time (and costs) are incurred in collecting suitable data. Tourism, as a multi-sectoral activity will present particular difficulties in generating data.

Multiplier studies are relevant for a period of time. Although they can be updated, there is no guarantee that the basic data used and the interrelationships will remain valid, e.g. that relative prices used remain constant. It should also be noted that multiplier studies are made of specific countries or regions, and the coefficients calculated reflect the particular data used. Therefore two seemingly comparable destinations, such as Barbados and Antigua, or Seychelles and the Maldives, may have very different multipliers.

Despite these cautions, multiplier analysis is a technique which is constantly being refined as more experience of its usefulness and limitations is gained. Compared with input–output analysis it is relatively cheap to use and can generate results quickly. The information on intersectoral linkages arising from tourist expenditure information and the impacts of tourism expenditure in certain sectors of the economy can be very useful to support planning and policy decisions. For example, knowing where tourist expenditures have the most impact on the economy or where import leakages are greatest, provides valuable information for planners. Despite the many limitations of multiplier analysis, it is still the most widely used technique to measure the impact of tourism.

Leakages

International tourism will generate imports. Tourists are short-term stay visitors who bring with them certain expectations relating to accommodation, food, hygiene, etc. To meet these expectations many developing countries have to import goods and services in order to encourage and develop tourism. Payments for these goods and services to support the tourism sector are said to be 'leakages', i.e. part of the tourist expenditure leaks out of the economy to pay for necessary imports. Very few countries, if any, have the resources and means to supply total tourism demand. It is necessary, therefore, to examine the import pattern of the tourism sector to see whether imports can be limited and substituted by domestic production.

Encouragement of domestic production will not only reduce the leakages of foreign exchange, but generate employment and income. The less developed the country or the more open the economy, the greater the leakages are likely to be. An open economy is one which is highly dependent on imports to sustain its activity. In some of the Caribbean island economies, leakage factors of over 50 per cent are common, i.e. 50 cents in every dollar earned is leaked outside the economy. It is a continuing problem and one which economic impact studies can help policymakers identify.

The foreign exchange earnings derived from tourism are overstated because they are gross not net figures. Despite this overstatement, for many countries the tourism sector is a major opportunity to earn foreign exchange. Efforts are made to maximize the impact of these earnings by reducing the need to import goods and services. Because import substitution possibilities are not immediately available does not mean that they cannot be realized in the future. Planning must take into account what is possible. To identify possibilities is the first stage in reducing dependence on a high level of imports.

Contribution to government revenues

Contributions received by government from the tourism sector may be direct or indirect. Direct contributions arise from charging taxes on income; for example, private and company incomes generated by tourism employment and business. Indirect sources of income will mainly comprise the range of taxes and duties levied on goods and services supplied to tourists.

In order that governments might raise revenue there has to be some level of economic activity. As tourism activity increases we can expect it to generate employment, and income. In many developing countries the identifiable labour force is small and the majority of employment is found in agriculture and government service. This employment base often means that identifiable incomes on which taxes can be levied is not the major source of government revenues. Government revenues in most developing countries are derived from indirect taxes, e.g. on land, on crops, on imports. When tourism is a prominent source of employment it does provide an opportunity for government to widen its tax-generating base. In developed countries where the workforce is clearly defined and where company registration policies are in place, government revenue tends to be generated from company and private incomes and indirect taxation is much less significant.

The ability to generate revenue by direct taxation on individual and company incomes should not be overstressed. High levels of taxation will act as disincentives to investors and might deter reinvestment. In some countries where tourism is an important activity, it has been decided not to impose any income or company tax, or to keep the latter at very low levels, such as in the Bahamas. Where this policy is adopted, then government must find alternative ways of raising revenue and this is usually through indirect taxation.

There are a number of ways in which indirect revenues may be generated. These would include 'tourism taxes', i.e. taxes levied on goods and services bought by tourists. A bed tax – a percentage levied by government on the sale of a night's accommodation – will be paid by all users, but in specific regions tourists will be the main users. Indeed, the implementation of the levy originally may have been seen as a means of raising revenue from tourists. Similar reasoning can be applied to the imposition of airport taxes.

In many developing countries governments earn a substantial proportion of their revenues from duties levied on imports. Where the tourism sector is a major importer of goods and materials, this can generate considerable revenues. However, it should be remembered that although import duties are a revenue for government, they are a cost to the importer. Heavy duties will obviously have an effect on prices, which will affect the price competitiveness of a destination. In some countries, even where high levels of duty exist government may still not release foreign exchange for imports. This has recently been the case in, for example, Nigeria and Ghana.

Where tourism is an important sector of the economy, it may provide three main opportunities to contribute to government revenues. First, by direct taxes on personal and company incomes; secondly, by duties on imports; and thirdly, by government charging for the services it provides. These services for tourism can vary between countries. Some governments, such as those of India, Pakistan, Bangladesh and China, operate commercial services for tourists through specialist agencies, sometimes called tourism development corporations. There are historic reasons why this approach may have been adopted. In the four countries cited, government had to provide commercial services due to the inability or unwillingness of the private sector to offer them. Examples include the provision of transport services, handicraft centres and in some cases travel agencies. In most developed countries, governments tend not to provide these commercial services but rather leave them to the private sector.

However, in all countries governments provide general services which benefit tourism, e.g. communications, health and police services. It is perhaps this 'hidden' investment which many people fail to realize. Government has a very supportive role to play in the way in which tourism develops. For example, investment in servicing land for building purposes, the provision of airports, and training facilities. It is also the case that often these facilities, although benefiting tourism, may not be provided for the tourism sector but rather for general development purposes.

Most countries, developed and developing, offer investment incentives to potential investors. Often the cost effectiveness of these measures has not been evaluated. It is suspected that the generosity of these incentives in some cases may outweigh any revenue potential for government. The use of tax holidays and duty drawbacks may well help to establish and develop a tourism sector, but it does not necessarily raise the revenue potential for government.

Tourism can substantially contribute to government revenues, but there is a problem of measurement. One difficulty is in defining what constitutes 'tourism'. Many of the revenue contributions we have noted – import duties, bed taxes, etc. – can be derived from tourism-induced transactions, but they are also generated by non-tourism transactions. There is again the problem of trying to identify the flow of revenue raised from tourism activity. Surveys and multiplier studies can be used to disaggregate expenditure flows and to trace the contributions which are directly from tourism. But tourism expenditures increase general economic activity and this induced activity will also create revenues for government. Government revenues from the tourism sector will vary according to a range of factors, not least being the extent and structure of tourist activity. When a country is heavily dependent on tourism then fluctuations in demand, for whatever reason, will have immediate impact on government budgets. Shortfalls in revenues may well cause governments to alter or suspend development objectives. By measuring the tourism revenue contribution, governments will be more aware of their dependency and vulnerability on this source of income. Although such revenue is difficult to calculate, many governments are major beneficiaries from taxes on tourism activity.

Employment and income

There is considerable debate about how best to measure the employment and income impacts generated by tourism. In most developed countries good statistical information is available on employment and the number of people employed at any one time, but this information does not extend to cover the tourism sector. Despite this good database there are still difficulties in making an estimate of employment in tourism reflecting the fact that tourism is a multi-sectoral activity. Our best estimate of tourism employment in the UK is that approximately 15 per cent of the workforce is currently employed in tourism-related activities. In developing countries where employment is often in informal activities, e.g. beach trades, or in casual work in agriculture, it is difficult to estimate the number of people employed and within that total employment of the number of people involved in tourism.

In most countries, estimates of employment and income from tourism are made from sample surveys, from multiplier studies or from input–output tables. An additional economic consideration at national level is whether jobs and incomes generated by investment in tourism are greater or lesser than if a similar amount of investment had been used in other sectors. For the economist, the concept of efficiency or cost effectiveness is perhaps of prime importance. For the tourism planner it may be the number and quality of jobs which are of significance. For the tourism manager at the operational level, the main concern will probably be whether trained and effective people are available to fill job vacancies. It is therefore possible to examine the employment impact of tourism from a number of different perspectives. Basic to any enquiry into tourism and employment is the means of measuring employment created.

Measurement of employment

Employment generated by tourism is categorized into direct and indirect. Direct employment is defined as jobs which are specifically created by the need to supply and serve tourists. The obvious example is those jobs created by the opening of a tourist hotel. Tourism, however, requires a large input from the construction sector, and those workers employed on building tourism facilities constitute a backward linkage from the tourism sector. These jobs in relation to tourism may be regarded as being indirect in the sense that they will be diverted to other sectors of the economy requiring construction services work when tourism reduces. In countries where tourism is a dominant sector of the economy, it is now usual to find this backward linkage effect constituting an important aspect of total construction sector output.

The disparate nature of tourism activity makes it difficult to estimate the employment impact. Even in developed economies such as the UK the actual number of jobs 'in tourism' is estimated. A favoured 'short cut' is to regard the hotel and catering subsector as being a proxy for the tourism sector. Such a short cut may seriously underestimate the total number of jobs in the tourism sector as a whole. It may also overestimate jobs because many employers in hotels and catering businesses do not provide services for tourists, e.g. industrial catering companies, hospital caterers.

In the absence of national employment records, the only realistic way of estimating employment generated by tourism is by undertaking specific surveys, usually on a sample basis. This does not overcome the problems of which activities constitute tourism or of tracing the indirect effects of specific tourism jobs on demands for output and additional jobs in supplier industries. In the latter case, special surveys will have to be made to make some estimate of demand which arises from the tourism sector, and what proportion of employment is attributable to that demand. Surveys of tourism expenditure will provide indicators to the areas where money is spent and on what. In the same way that income generated by tourist expenditure is capable of being expressed as a multiplier coefficient, so is employment creation. An employment survey will provide employment numbers and can also be used to yield qualitative data on the type of jobs, and perhaps tell us something about the employee. This type of survey is a basic requirement for a manpower planning exercise.

The efficiency, i.e. the cost effectiveness, of job creation in tourism is of interest to the economist. Tourism is often described as a labour-intensive activity. As a simple expression this can be interpreted as meaning that per unit of capital employed, tourism creates more jobs than a similar unit of capital invested in another sector. This relationship is often expressed as being the 'cost per job' in one sector compared with another. In those industries with large-scale operations or technologically sophisticated processes, large investments might create few jobs. An oil refinery is a standard example, where heavy capital investment is required to process the oil but generates few jobs. A similar investment in agriculture or light manufacturing sectors would generate more jobs, i.e. the cost per job generated will be lower and labour intensity greater.

Labour intensity should be distinguished from levels of productivity. The fact that tourism generates more jobs per capital unit invested tells us nothing about the levels of efficiency of work or performance. This is best done by constructing capital output ratios for various sectors. These are imperfect indices, but they do provide some indication of comparative investment output performance.

In many developing countries with growing populations and high levels of unemployment, productivity of labour may not be a prime consideration. As labour is in abundant supply and cheap, it can be substituted for capital in many sectors including tourism. If one of the main features of development strategy is to create jobs, then the nature of tourism as a service activity enhances the possibility of substituting labour for capital. Why import automatic door-opening mechanisms for hotels if jobs can be created by employing a doorman? Why have in-room drinks cabinets if an extended room service will create jobs? These jobs will in turn generate incomes. When considering job creation, one should not completely dismiss the question of labour productivity; cost levels have a direct effect on profitability. This will determine the long-term viability of the company and also relate to whether or not extra investment can be induced. Productivity in the tourism sector is of particular concern in the developed countries.

Types of jobs

Tourism employment is often described as being low skilled or menial. In many countries tourism employment is dominated by women. These comments may or may not be true for each particular destination. What is likely is that employment will be affected by seasonal demand. Out-of-season employee layoffs are common and this has serious implications for workers and their families. Where seasonality is a prevalent feature, then it may well influence planners' attitudes to the desirability of creating (seasonal) tourism jobs as against non-seasonal jobs in other sectors of the economy. It should be noted, however, that for many people, part-time or seasonal work is a preferred option.

The problems of seasonal demand and low-skilled jobs are matters which are legitimate areas for policy consideration. Seasonality can be regarded as a marketing problem. There are two types of seasonality. First, institutional seasonality, i.e. seasonality which occurs because of practices in tourist-generating countries. For example, most holidays in the UK are taken in June, July and August (the summer months), when people either stay at home or travel overseas in search of good climates. Secondly, seasonality can also be a feature of tourist-receiving countries where, for example, climatic changes will make certain times of the year unattractive for visiting tourists.

The question of low-skilled jobs is no different in tourism from where it exists in other sectors. In many tourism areas there may be no other job opportunities. In tourism there is a growing number of highly skilled and well-paid jobs in, for example, large multinational companies, new technology, aviation, and in the marketing of tourism resources and attractions. Every productive sector will have a hierarchy of jobs. The real challenge in tourism is to ensure that nationals can progress up that hierarchy of employment. This again is a policy area, but policies cannot be developed without data to provide a profile of jobs. This profile will help to identify needed skills and where and how these skills might be developed. Without this approach, the need to employ foreign experts over an extended period of time will not only constitute a leakage from the economy, but may give rise to social and political unrest.

Much of the required training for human resource development can be identified from data reflecting the number and types of jobs created in the tourism sector. Without such data it is impossible to develop specific training courses and perhaps specialist training centres which can meet the perceived needs of the tourism sector. In many cases, agencies like the World Tourism Organization and the United Nations Development Programme can contribute expertise and technical assistance.

In an international sector like tourism, it is not simply a matter of job creation, but also the availability of qualified persons to take up these jobs. To the tourism planner, job creation is a quantitative factor; to the tourism manager, the concern is likely to be more qualitative. Both aspects are interdependent. So in considering employment in tourism one is concerned with quantitative and qualitative aspects. The area of human resource planning is one of growing significance in tourism.

Generation of income

The income effect of tourism has been described by reference to the multiplier concept. It is difficult to judge whether income effects arising from tourism employment are greater or lesser than in other sectors. What is known is that tourism activity, which often takes place in rural areas, may also make use of locations, e.g. mountains, jungles, beaches, which have limited alternative economic uses. In these cases, tourism generates a local or regional income *in situ* which no other activity may be able to do.

In economic terms, tourism can generate many benefits, including employment and income, and perhaps improved infrastructure as a consequence of tourism development. In social terms, tourism activity in otherwise economically underdeveloped regions may provide a means of maintaining a level of economic activity sufficient to prevent migration of people to more developed areas of a country. In some of the remote areas of Scotland, such as the Hebridean islands, tourism has helped to diversify rural incomes and sustain communities. Similar experiences are to be found in mid-Wales, and Devon and Cornwall in England. In the Caribbean, e.g. Bahamas, Antigua, and in the Pacific, e.g. Fiji, Tonga, tourism has become the dominant economic activity.

In most developing countries tourism is given government support because of its potential to earn foreign exchange. At the national level this potential might be given the highest priority. At sub-national level, tourism may have priority in one region but not in other. It is not always the case that national and sub-national priorities coincide. In the context of a developed country, in the immediate postwar years the British government encouraged tourism because of its potential to earn foreign exchange and to help reduce the deficit on balance of payments. Increasing emphasis is now being placed on the role of tourism as an employment and income generator in areas of the country where few alternative activities exist.

It may also be noted that in many developing countries tourism-generated incomes are often higher than average income levels. This factor has a number of implications. For the individual, tourism employment often provides not only a higher income level, but also much more pleasant working conditions when compared to much of the alternative work available. The regional economy may be stimulated by higher spending and government may benefit via taxation. For the economy as a whole, higher earnings in the tourism sector can lead to a labour drift from the land or from other sectors and a subsequent need to increase wages in other sectors to prevent further labour drift. The creation of tourism employment and income within a country can engender major policy issues.

The employment and income effects of tourism are interlinked; they are part of the total impact of tourism. Their singular importance is that they trigger the multiplier effect. Income and employment, although treated as statistical concepts, have wider implications. The nature and type of tourism employment has social and cultural implications; the very fact of having a job in tourism may give rise to changes which are essentially social in nature. These changes provide policy issues which may be critical to further development in the sector (Chapter 6).

Regional development

The regional impacts of tourism are often one of the major attractions for economic planners. Tourism can make use of historical and cultural sites, e.g. the Boroburdur Temple Complex in Java, Indonesia; a scenic, natural landscape, e.g. Scotland; historic cities, e.g. London; and natural climate advantages, e.g. Gold Coast in Queensland, Australia – all provide focus for development. Many of these locations have, for different reasons, few alternative economic development possibilities. In the case of Scotland, for example, where tourism is now the dominant sector in the economy, many of the most touristically attractive regions, such as the Highlands and Islands, have very poor agricultural soils, difficult climates and poor infrastructure. For these reasons alternative development, for example light industry or general manufacturing, is not viable. Tourism helps not only to stimulate economic activity in such regions, but perhaps is the only realistic alternative to low-income agriculture.

In the developing world, economic planners are putting more emphasis on how to create and stimulate rural incomes. It is usually the non-urban areas where the poorest people are to be found. If tourism can develop using natural infrastructure and climatic advantage, it often is a cost-effective way of meeting national development objectives.

Summary

Despite these important economic advantages from tourism, there is a growing concern that as tourism is essentially an international exchange of people, and people bring with them their social preferences and prejudices, some inter-cultural conflict may develop. In Chapter 6 some of the non-economic impacts of tourism are examined.

Further reading

Bull, A. (1995) *The Economics of Travel and Tourism*, 2nd edn, Pitman, London

Cooper, C., Fletcher, J., Gilbert, D. and Wanhill, S. (1993) *Tourism; Principles and Practice*, Pitman, London

Johnston, P. and Thomas, S. (eds) (1992) *Perspectives on Tourism Policy*, Mansell, London

Lundberg, D. E., Stavenga, M. H. and Krishnamoorthy, M. (1995) *Tourism Economics*, John Wiley, Chichester, UK

6 Social and cultural aspects of tourism

Introduction

The objective of this chapter is to identify some of the major social and cultural impacts on a society which can result from the development of, or an increase in, tourism. Society can refer to a country, region or specific location and to that group of people who collectively live in a location. Over a period of time, a society will develop its own tradition, attitudes and a style of life which may be more or less distinctive. It is this way of life which is usually incorporated in the word 'culture'.

There is now a well-developed literature on social and cultural impacts of tourism. Many research studies are highly specific, and may therefore be of more academic interest rather than of relevance to policymakers. However, experience in many different countries does constitute general phenomena relating to tourism. In many cases, the regularity with which these phenomena are reported allows policymakers to anticipate certain social and cultural impacts from future planned development of tourism.

It is not the purpose in this chapter to discuss social and cultural impacts of tourism in terms which are meaningful only to sociologists and anthropologists. The intention is to denote 'areas of concern'; that is, to consider some of the non-economic impacts of tourism, what effect they may have on a society, and what problems may arise. Concentration will be on general impacts. This does not preclude the probability that some tourist destination areas might have unusual and highly specific impacts.

It is also worth noting that it is easy to exaggerate impacts arising from tourism. For example, certain areas of a country may never be visited by tourists. Tourist visits to very large countries such as India tend to be concentrated in certain areas or tourist circuits. Therefore, to refer to 'the social and cultural impact of tourism on India' is misleading. Tourism tends to be localized and therefore impacts tend to be localized initially. Whether impacts cause changes, and whether these changes spread through society, will be influenced by a wide range of factors, such as the size of country, general spread of tourism activity, and basic cultural and religious strengths.

It is unfortunate that many of the writers on the social and cultural impacts have tended to react negatively to tourism development. These negative reactions should be viewed in the same way that economic disbenefits are – they are problems which require management solutions.

They will not go away and might intensify. As tourism is a great international exchange of people, it is as important to plan for human satisfaction as it is for economic needs.

Until the mid-1970s most studies of tourism concentrated on measuring the economic benefits; little emphasis was given to a prime characteristic of international tourism – the interaction between tourists and the host community. From the mid-1970s onward, more scholars and practitioners in tourism gave increasing attention to the relationship between host and guest, and particularly to the non-economic effects induced by that relationship.

Closer study of this relationship has made us more aware of the social, cultural and environmental problems which can arise from tourism, and particularly from an over-rapid growth in visitor arrivals. Many of these problems can now be anticipated and therefore considered in relation to a policy and planning framework. It should, of course, be noted that many of these problems are not new. In the Caribbean, Asia and Africa there are many examples of newly independent countries which have 'inherited' mature tourism sectors: Jamaica, Barbados and more recently Zimbabwe may be mentioned in this respect. In these countries, many of the problems of the tourism sector are not of recent origin, and may cause particular difficulty in finding management solutions.

Despite these difficulties, governments have ultimately to find a means of managing, if not completely eradicating these problems. This is particularly the case where tourism-related problems impact on the sociocultural values of the society or on the environment. These wider concerns are the responsibility of government, and it may be that government is the only agent able to introduce the required remedial actions. In the following, it is intended to examine the main areas where tourism can influence the sociocultural norms of a society.

Many of the social and cultural effects of tourism are portrayed as being essentially negative; early studies by de Kadt (1976) and O'Grady (1981) have both detailed cases where tourism has caused major changes in the structure, values and traditions of societies. There is continuing debate as to whether these changes are beneficial or not; the interests of society and the individual are not necessarily similar. There is little doubt, however, that where international tourism is of any significance in a country, it does become a major 'change-agent'.

It is not surprising that international tourism should induce such changes, because tourists usually remain in the host country for a very short time. They bring with them their traditions, values and expectations. They travel in what Eric Cohen has termed an 'ecological bubble':

A tourist infrastructure of facilities based on Western standards has to be created even in the poorest host country. This tourism infrastructure provides the mass tourist with the protective 'ecological bubble' of his accustomed environment.

In many countries, tourists are not sensitive to local customs, traditions and standards. Offence is given without intent. In a sense, foreign visitors do not integrate into a society, but rather confront it. Where large numbers of tourists, often of one nationality, arrive in a country, reaction is inevitable.

Reaction may take two forms: either a rejection of foreign visitors by locals, or an adoption of the foreigner's behavioural patterns to constitute a social 'demonstration effect', where local people copy what foreigners wear and do. In both cases, problems will arise. An ongoing point for discussion and action is how to make tourists aware of local customs, traditions and 'taboos'. Is the information and educational process only a function of low-volume tourism, as for example in Western Samoa, and Bhutan, or can it be adopted for high-volume visitor flows, e.g. India, Thailand? Very little attention has been given to the relationship between the scale or volume of tourism and its impacts on societies. This relationship is subsumed into the question of the carrying capacity of a destination, but as considerations of social and cultural impacts are essentially qualitative rather than quantitative judgements, it is a difficult area to analyse. For example, the Seychelles has established a growth limit of 4000 bed spaces in its tourism sector development plan. Why is it 4000 rather than 5000 or perhaps even 3000? To some extent the capacity limit is determined by individual locations and the availability of infrastructure; but there is also a strong but indeterminate notion of the possibility of overcrowding in some locations.

Effects on social behaviour and values

When tourists enter the host country, they do not just bring their purchasing power and cause amenities to be set up for their use. Above all, they bring a different type of behaviour which can profoundly transform local social habits by removing and upsetting the basic and long-established norms of the host population.

Tourism is a 'total social event' which may lead to structural changes in society. These changes can now be seen in all regions of the world.

During the tourist season, the resident population not only has to accept the effects of overcrowding, which may not exist for the remainder of the year, but they may be required to modify their way of life (increase in seasonal work, shift working) and live in close contact with a different type of visiting population, mainly urban, who are there simply for leisure. This 'coexistence' is not always easy. It often leads to social tension and xenophobia, particularly noticeable in very popular tourist areas or where the population, for psychological, cultural or social reasons, is not ready to be submitted to 'the tourist invasion'.

The 'demonstration effect' results from the close interaction of divergent groups of people, and manifests itself by a transformation of values. Most commonly it leads to changed social values resulting from raised expectations among the local population aspiring to the material standards and values of the tourists. Not unnaturally, changing social values lead to altered political values, sometimes with unsettling consequences. A decline in moral and religious values is also not uncommon and may show itself through increased crime levels. Not only are local attitudes changed, but the targets and opportunities for criminal activity are increased.

As tourism is essentially a human activity, it is desirable to avoid conflict between visitors and the host community. The behavioural patterns of the visitors must be acceptable or tolerable to the host community. The resilience of the host community to accept tourism is subject to numerous qualitative parameters: the socioprofessional structure of the local population; level of education and knowledge of tourism; standard of living; and strength of existing culture and institutions. What is needed is recognition that the local population is part of the cultural heritage which merits protection as much as other aspects of the tourist destination, e.g. the environment.

Human relations are important, since the excesses of tourism may have very damaging repercussions: the transformation of traditional hospitality in many countries into commercial practice results in economic factors superseding personal relationship. Further effects may be the appearance of consumerist behaviour, relaxation of morals, begging, prostitution, drug-taking, loss of dignity, frustration in failing to satisfy new needs. Nevertheless, it would be wrong to blame tourism for all these problems, which are linked also to social changes affecting communities in the process of modernization. Tourism accelerates the process, rather than creates it.

Cultural impacts

Tourism may generate social costs, often difficult to estimate, but which are no less serious for that reason. An example is the threat to traditional customs specific to each country and sometimes to particular regions. However, tourism may become the guarantor of the maintenance of certain original traditions which attract the holidaymaker. It is important to protect and maintain the cultural heritage and deal with connected problems: the illegal trade in historic objects and animals, unofficial archaeological research, erosion of aesthetic values and of a certain technical know-how, disappearance of high-quality craft skills, etc.

The commercialization of traditional cultural events may lead to the creation of pseudo-culture, ersatz folklore for the tourist, with no cultural value for the local population or the visitors. The same applies where the craftsman is concerned. The issue is the potential conflict between the economic and the cultural interests, leading to culture being sacrificed for reasons of promoting tourism, i.e. creating an additional economic value at the price of losing a cultural value. However, the exposure of resident populations to other cultures due to tourism would appear to be an irreversible process. On a social level, well-organized tourism can favour contacts between holidaymakers and the local population, will encourage cultural exchanges, will lead to friendly and responsible enjoyment and finally, will strengthen links between countries.

From the viewpoint of tourism planned to respect the physical and human environment, other positive advantages can be mentioned. The most significant are given below:

1 Tourism constitutes a method of developing and promoting certain poor or non-industrialized regions, where traditional activities are on the decline, e.g. tourism replacing sugar cane cultivation in many Caribbean countries. The development of tourism provides an opportunity for a community to remain intact and to slow the drift to urban environments. The retention and continuation of communities *in situ* is often the best

way to conserve tradition and lifestyles. The income and employment opportunities arising from tourism provide a stability to community life.

2 Tourism accentuates the values of a society which gives growing importance to leisure and relaxation, activities which demand a high-quality environment, e.g. Scandinavian countries.

3 With proper management, tourism can ensure the long-term conservation of areas of outstanding natural beauty which have aesthetic and/or cultural value, e.g. National Parks in the USA, Ayers Rock in Australia.

4 Tourism may renew local architectural traditions, on the condition that regional peculiarities, the ancestral heritage and the cultural environment are respected. It may also serve as a springboard for the revival of urban areas, e.g. Glasgow, Scotland.

5 Tourism contributes to the rebirth of local arts and crafts and of traditional cultural activities in a protected natural environmental setting, e.g. Highland Games, Scotland; Prambanan Ramayana open-air cultural centre, Jogyakarta, Indonesia.

6 In the most favourable of cases, tourism may even offer a way to revive the social and cultural life of the local population, thus reinforcing the resident community, encouraging contacts within the country, attracting young people and favouring local activities.

It has been noted that the economic impacts of tourism are often observed in the short-term if not immediately. Tourists can be seen arriving at airports and spending money. The social and cultural impacts take very much longer to appear and, as qualitative changes, may be subtle and difficult to measure. In some cases, little is done to monitor these changes until one day they explode into a violent expression of discontent. Such outbursts will deter tourists from visiting a country or even a region, and often undo years of patient (and costly) image building. The need is to identify potential conflicts and to defuse situations before they occur.

In many cases, the seeds of discontent and antagonism are seen at the preplanning stage. Insufficient or no attention is given to local views, needs and susceptibilities. The errors and omissions of planners become frustrations which are linked to tourism. Tourism is an abstract concept for many residents in developing countries. Tourists are not abstract – they are present in the society and can become the focus for local resentment. This must be avoided, not only for the sake of tourism and tourists, but also for the local community.

Concern with host–guest relationships has become more prevalent in the tourism literature. The notion of sustainability has been applied to tourism. Planners are becoming more aware of the need to see tourism development within a long-term perspective. It is no longer sufficient to view tourism development in simple terms of costs and benefits. Increasingly, attention is being given to the acceptability of the type and scale of tourism development to the host community. Hence emphasis is being given to involving the host community in both the planning and management of tourism development. It is a difficult issue to resolve because in many developing countries the concept of the community and community leadership is very different from that understood in Western, democratic countries.

It should be noted that tourism is a discretionary purchase. Tourists must be persuaded to visit a country, they cannot be coerced. If a country has acquired a reputation for an antagonistic attitude towards tourists, visitor arrivals will eventually decline, no matter how justified that feeling may be. In relation to tourism planning, protecting the interests of the local community is as important as ensuring the long-term welcome and acceptance of tourists; both objectives are interlinked.

Identifying sociocultural impacts

There is a growing volume of literature relating to the sociocultural impacts of tourism. Many of the impacts noted are similar. Despite these similarities, it is not possible to use results from one study in a specific location as the basis for a general conclusion. There are a very large number of factors which can influence sociocultural impacts, and similar factors might provide different responses in different locations. The reason for this diversity is that we are considering tourism impacts on societies, i.e. groups of people comprising communities in particular locations. These societies have developed their own cultures and lifestyles, factors which will influence attitudes towards tourism.

As noted previously, international tourism, certainly more than domestic tourism, tends to confront a host community rather than integrate into it. The main reason is that tourists are short-stay visitors carrying with them their own cultural norms and behavioural patterns. They are usually unwilling to change these norms for a temporary stay – and may be unaware that these norms are offensive or unacceptable to the host community.

A further difficulty can be the existence of a language barrier which itself may be a major factor limiting visitor understanding of the host community. Language barriers create their own cocoon, limiting social interchange between tourists and residents. These difficulties will create problems, and require some form of tourism 'education' for visitor and host. The main thrust of tourism 'education' has been the provision of information for the tourist, giving, for example, ways of behaviour unacceptable to local people, dress codes, and expected courtesies. Examples of information given to tourists on arrival can be found in Sri Lanka and Western Samoa. Hotels in Iran often have pictures of Iranian women garbed in traditional dress, emphasizing the need for women to wear modest clothing in that country. Attempts to inform tourists of behavioural norms are being balanced by attempts to educate communities to the cultural differences tourists bring with them. The host communities must appreciate they are there to welcome their paying guests. Increasingly 'tourism awareness' campaigns seek to inform local people of the benefits that tourism can bring and about different cultural behavioural patterns, e.g. Zambia and Malaysia. In many countries, including the UK, tourism is featuring as part of the school curriculum.

Perhaps the most difficult problem in identifying sociocultural impacts is that they can take a very long time to emerge. Unlike the economic effects of tourism which are readily seen, changes in society may be imperceptible but cumulative. It may also be very difficult to identify tourism as the cause of these changes as opposed to other influences, e.g. radio, newspapers, television. For example, is the 'social demonstration effect' solely attributable to what tourists are seen to do? Or may it be influenced by general media reporting? If changes in society are evolutionary rather than revolutionary, then tourism planners must have a system of monitoring these changes and reacting to them when necessary.

In considering the impact of tourism on a community, we need to know something about the volume of tourist arrivals, seasonal dispersion and intensity of location. The greater the volume of tourist arrivals, the greater the impact on a location. In some areas, the tourist–resident ratio is very high, and when this ratio is intensified by a seasonal demand factor it can cause very great stress on local economies and communities. Access to shops, transport, beaches and specific tourist attractions may be subject to overcrowding, delays, queuing and, often, rises in short-term prices. Where residents use or share facilities with tourists, there can be a gradual build-up of resentment, frustration and eventual aggression. These problems can be increased by the type of tourists arriving at a destination.

Some groups of tourists are more insensitive to local cultures than others. Often large low-income groups based on cheap package tours can bring particular problems. This is not to hypothesize that all low-income groups are badly behaved and insensitive to local traditions and customs. Certain ethnic groups might also exhibit characteristics which are unacceptable in a particular location or country. Where problems are clearly associated with groups of tourists from a particular country or, perhaps, sent by a particular company, action should be taken to curb the problem.

It should be apparent that certain volumes of tourist arrivals, or particular types of tourist groups, will be unacceptable in some locations. Tourism planners should attempt to 'influence' the type of tourism demand in the same way that attempts are made to 'protect' aspects of tourism supply, e.g. certain attractions and locations. For some developing countries, these problems are particularly difficult to overcome because tourism sectors, with all their specific characteristics, have been inherited from colonial times. Not all of this inheritance is bad, but where the sector is a major economic contributor to the country, it may be difficult to make necessary changes without endangering existing economic benefits. Management changes and actions may have to be introduced over a long period of time.

One of the problems of changing the type of tourism activity is that tourists and residents often have a very different view of a country and its society. A country's tourism 'image' may be the creation of a travel company, keen to stress those aspects of a country which it believes may persuade tourists to buy holidays in the destination. So what might be regarded as 'quaint' aspects of life by a tourist might be seen as a symbol of 'backwardness' by residents. Religious rites and ceremonies treated as a 'holiday experience' by tourists can represent a fundamental aspect of life for residents. In a similar vein, alcohol, promiscuity, gambling and begging may be regarded differently by tourists and residents. These are only a few generalized examples of changes which can arise from tourism.

It is appropriate to stress that tourism development can bring with it beneficial sociocultural impacts. The interchange of ideas, cultures and perceptions can do much to dispel ignorance and misunderstanding. The development of youth tourism, in particular, will tend to generate long-term advantages, not only in relation to repeat journeys, but in a wider understanding of cultural differences.

Domestic tourism will avoid most if not all of the sociocultural aspects relevant to international tourism. As domestic tourists are usually citizens of the country their cultural background will allow them to assimilate into the visited destination. Often language and religion constitute no barriers to travel or communication. In some countries, such as Iran, Pakistan and Oman, emphasis is given to attracting tourists from Islamic countries and also on creating cultural tourism where visitors are likely to be more sensitive to the norms of the host societies.

It is not too difficult to identify some of the sociocultural problems linked to tourism. What is of more concern is how such problems can be dealt with within the further development of the tourism sector. Given the disparate nature of the problems, it is only possible to suggest a general approach to developing a management strategy to control the social and cultural aspects of tourism.

A management strategy for social and cultural impacts

There are three broad aspects to developing a management strategy. First, the sounding of representative opinion at the location of any proposed development should be incorporated into the planning process. Secondly, representative opinions on the current impacts of tourism should be surveyed on a continuing basis. Thirdly, other countries' experiences in these aspects of tourism should be studied for longer term guidance.

Defining 'representative' opinion is not in itself an easy task. In most communities there exist pressure groups which may be supportive of, or antagonistic to, tourism. Pressure groups are skilled at using social and political systems to further their own aims. In developing countries, societal structures may be quite distinct from those existing and functioning in developed countries. Access to radio, television and the press may be limited in some countries, and participative democracy might not exist. In these circumstances it may not be possible to introduce a representative consultative process.

It may also be the case that societal structures vest the responsibility for community views onto a single person – a tribal chief, landowner or institutional organization. In trying to sound out local opinion about a tourism development, care must be taken to use confirmed representatives. It should also be remembered that 'opinion' is often speculative; to ask a person without any knowledge or experience of tourism to anticipate changes that may or may not arise from a proposed development is not likely to be very convincing or useful.

It is good planning practice to try to obtain the views of a community before development takes place. It will provide tourism planners with information about the likely acceptability of any proposed development, what views are held by the local community, and whether or not any fears can be allayed by the development of an appropriate management strategy.

Summary

In many locations, tourism is already in existence and the need is to discover what residents' views of tourism are. In this case, the enquiry aims to record and then to monitor the residents' perceptions of the impacts of tourism. Once these opinions have been collected, they can be tested for validity, as there are many factors which can influence a residents' view of tourism and its impacts on a locality.

To be of use to tourism planners, surveys of opinion have to be properly structured and stratified. As a continuing exercise, they can produce a stream of data, perhaps qualitative but nevertheless, important, as a means of trying to harmonize tourism development within a community. The basis for any management strategy is information. Measures should be taken to introduce preplanning and monitoring surveys as noted above.

References

de Kadt, E. (1976) *Tourism – Passport to Development?*, Oxford University Press, Oxford

O'Grady, R. (1981) *Third World Stop-over*, World Ecumenical Council of Churches, Bangkok

Further reading

Cohen, E. (1972) Towards a Sociology of International Tourism, *Social Research*, **39**(1), 172

Harrison, D. (ed.), (1992) *Tourism and the Less Developed Countries*, Belhaven Press, London

Murphy, P. C. (1985) *Tourism: A Community Approach*, Methuen, London

Smith, V. L. and Eadington, W. R. (1992) *Tourism Alternatives: Potential and Problems in the Development of Tourism*, University of Pennsylvania Press, Philadelphia

Theobald, W. (1993) *Global Tourism – The Next Decade*, Butterworth-Heinemann, Oxford, UK

Wall, G. and Matheison, A. (1982) *Tourism: Economic, Physical and Social Impacts*, Longman, Harlow, Essex, UK

7 Tourism and the environment

Introduction

There is current and growing concern about the impact that some forms of
tourism developments are having on the environment. There are examples
from almost every country in the world, where tourism development has
been identified as being the main cause of environmental degradation. In
Spain, overbuilding of tourist accommodation in coastal areas has caused
water pollution. In India, the Taj Mahal is suffering wear and tear from
visitors. In Egypt, the pyramids are also threatened by large numbers of
visitors. It should be noted that it is not only tourism development which
degrades an environment. Poorly planned industrial and agricultural
expansion have also had disastrous consequences in some locations.

It is now recognized that the world is facing major environmental
degradation. International attention is being given to acid rain, ozone layer
depletion and consequent global warming. In many countries, poor
agricultural practices and overpopulation is destroying fertile land. Unwise
use of chemical and fertilizers is polluting water sources. Urbanization is
threatening recreational space. What was recognized as local problems are
now attracting global attention. Although tourism development is not
responsible for these problems, it has become a major contributor in some
countries and without a management scheme to control the problems,
tourism will suffer.

Governments are making greater efforts to limit degradation through
encouraging 'environmentally friendly' practices and sometimes prohibit-
ing others. In relation to tourism, experience demonstrates that large
volumes of visitors tend to create proportionally larger environmental
impacts than smaller numbers of visitors. There has been a growing concern
to limit the numbers of tourists at certain destinations and sites. The concept
of an optimum carrying capacity has been given more attention. There is no
doubt that the way in which tourism uses the environment today will have
consequences for its future use – and perhaps availability. More emphasis is
being put on developing small-scale tourism as a more 'environmentally
friendly' alternative to mass tourism. In practice, 'alternative' tourism is a
spurious term; it is a form of market segmentation which matches particular
supply and demand conditions. For many countries, small-scale tourism
may be appropriate to certain locations, but is not regarded as a serious

alternative to large-volume visitor arrivals. In the developing countries in particular, large volumes of visitors are essential to generate economies of scale and provide the impetus for development.

Large-scale tourism should not be equated with environmentally unfriendly development. It requires careful planning to ensure that both environmental and social considerations are evaluated at the planning stage. As a consequence of global environmental concerns, tourism planners are now more aware of their responsibilities to future generations for the careful use of the environment.

In its broadest definition, environment refers to the physical environment which is comprised of natural and built components. The natural environment is what exists from nature – climate and weather, water features, topography and soils, flora and fauna, etc. – and the built environment is the man-made physical features, mainly all types of buildings and other structures. However, it must be understood that in comprehensive environmental analysis, sociocultural and economic factors of the environment are included and, in fact, it is often difficult and undesirable to try to separate the socioeconomic and physical components of the environment.

The relationship between the environment and tourism is a very close one. Many features of the environment are attractions for tourists. Tourist facilities and infrastructure comprise one aspect of the built environment. Tourism development and use of an area generate environmental impacts. It is essential that these relationships be understood in order to plan, develop and manage the resources concerned properly.

The Manila Declaration of the World Tourism Organization, adopted in 1980, emphasizes the importance of both natural and cultural resources in developing tourism, and the need to conserve these resources for the benefit of tourism as well as residents of the tourism area. The Joint Declaration of the WTO and United Nations Environment Programme, which formalized inter-agency coordination on tourism and the environment in 1982, states

The protection, enhancement and improvement of the various components of man's environment are among the fundamental conditions for the harmonious development of tourism. Similarly, rational management of tourism may contribute to a large extent to protecting and developing the physical environment and the cultural heritage, as well as to improving the quality of life. . . .

Considerable research has been accomplished during the past 20 years on the environmental impacts of development, including some research specifically on the impacts arising from tourism. So it is now possible systematically to evaluate these impacts and recommend ways to deal with them, including 'preventive' measures of environmental planning or by remedial measures. However, this is still a relatively new field of study. There is a need for continuing research, especially on the environmental impacts of various types of tourism development in tropical environments and in ecologically sensitive and vulnerable areas, such as small islands, reefs and desert oases.

There are two main environmental concerns. One is the impacts generated by the tourism development itself, and the other is maintenance and, where necessary, improvement of the overall quality of the tourism area. They are reviewed separately in this chapter.

Types of environmental impacts

Tourism can generate both positive and negative environmental impacts, depending on how well development is planned and controlled. The principal impacts are outlined below. They will not all occur in one area as their incidence depends on the type and scale of tourism development and the environmental characteristics of the area.

Negative impacts

Water pollution

If a proper sewage disposal system has not been installed for a hotel, resort or other tourist facilities, there may be pollution of ground water from the sewage; or if a sewage outfall has been constructed into a nearby river or coastal water area but the sewage has not been properly treated, the effluent will pollute that water area. This is not an uncommon situation in beach resort areas where the hotel has constructed an outfall into the adjacent water areas which may also be used by tourists for swimming, e.g. Pattaya Beach Resort area, Thailand. The use of the Blue Flag symbol by the European Community to designate clean beaches and water areas is one attempt to inform potential users of beach environments of relative standards of cleanliness.

Air pollution

Tourism is generally considered a 'clean industry', but air pollution from tourism development can result from excessive vehicular traffic used by and for tourists in a particular area, especially at major tourist attraction sites. This problem is compounded by improperly maintained exhaust systems of the vehicles. Also, pollution in the form of dust and dirt in the air may be generated from open, devegetated areas if the tourism development is not properly planned and developed, or is in an interim state of construction.

Noise pollution

Noise generated by a concentration of tourists, tourist vehicles, and sometimes by certain types of tourist attractions such as amusement parks or car/motorcycle racetracks, may reach uncomfortable and irritating levels.

Visual pollution

Poorly or inappropriately designed hotels and other tourist facility buildings may be incompatible with the local architectural style or scale. Badly planned layout of tourist facilities, inadequate or inappropriate landscaping, excessive use of large and ugly advertising signs, and poor maintenance of buildings and landscaping can result in an unattractive environment for both tourists and residents.

Overcrowding and congestion

Overcrowding by tourists, especially at popular tourist attractions, and vehicular congestion resulting from tourism-generated environmental problems, can lead to resentment on the part of the residents of an area.

Land use problems

According to good planning principles, tourism development should not pre-empt land which is more valuable for other types of use such as agriculture, residential or recreation occupation, or perhaps should remain under strict conservation control.

Ecological disruption

Several types of ecological problems can result from uncontrolled tourism. Examples are over-use of fragile natural environments by tourists leading to ecological damage; for example, killing or stunting the growth of vegetation in a park/conservation area by many tourists trampling through it; collection of rare types of seashells, coral, turtle shells or other such items by tourists (or by local persons for sale to tourists) which depletes certain species; breaking and killing of coral by boats and boats anchors and divers (coral requires decades for regeneration); undue filling of mangrove swamps, which are important habitats for sea life and water circulation.

Environmental hazards

Poor siting and engineering design of tourist facilities, as with any type of development, can generate landslides, flooding and sedimentation of rivers and coastal areas resulting from removal of vegetation, disruption of natural drainage channels, etc.

Damage to historic and archaeological sites

Overuse or misuse of environmentally fragile archaeological and historic sites can lead to damage of these features through excessive wear, vibration and vandalism.

Improper waste disposal

Littering of debris on the landscape is a common problem in tourism areas because of the large number of people using the area and the kinds of activities they engage in. Improper disposal of solid waste from resorts and hotels can generate both litter and environmental health problems from vermin, disease and pollution, as well as being unattractive.

Positive impacts

Tourism, if well planned and controlled, can help maintain and improve the environment in various ways as indicated below.

Conservation of important natural areas

Tourism can help justify and pay for conservation of nature parks, outdoor recreation and conservation areas as attractions which otherwise might be allowed to deteriorate ecologically.

Conservation of archaeological and historic sites

Tourism provides the incentive and helps pay for the conservation of archaeological and historic sites (as attractions for tourists) which might otherwise be allowed to deteriorate or disappear.

Improvement of environmental quality

Tourism can provide the incentive for 'cleaning up' the overall environment through control of air, water and noise pollution, littering and other environmental problems, and for improving environmental aesthetics through landscaping programmes, appropriate building design and better maintenance, etc.

Enhancement of the environment

Although this is a more subjective benefit, development of well-designed tourist facilities may enhance a natural or urban landscape which is otherwise dull and uninteresting.

Improvement of infrastructure

Local infrastructure of airports, roads, water and sewage systems, tele-communications, etc., can often be improved through development of tourism, providing economic as well as environmental benefits.

Environmental planning process

The best way to avoid negative environmental impacts and reinforce positive impacts is to plan tourism properly, using the environmental planning approach, before development. This planning must take place at all levels – national, regional and site-specific areas for hotels, resorts and tourist attraction features. It should be done in a comprehensive manner and be integrated with the overall planning of the area. An environmental impact assessment is required for the final plan. It is worth while examining this process and some of the basic environmental planning policies and principles which can be applied.

Environmental planning follows the same process which is used for development planning, but more emphasis is placed on considerations of the physical environment and sociocultural requirements. The process involves the steps outlined below.

Establishing development objectives

The general objectives of developing tourism must be decided as a basis for planning. These must necessarily be preliminary until they are determined as realistically compatible with one another. Environmentally oriented objectives in a regional plan, for example, often include developing tourism in such a manner that no serious negative impact results, and using tourism as a means of achieving conservation objectives such as preservation of cultural monuments and development of national parks.

Survey of the existing situation

This survey includes all aspects of the existing situation, particularly the detailed characteristics of the environment. For example, in a beach resort area the survey would include the climatic and weather patterns of rainfall, temperatures, humidity, sunshine and winds; land and underwater topography; extent and quality of the beach; beach erosion; near-shore water current flows, etc. Investment would cover historical and existing land use, settlement and transportation facility patterns, cultural and archaeological sites, land tenure patterns, and any existing development plans for the area. The socioeconomic characteristics of residents would be considered.

There is now an increasing awareness of environmental auditing, but it is by no means a general practice. The audit had its origins in manufacturing industry where the technique was developed to measure a company's compliance with environmental regulations and controls. The European Union uses the following definition:

A management tool comprising a systematic, documented and periodic evaluation of how well organizations, management and equipment are performing with the aim of safeguarding the environment by facilitating management control of environmental practices and assessing compliance with organizational policies, which would include regulatory equipment and standards applicable.

Few tourism companies have adopted this practice, although some hotels have done so. It may be that as governments become more concerned for environmental issues, legislation will be used to enforce standards.

There is no single approach to environmental auditing. The methodology selected will depend very much on the nature of the tourism business and the location of the activity. Some countries, such as Singapore, have very high standards of environmental legislation and control, whereas other countries have virtually none. As tourism now is becoming closely linked to the concept of sustainability, it is inevitable that more use will be made of environmental auditing as a planning and control technique.

Analysis or synthesis

The planning process includes several types of interrelated analyses such as the market analysis and alternative projections of number and type of tourist arrivals, accommodation and other tourist facilities needed. Other factors may include socioeconomic impact of tourism development; types of tourist attractions to be developed; type and extent of transportation facilities and service required. The physical environmental characteristics are analysed to determine the carrying capacity of the area, the environmental impacts of alternative types and levels of tourism development, and how best the development can fit into the environment. This analysis should also include an overall resource evaluation and assess optimum use for particular areas so that tourism does not pre-empt more important options. A useful approach in summarizing the analysis is to prepare, in written and in map form, the major opportunities and problems for tourism development in the area.

Plan formulation

The best approach is to formulate, in outline form, alternative plans and evaluate these alternatives with respect to how well they meet the development objectives. This evaluation may determine that some of the development objectives are not realistic or are not compatible with one another and need to be modified. The best alternative plan, or combination of alternatives, is selected and refined to become the final plan. A detailed environmental assessment should be made of the final plan.

Recommendations

Recommendations are prepared on all aspects of the planning programme.

Implementation

Based on the plan, implementation can commence, utilizing various organizational, marketing, legal and financial techniques. Part of the implementation may require zoning and development controls.

The Tourism Development Zone seeks to identify attractions in a geographical area which can sustain tourist interests. The attractions can be natural or man-made. The concept transcends administrative and political boundaries and seeks to develop and manage a geographical area based on its tourist attractions. An example would be Loch Lomond in Scotland, which is zoned for tourism and recreational development but incorporates several local government authorities. In some countries, e.g. Namibia and South Africa (Northern Cape Province), transnational parks are being developed.

Carrying capacity of the planning area

From the environmental standpoint, one of the most important analytical techniques is determination of the carrying capacity of the planning area. Overdevelopment and overuse by tourists is perhaps the major source of environmental degradation. Places which offer the greatest tourism potential, such as small islands, coral reefs, coastal/beach areas, oases in arid lands, and some mountain and lake environments are particularly vulnerable to overuse and overdevelopment. Also, man-made features are often quite sensitive to overuse.

It is possible to calculate the carrying capacity for finite space, e.g. stadia, buildings. Football, other sports stadia and places of entertainment in the UK have capacity limits determined by police and fire planning authorities. The main difficulty is in trying to determine the carrying capacity of people in open spaces. In practice these capacities will not be determined by physical space alone but by other constraints, e.g. infrastructure, including road access, water supply, sewerage, etc. Subjective factors such as visual pollution and noise intrusion will be other considerations. There is no single formula applicable to determining carrying capacity. This must be determined by a combination of objective and subjective evaluation conditioned by planning experience.

If carrying capacities are determined as part of the planning analysis and used in formulating the plan, a basic cause of environmental problems can be eliminated. General capacity standards have been established for many facilities and areas, but each specific place must also be evaluated with respect to its particular capacity characteristics.

Some environmental planning policies and principles

Environmental planning policies and principles have evolved which have a wide application in tourism, although they are not necessarily applicable to all areas. Some basic policies at the national and regional levels are as follows:

1 Develop tourism in a carefully planned and controlled manner and, where warranted, establish an upper limit on growth, as Bhutan has done, at least for certain time periods.
2 To use tourism as a means for environmental conservation and to help justify and pay for conservation of places, and for maintenance of overall environmental quality, e.g. the Borobudur Complex, Java, Indonesia; National Parks, USA.
3 To use selective marketing techniques to attract environmentally-oriented tourists who respect the environment and are conservation minded in using it, e.g. viewing mountain gorillas, in Rwanda.
4 Maintain a moderate rate of tourism growth to allow sufficient time to plan and develop the area, and to monitor environmental impacts (and also give residents time to adapt if this is a new activity in the area), e.g. the Seychelles has limited expansion of hotel room numbers.
5 Concentrate tourist facilities in certain areas (often in the form of resorts), to allow for the efficient provision of infrastructure, thus reducing the possibility of pollution and providing the opportunity for integrated land-use planning and application of development controls, to contain any negative environmental impacts. The concentration approach is especially applicable in large-scale mass tourism areas, e.g. Nusa Dua complex, Bali, Indonesia.
6 Phase development so that when one area (or tourist attraction) becomes saturated a new area can be developed to distribute tourists better, e.g. resort development in the Maldives.

7 Use various techniques to reduce seasonal peak use of facilities and attractions when saturation levels are exceeded, e.g. peak pricing policies in Caribbean islands.

8 Consider alternative tourism development strategies, such as:
   (a) quality tourism which implies highly controlled development and selective marketing attracting affluent tourists with high expenditure patterns, e.g. Bermuda
   (b) special interest tourism which requires limited specific infrastructure and is selectively marketed to relatively small numbers of tourists, e.g. marine diving, nature safaris; cultural tours; e.g. 'walking safaris', Zambia
   (c) village tourism which involves development of small-scale facilities and services located in or near villages, owned and operated by the villagers, and catering for a specialized market who want to experience village life, e.g. original development of village tourism in Senegal
   (d) farm or ranch tourism with tourists staying on the farm or ranch and engaging in local activities, e.g. game ranches, Namibia; farm holidays in the UK
   (e) home visit/professional exchange tourism with tourists staying with local families and persons with similar professional interests, e.g. home-stay programmes, Jamaica.

There are several environmental planning principles which should be applied to development of hotel and resort sites. In summary form, these principles include the following.

1 Preservation of any important or interesting historic, cultural and archaeological sites.

2 Preservation of any important or unusual nature areas, such as ecologically important swamps, wildlife habitats, significant vegetation, unusual geological formations, etc.

3 Preservation to the extent possible of major trees and incorporation of them into the site plan.

4 Designation for limited or no development of areas with environmental constraints, such as steep slopes, susceptible to flooding, and unstable soil conditions; these can often be used for parks and open spaces in the site plan.

5 Application of principles of functional relationships among different use areas, e.g. hotels located near or within walking distance of beaches or other major attractions, centralized commercial facilities, etc.

6 For resort development in rural areas, generous use of open space and landscaping to create a park-like setting with emphasis on natural features of the site.

7 Integration of the road network with the land-use patterns and major attractions, and use of footpath systems and electric car/shuttle bus service within the resort where possible.

8 Careful site planning so that views and outlooks are maintained and unpleasant wind patterns are not generated.

9 Special environmental analysis and design of any development such as boat piers which extend into the water area.

10 Application of appropriate development standards (these are often in zoning regulations), including the following types:
  (a) maximum allowable density of accommodation units per acre or hectare so that the site is not overdeveloped and sufficient space is available for landscaping and recreation; the actual density will depend on the type of hotel/resort and local environmental characteristics
  (b) maximum allowable amount of land coverage by buildings and other structures in order to maintain the natural character of the site and provide sufficient space for landscaping
  (c) maximum allowable height of buildings, so that buildings fit well into the environment
  (d) sufficient setback of major buildings from the beach, in order that the natural appearance of the beach/coastline is maintained, the possibility of damage to buildings from beach erosion is lessened, and adequate beach area for tourist and general public use is available
  (e) sufficient setback of major buildings from roads, major attraction features and other buildings (provision of public access to beaches and other major attractions is important for social reasons)
11 Application of appropriate infrastructure standards pertaining to:
  (a) portable water supply system
  (b) sanitary sewage disposal system
  (c) sanitary solid waste disposal
  (d) adequate telecommunications system
  (e) proper road and footpath construction and maintenance
  (f) adequate off-street parking areas with landscaping.

Architectural design

Appropriate architectural design of tourist facilities is essential to achieve integration into the natural environment. Although architectural design cannot and should not be legislated for, flexibility must be allowed for the architect to exercise his creativity. However, certain basic principles can be applied. Architectural design should reflect the natural environment; for example, emphasis on indoor–outdoor relationships in tropical and sub-tropical areas and use of indigenous and natural building materials to the extent possible. The design should represent the regional traditional or historic architectural styles and motifs, with emphasis on appropriate roof configurations even though the facility interiors may be functionally modern. Exterior colours generally should be subdued and compatible with the colour range of the surrounding natural environment, and non-reflecting surfaces utilized. Signage should be strictly controlled.

Suitable landscaping is an important component of any tourist facility development, and is essential for rural resorts in order to provide an attractive visitor environment and integrate the development into the natural setting. There are also principles of landscaping in tourism environments which are used by landscaping architects.

Energy conservation techniques should be incorporated into the design of tourist facilities. Much tourism takes place in tropical and arid areas, such as in many parts of South Asia, where solar energy devices can be effectively used. For example, in several Pacific Island countries, solar energy is used for water heating in hotels. More generally, careful siting and architectural design of buildings can greatly reduce the amount of room heating or air conditioning required.

On some sites, tourist facility development will unavoidably disrupt the natural ecosystem balance. In such situations, the environmental plan should recommend ways to establish a new ecological balance and stability in order to avoid future environmental problems.

Environmental planning of tourist attractions

Planning for nature parks and conservation areas is a specialized type of planning. It must be based on a thorough environmental analysis of wildlife, vegetation and geological and scenic features, and the different ecosystems. A decision must be made whether it is to be a multi-purpose conservation and recreation area such as a national or regional park, or a strict conservation zone such as a nature reserve. Within larger parks and reserves, a management plan including zoning is necessary to identify appropriate areas for visitor facility development and other places within which visitor use is more controlled. A land-use decision must be made whether to allow overnight accommodation and other intensive uses within the park, and whether these are to be located outside but near to the park entrance. In any case, intensive use facilities should not be located near to major park features although views of these features can be incorporated into the facility planning. In nature parks, careful management of visitor use is important so that elements of the natural environment are not damaged or destroyed.

Environmental planning for cultural features, such as historic and archaeological sites in rural areas, particularly, must give consideration to maintaining an open and natural setting around the site so that the feature can be fully appreciated and not degraded by nearby unsuitable development. A good example of recent planning for a major cultural monument is that of Borobudur in Java which was reconstructed and is now being developed as a national archaeological park. The conceptual approach to planning this park is maintaining an open setting near the monument, placing visitor facilities further away but within walking distance, and controlling land use in the entire vicinity.

Environmental impact assessment

With the increasing concern about the environmental impacts of development, the Environment Impact Assessment (EIA) has been formulated to assess the impacts of proposed developments including tourism projects. EIAs are designed to follow a particular format and can be incorporated into the project approval procedure. The EIA is a very useful technique to ensure that the environmental impacts of proposed projects have been evaluated and provide the basis for making any necessary adjustments to the project plan.

A basic model for environmental impact is presented here to provide a guideline. This list does not include economic or sociocultural factors because they have been discussed in detail in Chapter 6.

Environmental impact checklist

Each factor listed below is evaluated in terms of possible type and extent of impact:

1 Air pollution.
2 Surface water pollution, including rivers and streams, lakes and ponds and coastal waters.
3 Ground water pollution.
4 Pollution of domestic water supply.
5 Noise pollution, generally and at peak periods.
6 Solid waste disposal problems.
7 Water drainage and flooding.
8 Ecological disruption and damage, including both land and water areas and plant and animal habitats.
9 Land-use and circulation problems within the project area.
10 Land-use and circulation problems created in nearby areas by the project.
11 Pedestrian and vehicular congestion, generally and at peak periods.
12 Landscape aesthetic problems.
13 Electric power and telecommunication problems.
14 Environmental health problems such as malaria and cholera.
15 Damage to historic, archaeological and cultural sites.
16 Damage to important and attractive environmental features, such as large trees.
17 Generation of erosion and landslide problems.
18 Likelihood of damage from environmental hazards such as earthquakes, volcanic eruptions and hurricanes.

After each impact factor has been individually evaluated, a useful technique is to prepare an evaluation matrix which summarizes and synthesizes the impacts, so that a comprehensive evaluation can be made of all the factors.

Summary

The approach to evaluation of environmental impacts as well as socio-cultural impacts being increasingly applied now is to view them as costs and benefits, even though they are more difficult to quantify than economic costs and benefits. An evaluation can then be made of the total economic, environmental and sociocultural costs and benefits of a tourism project (or of tourism development generally in a country or region) to arrive at a meaningful total assessment of the project.

Even though an environmental assessment is made, together with any necessary adjustments to the plan, and impact control measures are applied, periodic monitoring of environmental impact should take place in order to detect any problems which might arise.

As tourism is constantly changing and often increasing at a rapid rate, monitoring of its impacts is a continuous process. Irrespective of the scale of tourism development, good management is required to minimize its negative effects. Tourism planning therefore must incorporate a vision of future development and also a mechanism for its control.

Further reading

Cater, E. and Lowman, G. (eds) (1992) *Eco-Tourism: A Sustainable Option*, John Wiley, Chichester, UK

Gunn, C. (1988) *Tourism Planning*, 3rd edn, Taylor and Francis, Washington, D.C.

Inskeep, E. (1991) *Tourism Planning*, Von Nostrand Reinhold, New York

Jenkins, C. L. and Inskeep, E. (1986) Lecture Programme on Tourism Development Planning, WTO, Madrid

Krippendorf, J. (1989) *The Holidaymakers: Understanding the Impact of Leisure and Travel*, Butterworth-Heinemann, Oxford, UK

Middleton, V. T. C. (in press) *Sustainable Tourism*, Butterworth-Heinemann, Oxford, UK

Pearce, D. (1996) *Tourism Development*, 2nd edn, Longman, Harlow, Essex, UK

Price, M. (1996) *People and Tourism in Fragile Environments*, John Wiley, Chichester, UK

Seaton, A. V. et al. (1994) *Tourism: The State of the Art*, Pt 6, John Wiley and Sons, Chichester, Sussex, UK

WTO/UNEP (1982) *Joint Declaration on Tourism and the Environment*, Madrid

8 Tourism trades

Introduction

The purpose of this chapter is to describe the parameters of the tourism industry and to establish the role of the tourism trades, how they relate to each other, the size, influences and trends that sustain them.

Is there a tourism industry? There is a school of thought that suggests that tourism does not exist as an industry since it comprises a large number of independent sectors, many of which are not significantly dependent on tourists or their movements for their existence. In fact, tourism is best viewed through an appraisal of the demand side and the way in which the tourist spend is spread throughout a wide range of primary, secondary and tertiary industries and services as the tourist travels around.

The tourist spend in turn has an effect on the social and economic structure of the stopping places *en route* and at the destinations where the tourists make purchases. Businesses are set up to feed and accommodate them, retailers stock postcards and souvenirs and local government will eventually become involved to provide car parks, entertainment and many other facilities which will improve and ensure the quality of the experience.

As the tourist destination succeeds, the tourist spend is spread more widely throughout the community, creating an economic multiplier; for example, bringing more workers to the area who in turn will need more houses, more shops and services, and then more teachers for their children. Shops and petrol stations will multiply and there will be more taxi and public transport services. This very enlargement can serve to improve the tourist facilities, the choices for the visitors and increase the attraction of the destination. It will also improve the facilities and economy for the local residents.

The converse is equally true. If there is a decline in tourism numbers and spend, a destination will fall into decline. Shops will close, transport services contract and unemployment increase. If international tourists were to fail to arrive in London, more than half the hotels and theatres would have to close, making the city a poorer place for the residents and far less attractive to the domestic tourist.

International tourism spending is an export earning, yet unlike any other 'export' the spending tourists deliver themselves to the product, and while earnings from international tourism are classified as 'invisible earnings', the effect of any significant fall in such earnings would be all too visible!

Table 8.1 Tourist expenditure breakdown, 1994

	Overseas		Domestic		Total	
	(%)	£(m)	(%)	£(m)	(%)	£(m)
Accommodation	36.1	3581	37.0	5 385	36.7	8 966
Eating out	22.0	2182	24.0	3 450	23.1	5 632
Shopping	24.5	2430	14.0	1 945	17.9	4 375
Travel within UK	8.0	794	17.0	2 585	13.8	3 379
Services, etc.	7.1	704	1.0	112	3.3	816
Entertainment*	2.3	228	6.0	850	4.4	1 078
Other	-	-	1.0	170	0.7	170
Total†	100.0	9919	100.0	14 495	100.0	24 414

* Entertainment includes visits to tourist attractions, historic houses, theatres, etc.
† Totals may not add up because of rounding.

Source: Overseas – *International Passenger Survey*, Department of National Heritage; Domestic - *United Kingdom Tourism Survey*, English Tourist Board, London. See also *Tourism Intelligence Quarterly*, BTA/ETB, Jan. 1996.

Tourist expenditure breakdown

The Office for National Statistics' International Passenger Survey (IPS) collects information on earnings and expenditure for the travel account of the UK's balance of payments. In 1992, as in 1986 and 1979, a trailer questionnaire was designed to collect a detailed breakdown of the overseas visitor spending in Britain.

Similarly the United Kingdom Tourism Survey (UKTS), sponsored by the national tourist boards of England, Scotland, Wales and Northern Ireland, collects annually detailed expenditure of domestic tourism spending.

More than a third of the total turnover of the tourism industry is accounted by the accommodation sector. The spending pattern of both domestic and international tourists on accommodation and eating out is similar but their spending patterns on shopping and travel within the UK are different – for details see Table 8.1.

Expenditure of domestic tourism on accommodation includes an estimate of £745 m on package trips. The definition of package trip is a trip where a single price for accommodation plus some form of transport and other services such as sightseeing or eating out or theatre tickets are included.

Tourism is Europe's largest trade and its success or failure has a very direct effect on employment levels throughout many industries (Chapter 5). However, success will usually bring with it problems of seasonality and quality control, such as: How do ski resorts survive in the summer? How do seaside resorts flourish in the off-season? Is there enough to do when we get there? It is in meeting the need for sustained levels of productivity and customer satisfaction that two key factors of tourism can be identified. First, the key role the regional or local government plays as a primary host and partner with the private sector in tourism enterprise. Secondly, the fact that the markets for tourism products are remarkably segmented, offering an unlimited opportunity for new product development that can help to overcome seasonality and meet new market demands.

The public authority is both regulatory referee and operator. In practice, the public sector is very often the largest operator of commercial services in transport, ports, airports and other infrastructure services; in the USA, for example, government owns and operates some of the largest national parks in the world (Chapter 11). Even where these operations are privatized, the public sector has a large degree of legislative control over their operations and activities. The public sector is often the initiator, or builder and operator of theatres, cultural centres, conference and exhibition facilities and leisure and sports centres. They are the guardians of the local environment; protectors of the heritage. As well as keeping the streets clean and providing public lavatories, they may also operate and maintain a wide range of museums, art galleries and historic properties which can be substantial destination attractions.

The trade contributors to the tourism industry can be structured in terms of their direct interdependence and the level of direct earnings from tourism. The primary tourism trades are: transport, travel trade, accommodation and catering, and tourist attractions. These comprise the means of travel, the support systems and the reasons for travelling. The secondary trades are those that benefit directly from the tourist spend, usually at the destination,

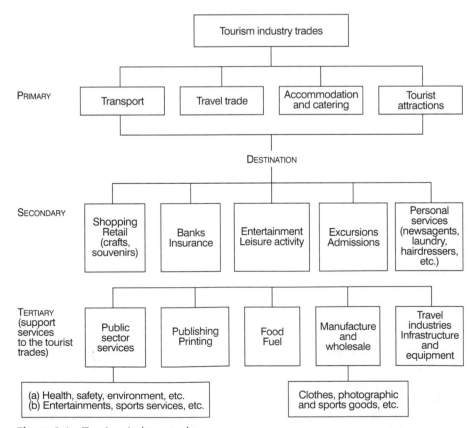

Figure 8.1   Tourism industy trades

but not always, and the tertiary trades are those that benefit indirectly as a result of tourism spend such as credit card companies, publishing and printing, wholesalers and manufacturers who supply the tourism trades, and many others whose activity is supportive of the tourism infrastructure (Figure 8.1).

The public sector not only has a significant role in the provision of tourism services, but it also receives remuneration from the tourist in the form of payment for services provided, whereas at the destination contributions to public sector taxes are indirect through local rates from business, and personal taxation. Local and national governments also receive direct revenue from sales taxes and, for example, airport and departure taxes.

The indirect, direct and personal travel and tourism taxes shown in Table 8.2 do not reflect the entire picture of taxes contributed by the industry worldwide. Many countries and cities apply user charges and fees at airports and border crossings. In 1994, the International Air Traffic Association (IATA) had tracked over 900 such taxes that are levied on travellers.

Looking only at the indirect tax contribution, travel and tourism was responsible for 11.7 per cent of all indirect sales and VAT taxes collected in 1991. As the world's largest industry, travel and tourism is also one of the world's largest tax contributors.

The levels of investment are often a good indicator of the industry outlook for growth. According to the World Travel and Tourism Council (WTTC), in

Table 8.2 Travel and tourism taxes – estimated 1996 revenue (US$, billions)

	Indirect	Direct corp.	Personal	Total
Australia	4.60	1.23	5.31	11.13
Austria	4.85	0.33	1.79	6.97
Belgium	4.51	0.79	5.17	10.47
Canada	9.11	1.34	6.84	17.29
Denmark	3.37	0.36	2.37	6.10
Finland	2.05	0.17	1.81	4.02
France	27.13	2.98	11.62	41.73
Germany	34.47	1.39	10.97	46.83
Greece	1.97	0.19	0.47	2.62
Iceland	0.13	0.01	0.04	0.18
Ireland	0.90	0.11	0.72	1.74
Italy	13.65	3.01	21.58	38.24
Japan	41.65	2.84	26.99	75.48
Luxembourg	0.37	0.08	0.20	0.65
Mexico	3.04	0.99	1.00	5.04
Netherlands	4.86	1.41	4.68	10.95
New Zealand	0.78	0.17	0.93	1.97
Norway	2.18	0.35	0.71	3.25
Portugal	2.09	0.42	1.08	3.60
Spain	10.93	2.60	8.67	22.20
Sweden	3.12	0.30	0.09	3.51
Switzerland	2.26	0.29	1.00	3.56
Turkey	1.25	0.17	0.94	2.36
UK	18.68	8.01	12.95	39.64
USA	52.81	12.88	66.89	132.57

Source: *World Travel and Tourism Council*, 1996.

1996 the EU's travel and tourism capital investment is estimated at 14.6 per cent of total investment, or ECU 197 bn (US $236 bn). Long term the outlook is even stronger, with investment in travel and tourism growing by 35.5 per cent in real terms to a total of ECU 366 billion (US $426 bn) by 2006.

In 1995 travel and tourism in the EU was estimated to generate 19.4 million direct and indirect jobs across a broad spectrum of activities.

Investment in tourism, whether by the public or private sector, can also be a significant generator of jobs. For example, Stephen Wheatcroft, an aviation economist, has calculated that a US $150 m investment in a Boeing 747 carrying 400 passengers will create 400 jobs, while an equal investment in a 1500-bedroomed 4/5 star hotel will generate up to 3750 jobs (Wheatcroft, 1994).

Primary trades

There are four primary tourism trade sectors: transport; travel trade; accommodation and catering; and tourist attractions.

All four sectors to a greater or lesser degree are interdependent. Transport, accommodation and catering acting as the tourism 'hardware' and tour operators/agents, tourist attractions and recreation activity fulfilling the role of 'software' in so far as they usually provide the reason and the catalyst for tourism to take place and for the use of the transport and accommodation.

Each sector comprises a multitude of commercial enterprises with a small number of dominant companies and many small and medium-sized enterprises. For example, according to Kleinwort Benson (1995), the key operators in the hotel sector in the UK were represented in 1994 by 57 publicly quoted companies, who accounted for 1357 hotels offering 122 548 bedrooms. Although there has been no accurate count of the accommodation stock in the UK, it has been estimated that there are more than 100 000 establishments in business as tourist hotels and accommodation units.

According to the UK tourist boards, the number of hotels in England, Scotland, and Wales in 1992 was more than 26 000. Lodging accounts for around one third of the UK's total tourism jobs, followed by the transport sector with a 15 per cent share. According to the OECD (1994), the travel trade represents an estimated 3–5 per cent of total tourism jobs. It has also been estimated that for every 1 million passengers passing through an airport, more than 2500 jobs are created.

From time to time all the sectors of the travel trade come together in global, regional or local 'marketplaces'; these are travel trade exhibitions such as the annual World Travel Market in London or workshops organized by tourist boards or trade sectors, such as the conference market in 'Confex' or the British Association of Conference Towns meetings market in 'Confer'. Worldwide there are over 100 such trade events. These travel trade market-places enable tour operators to meet and discuss future business with transport and accommodation companies, and provide an opportunity for travel agents to review the new products that are available to them, and to collect tourist information literature for their reference files.

The rapid growth of tourism as a worldwide phenomenon has meant that all the associated travel trades need to think globally and to develop worldwide distribution systems for their products and services. Since the majority of travel and tourism businesses are small, this can be difficult and expensive to achieve. An example of how the opportunity has been grasped by the hotel industry is in the cooperative marketing activity of Best Western Hotels, a consortium of subscribing, usually small privately owned hotels, who share the costs of worldwide promotion and an international reservations system.

Transport

This sector comprises the providers of road (service buses and coaches, coach hire, car hire and cycles), rail (high-speed trains, inter-city, local services), air (scheduled, charter, private hire) and sea services (passenger shipping, ferries).

Transport provides the means of getting to the destination, or in some circumstances may be the tourism experience itself; for example, coach touring, cruising, certain long-distance rail journeys in special trains, and touring by private or rental car.

Transport systems, national and international, were usually introduced for business reasons, mostly domestic as were the original canals in the seventeenth century, followed quickly by rail systems. The railways were encouraged to appreciate mass tourism through the good offices of Thomas Cook who purchased their spare capacity for group excursions. The advent of the motor car and mass production gave individuals the opportunity to travel widely, causing an explosion of independent domestic markets. Similarly, the aeroplane increasingly expanded its passenger seating capacities, and flew longer distances at relatively modest fares, opening up mass tourism to worldwide markets.

Today, the investors in most forms of transport, when calculating the returns on capital, take account of the tourism use and revenue, either as a main market, or as an income generator for spare capacity. Public and private transport company schedules are often designed to maximize the benefits to be won from conveying tourists.

Whereas island nations fairly obviously are the largest markets for air travel, travel by private car tends to dominate (Table 8.3). Coach travel is still a significant mode of travel, with railways trailing some way behind, although this will have more to do with the limited high-speed routes available and the relatively high tariffs charged for long-distance high-speed rail travel. These figures are really more representative of a large and active domestic market which today the EU has virtually become. However, when other parts of the world are examined, the aeroplane as a deliverer of international tourists is very dominant – see Table 8.4, later.

For the consumer the choice of transport will usually be made on the basis of three factors: the time they have available, the price, and the quality in terms of comfort and associated service. In order to benefit from these choices the transport operators will offer a range of fares, dependent on the

Table 8.3   International trips from EU Member States by mode of travel, 1990*

	Car	*Plane*	*Coach*	*Train*	*Total*
Germany	55	27	25	11	65.2
UK	25	67	14	5	26.7
Netherlands	59	24	13	9	16.7
Belgium	52	23	14	9	16.5
France	38	49	18	13	14.8
Spain	35	35	25	8	7.2
Denmark	37	38	15	12	5.9
Greece	18	54	23	5	2.3
Portugal	45	28	24	8	1.8
Ireland	14	73	8	5	1.2
Luxembourg	62	12	19	7	0.4
Total					158.7

* All trips away from the domestic country for one night or more. This includes all aged 15 or over travelling on holiday, for business and other private reasons. It excludes educational travel. Figures for Italy were unavailable.

Source: European Travel Monitor, 1990.

peak demand times, and the comfort of the accommodation offered. In addition, other incentives may be offered, such as cheaper fares for advance payment with no refunds available, and seat quality upgrades for relatively small supplements at off-peak times.

Aspects of regulation/strength of government control – liberalization

The oil crisis of 1973 saw a rapid increase in the price of fuel and a temporary braking effect on the growth of tourism, and again a rapid rise in the price of oil in the early 1980s had a similar effect. Fuel continues to be a spectre at the feast of tourism, together with threats of war, the Gulf War for example, continually rising prices, creeping taxation – as in government taxes, and now in the form of carbon fuel taxation to curb excessive use of some fuels for environmental reasons.

The traveller by definition has no residence in the places visited and thus will have no vote and is unable to use the ballot box or any other democratic method to raise objection to what has become an increasing malaise of taxation on the tourist and traveller. Departure taxes demanded in designated currencies, not always the local currency, can leave a lasting bad memory, and if the journey has several stopovers, can amount to substantial sums.

Airport taxes, normally collected by the airline issuing the ticket, can seem to do a disappearing trick as part of the cost of travelling, but with several stopovers the applied taxes can add up to a substantial percentage of the overall cost of the trip.

In Europe, value added taxes are variously applied from nil up to 25 per cent on tourism services including transport. Attempts to apply equality throughout the EU have failed, and this creates unfair competition between Member States.

Hotel taxes may or may not be shown separately on the hotel invoice, but when taxes are shown they can often be the composite of a government tax, to which may be added a local *taxe de séjour* or sales tax, and usually applied before any VAT is added to the invoice.

Infrastructure costs/development time

Building and operating tourism infrastructure for transportation is very costly and often a lengthy process. The following are some examples of major infrastructure developments, giving an idea of the enormous costs and the time scales involved.

The Channel Tunnel has cost £10 bn to build – it was started in 1987 and completed in 1994. It is an impressive achievement, having been built without public sector funding and has broken new ground in construction and civil engineering technology. It now presents a serious competition to the ferry companies who have been dominant carriers of cross-Channel tourist demand for so many years. Today a simple straightforward three-hour journey between London and Paris by the Eurostar train service is challenging the supremacy of the airline services. These, while only taking a little less than an hour between the respective airports, have no control over the city centre to airport transfer services which may often take a longer time than the flight itself. In an effort to cut the Eurostar city-to-city schedules down even more, it is proposed to build a Channel Tunnel high-speed rail link from central London to the tunnel – this is estimated to cost £3 bn.

A joint public/private sector development to get more people to Heathrow Airport faster is the London Paddington to Heathrow rail link, begun in 1995 and opening in 1997, which will cost £300 m.

With a view to improving the quality of service offered at Heathrow London Airport, the BAA is proposing to build a fifth terminal. The terminal is forecast to cost £900 m and would enable Heathrow capacity to be lifted from 54 million passengers a year (1995) to 80 million by the year 2013. The new Frankfurt air terminal which opened in 1994 cost about £2.3 bn.

The Swiss are building two more tunnels under the Alps to assist the free flow of traffic between northern Europe and Italy. Work starting in 1996 will not be completed until 2007. The combined tunnel–bridge taking road and rail traffic between Denmark and Sweden, for which building has already begun, will not be completed for 10 years.

The ever rising costs of manufacturing and servicing aircraft, railway rolling stock and shipping are also a heavy burden on rapid expansion of services to meet demands. The cost of a modern jet aircraft today is between US$25 m and US$150 m, depending on the size and range, and up to eight crews per aircraft can be required to ensure maximum efficient utilization. The cost of the new P & O cruise ship is £300 m.

National Air Traffic Services (UK) handles 1.5 million aircraft movement annually, involving 100 million passengers. Improvements in techniques aided by new technology have helped to bring average take-off and landing delays at London airports down from 28 minutes to eight minutes over the last three years. This, however, has required an investment of £150 m a year, plus a new £350 m air traffic control centre.

Air travel

The world's airlines are estimated to have a total fleet of 17 000 aircraft operating over a route network of about 15 million km and serving nearly 15 000 airports.

IATA was formed in 1919 with five founder members and celebrated its fiftieth anniversary in 1995 with a membership of 229 airlines. During the four years 1990–1993 the cumulative operating loss of all IATA member airlines amounted to US $15.6 bn – more than the combined profit of members throughout the association's 50-year history.

IATA's clearing house dealt with US $7 m worth of interline transactions in its first year of operation in 1947. It settled US $21 billion in total claims in 1993.

IATA reports that since 1949 the total number of passengers carried by member airlines has grown from a few million to nearly 1 billion a year by 1993 and is still growing. The number of aircraft operated by IATA member airlines has grown from 2380 in 1952 to 9281 by 1993. Since 1949 the average number of seats per aircraft has grown from 32 to a peak of 187 in 1985, since when the average has fallen slightly to 184.

The development of transatlantic air travel has been a critical factor in expanding tourism both for Europe and latterly for the USA. In 1950 there were some 10 000 transatlantic flights carrying 300 000 passengers. By 1988 this had grown to 128 000 flights carrying 26 million passengers, with an enormous boost given in 1970 when the wide-bodied Boeing 747 was introduced on the route.

The Air Transport Action Group forecasts that European air traffic of 366 m passengers in 1994–95 will rise to over 500 m by 2000 and more than 800 m by 2010. In Europe, the Association of European Airlines claims that a favourable economic climate and fall in real average fares would lead to an average annual traffic rise on intra-European routes of 6.6 per cent over the five years to 1999. But it questions if European airport and traffic control systems could cope with this forecast growth.

Today one of the main inhibitions to expansion lies in airport congestion. A study commissioned by IATA in 1989 calculated that passengers lost due to congestion cost airlines US $5 bn that year, and subsequent predictions suggest that the figure would rise to US $6 bn by 2000. The environment is another factor that has seen many airlines employing managers specifically to identify environmental impacts, to overcome aircraft noise, develop fuel efficiency and coordinate operations with other interests to overcome congestion. British Airways has calculated that it is wasting 16 000 tonnes of fuel a year, worth £2.4 m, due to holding delays at Heathrow and Gatwick Airports.

A hub airport is one where passengers change aircraft for onward flights, known as interlining. London Heathrow is a good example of this with 90 airlines from 85 countries serving over 200 destinations. It serves nearly 48 m passengers a year, of whom 30 per cent are interlining. Frankfurt handles 32.5 m.; Paris–Charles de Gaulle 26.1 m.; Paris-Orly 25.4 m; Amsterdam 21.3 m; and London–Gatwick 20.2 m. In the case of Amsterdam's Schipol Airport, interlining passengers are an important factor, especially from the UK. In 1993, 43.4 per cent of all passengers arriving were interlining.

Table 8.4   Ten major tourist destinations – percentage of tourist arrivals by air

Australia	99%
Bahamas	99%
Dominican Republic	100%
Japan	99%
New Zealand	99%
Philippines	99%
Puerto Rico	100%
Singapore	99%
Taiwan	99%
US Virgin Islands	99%

Source: Wheatcroft (1994). *Stephen Wheatcroft, WTTC Forum*, 1993.

Regional airports are growing in importance. There are 56 members of the European Regional Airlines Association (ERAA). Liberalization under an EU Inter-regional Air Services Agreement has helped to increase the market for regional airlines. The members of ERAA, who carried 36 million passengers in 1993, have been enjoying a 14 per cent annual growth, which is twice the growth rate for the larger carriers flying traditional routes into leading hub airports. The development of quiet, short take-off jet aircraft has helped to make operating over short distances more economical than in the past. Local authorities owning and operating airports are now pursuing the regional airlines to operate services to the major hubs in order to put themselves on the map for business and tourism.

A 1992 Gallup Organization survey of US air travellers found that

1   The average flyer took 4.3 trips in 1992, up from 3.6 in 1991.
2   Thirty-seven per cent of trips taken were for business, a steep drop from 46 per cent reported in 1991.
3   Frequent flyers (more than 10 trips a year) were only 8 per cent of flyers, but accounted for 46 per cent of all trips.

To illustrate the domination of air transport as a deliverer of tourists Table 8.4 sets out the percentage of tourist arrivals by air (all the destinations listed receive more than 1 million visitors a year).

As the EU develops its single market aspirations, one of the major effects will be the liberalization and deregulation of air services which will bring about changes in the routes and fares charged by the European national airlines. Deregulation in the USA in the 1980s brought about lower fares and the consolidation of airlines operating domestic services. The EU aims to be the sole negotiator for all traffic rights between Europe and other regions of the world, rather than each member country negotiating its own traffic rights.

Road

Car ownership and the quality of the roads has an important role in the growth of tourism; the relatively recent development of integrated

Table 8.5   Volume of cars in European countries

	Cars per 1000 people	Average no. cars per km of road
Germany	466	62
France	422	36
Belgium	402	
Netherlands		65
UK	378	67

Source: *Roads Facts '95*, the British Roads Federation.

motorway systems throughout the UK and Europe has reinforced the trend for individual holidays.

Passenger travel within the EU has risen by 85 per cent over the past 20 years, mostly in the form of private car journeys, which account for 79 per cent of all travel (Table 8.5). Germany has 10 955 km of motorways with a further 2000 km planned, while France has 8100 km in use and 3000 km planned. The UK has 3141 km, with only 276 km planned. There are at present about 21 million cars in the UK, forecast to increase to 25 million by the year 2000, a factor which has to be set against a falling expenditure on road-building programmes. Europe now has more cars than the USA (Table 8.6).

Between 1970 and 1990 the world's passenger car registration grew at an average of 4.4 per cent annually. This is a good parallel with the growth of world tourism. However, as demand is expected to increase further, major infrastructure problems will have to be faced.

Car rental

Between 1970 and 1989 the car rental business grew at a rapid rate of almost 10 per cent per year, and although between 1990 and 1991 there was a sharp set-back in growth, it began to pick up again in 1993. A survey in the USA

Table 8.6   Growth of passenger car registration

Region	1970 (millions)	1990 (millions)	% Change (1970–90)	Average annual increase (1970–90)
Africa	2.91	8.8	202	5.7
Asia	12.25	56.1	360	8.0
Europe	67.93	184.3	171	5.1
North and Central America	97.87	165.7	69	2.6
South America	4.59	20.5	345	7.8
Oceania	4.88	9.4	92	3.3
World total	190.43	444.9	134	4.4

Source: *Motor Vehicle Manufacturers Association of the US.*

Table 8.7   Market share of the leading car rental operators in Europe, 1991

Company	% Market share
Avis	13
Hertz	11
Europcar	11
Budget	10
Euro Dollar	6
Others	49

Source: *Budget/EIU Special Report No. R451.*

in 1991 by the US Travel Data Center found that 17 per cent of the US adult population, or 32 million people, used a rental car in the 12-month period June 1990 to June 1991. Fifty-three per cent of the users of rental cars rented a car once during the year, 21 per cent rented twice, and 13 per cent rented between three and five times. The big four companies Hertz, Avis, Budget and National, all of whom are controlled by car manufacturing companies, operate in airports and control about 80 per cent of the airport market; 80 per cent of all US rentals occur at airports.

The position is somewhat different in Europe where, although the larger car hire companies control an estimated 70 per cent of the airport business, second-tier companies account for nearly 50 per cent of the total market (Table 8.7). Eurostat quote over 500 000 short-term rental cars with available rental periods of 4 to 5 days and strong growth (5 per cent) in recent years.

Bus and motorcoaches

There are three forms of bus travel for the tourist: public bus services, inter-city express services, and coach charter which is directly related to coach tours, transfers and sightseeing.

Greyhound operates in the USA as the country's only national coast-to-coast, inter-city bus system. Nevertheless most people who travel by Greyhound take short trips, with over 50 per cent of all passengers taking trips of less than 200 miles (320 km). In 1992 the company carried about 15.1 million passengers.

In the EU there are over 90 coach lines, running authorized regular long-distance services. It is believed that with recent deregulation, easing of general restrictions and the elimination of border crossing rituals this number is likely to increase.

Scheduled bus and coach services are highly price sensitive. So long as train services are quicker, but generally more expensive, there will remain a large market for long-distance coach services.

Coaches used for touring, sightseeing and transfers are under continual pressure from legislation and regulation; legislation to ensure that drivers do not work too long hours, and regulation on parking and access. Rome and Salzburg, for example, already refuse coach access to parking at some major historical sites.

Coaches are the most obvious cost-effective, environmentally friendly delivery transport. In the UK, 9 per cent of all travellers used coach/bus transport as the main method of travel in 1994 (UKTS). However, being relatively large and disgorging apparently substantial numbers of people they are too often seen to be one of the problems of tourist movement, rather than a solution that requires good management to achieve contented and satisfied tourists with the least disturbance to local residents.

SEA Tourism/Travel Research (quoted in *Travel Industry World Year Book 1994–95*) reported that in 1990 some 60.7 m motorcoach passengers spent US $13.8 bn on group tours in North America. About 77 per cent of the passengers carried were on one-day excursions. On the multi-day tours, each busload of people spent about US $4300 a day on food, accommodation and admissions. A market survey by the National Tour Association found that the average US motorcoach tour traveller is 66 years old and two-thirds are 65 or older.

Rail

Railways remain heavily subsidized in Europe and many other countries, but the policies of privatization and the increasing introduction of high-speed trains are dismantling protectionist barriers.

The railway was the first form of mass transportation and its ability to move large numbers of people over distances was the catalyst that opened up tourism for the masses. While this ability to move large numbers cheaply and efficiently was eventually overtaken in the 1970s by the airlines, railways are beginning to make a significant comeback where they operate at high speed over relatively short distances (Table 8.8).

Table 8.8   Trend in passengers carried on European railways, 1981–94

	Passengers (millions)				International traffic
	1981	*1987*	*1991*	*1994*	*1987*
Austria	150	150	174	190	
Belgium	167	142	145	143	2.4
Denmark	136	146	144	142	0.7
Finland		41	46	44	
France	687	773	822		5.5
Greece	10	12	12	11	0.1
West Germany	1110	994	1045	1494	3.9
Ireland	15	25	26	26	
Italy	396	394	438		2.9
Luxembourg	12	10	10		0.5
Netherlands	205	222	330	312	1.8
Portugal	213	228	223	201	0.3
Spain	176	190	316	352	0.7
Sweden			82	9	
Switzerland			271	264	
UK	723	732	745	708	1.2
Total	4000	4059	4829	3524	20

Source: *Eurostat (Trains Database).*

The ranges most suited to high speeds are 200–1200 km for day trains and up to 2000 km for night trains. In continental Europe the conventional rail network has meant that high-speed traffic can be developed progressively within a Europe that is well suited to integrating new and existing infrastructure.

High-speed rail projects first appeared in Japan in the 1960s, and only later in Europe. European high-speed rail traffic already accounts for 30 bn passenger-km or 11 per cent of total long-haul rail traffic. The launch of high-speed services has triggered a sharp rise in the rail share of traffic in France, Germany and Spain.

Since 1990 there has been a strong support for developing the high-speed rail network in Europe. A programme for a 23 000 km high-speed rail network has been drawn up, including 12 000 km of new lines and 11 000 km of upgraded lines for the whole of the EU at a cost estimated by the International Union of Railways of ECU 200 bn. The fastest trains on the European networks are the French 300 km-per-hour TGVs. There are plans to raise the top speed to 350 km per hour shortly, and by improving the technical quality of traffic control and signalling systems it is anticipated that speeds of up to 500 km per hour will be reached by 2010.

The Eurostar Channel Tunnel passenger services started operating in late 1994, offering high-speed services between London and Brussels and Paris, and are attracting traffic away from the airlines.

Whereas Europe and Japan are increasing the size of their high-speed rail networks, Canada is reducing its own network by 51 per cent, a move that is expected to save the taxpayer about C$ 900 million. In the USA, however, the age of the transcontinental train is returning, with Amtrak now operating three services a week from Miami to Los Angeles.

Shipping

For the traveller, shipping was for centuries the only means to travel between continents. Today there exist very few long-distance passenger services. This sector of transport is clearly divided between cruising, where the ship is the accommodation and virtually the destination as well between stopovers for shore excursions, and relatively short-distance ferry services.

There are ferry services operated throughout the world, some of them internationally famous primarily because of the vast numbers of people who use them as the only means of getting from an island to the mainland or across an estuary, and the exotic settings in which they operate, e.g. Kowloon–Hong Kong; Staten Island–Manhattan.

For the British, the cross-channel ferries have been a feature of independent car tourism to continental Europe (Table 8.9). The prime interest of the cross-Channel and North Sea ferry operators has been to build their traffic and maintain its loyalty in the face of the competition from the Channel Tunnel. Throughput at Dover Harbour rose from 14.4 million passengers in 1986 to 18.5 million in 1993. Around 150 million cross-Channel passengers a year are expected by the year 2000 compared with 65 million in 1990.

One way in which the cross-Channel operators are competing with the Channel Tunnel is to introduce high-speed ferries; for example Seacat

Table 8.9 The ferry market in the Western and Eastern Channels, 1988–90

	Passengers (thousands)			Cars and coaches (thousands)		
	1988	*1989*	*1990*	*1988*	*1989*	*1990*
Western Channel						
UK–Spain	96	127	150	31	43	52
UK–France	2 808	3 484	3 901	605	839	990
Total	2 904	3 611	4 051	636	882	1042
Eastern Channel						
UK–France	13 181	15 904	16 236	1877	2310	2220
UK–Belgium	2 612	2 701	2 808	330	371	421
UK–Netherlands	680	671	803	130	120	131
Total	16 473	19 276	19 847	2337	2801	2772

Source: *Lloyd's Annual Ferry Review*, 1992.

catamarans which can travel at 35 knots, considerably faster than conventional ferries, but susceptible to cancellation in bad weather.

Duty-free sales are critical to the profitability of the cross-Channel operators and to many other ferry operators throughout Europe. In 1991, ferry companies occupied seven of the top 13 places in the league table of leading duty-free outlets. The leading ferry companies, of whom the most successful operate in the Baltic, earn more from these sales than any airline and most European airports. The top eight companies accounted for US $960 m, around two-thirds of ferry revenue from duty-free sales in 1991, according to an Economist Intelligence Unit Report, No. R451. With the prospect of duty-free sales being abolished altogether for operations within the EU, by the year 1999, these ferry companies will be badly affected and it is estimated that fare increases of up to 22 per cent will be required to replace duty-free revenue contributions to income and profitability.

Table 8.10 World cruise purchases, 1990

	No. passengers	
Country	(thousands)	%
UK	186	4
Germany (West)	184	4
France	112	3
Italy	75	2
Rest of Europe	110	2
Total Europe	667	15
USA and Canada	3640	82
World total (inc. others)	4461	100

Source: *EIU Special Report No. 2104 – The World Cruise Ship Industry*, 1990.

There has been a significant increase in cruising in recent years, with the North American market dominating (Table 8.10). In terms of passengers carried, Florida-based Carnival Cruise Lines and Royal Caribbean Cruises are the largest operators. Within each of the larger companies are subsidiaries or associated operators; however, the seven main players in world cruising provide some 70 ships and a capacity of over 81 000 passengers. In 1992 only 37 cruise ships from the major companies operated in the Mediterranean, but in the main these are smaller, lower capacity ships and tend to be used on short cruises.

The UK cruise industry is expanding very rapidly, with 264 000 cruise holidays taken in 1993, a figure that is expected to grow substantially. This anticipated growth in the cruise market has seen an investment of £300 m by P & O cruises in a new liner launched in 1995.

Travel trade

The travel trade is the smallest of the primary tourism industry sectors. In Britain and other European originating countries, it is highly concentrated on a limited mass product of outward package holiday travel to a highly concentrated number of mass market destinations in the sun and sea resorts.

The trade plays only a minor role in the domestic holiday market, and in the intra-European movement the majority share of the traffic is private car travel, individually organized, with considerable use of non-commercial accommodation. Even in the case of Britain, whose island position makes some form of public transport inevitable, 50 per cent of outbound travel is organized individually and not through package tours.

It is principally in package tours for a mass market, long-distance travel package tours and specialist areas where the travel trade plays its most significant role. Tour operators and travel agents can play a most important part in promoting and developing special destinations. This position is different in the USA where, although a substantial proportion of tourism is domestic, there is a greater use of domestic airlines to cover the longer distances involved.

The travel trade comprises two broadly interdependent sectors, tour operators and travel agents, with a number of integrated subsectors such as hotel and theatre booking agencies and representatives, incoming handling agents, tour guides and tour managers, airline seat brokers, and incentive travel houses.

Travel agents and tour operators are the promoters and 'enablers' of the tourist product. The tour operator puts together the transportation, accommodation, sometimes with meals, and sightseeing and other features in a 'package' and is essentially the wholesaler and risk taker. The travel agent retails the package, usually at a 'high street' location from brochures produced by a wide range of tour operators and earns a commission on the sales. Generally the tour operator will advertise his products in the national newspapers and on television, whereas the travel agent, sometimes with tour operator financial support, will more often promote the same product through local newspapers and local radio.

Table 8.11   Full-service US retail travel agents, 1985–92

Year	Locations*	% Increase
1992	32 147	0.2
1991	32 066	(−0.3)
1990	32 077	2.4
1989	31 320	3.1
1988	30 351	3.7
1987	29 264	2.2
1986	28 629	5.3
1985	27 193	4.4

* Excludes satellite ticket printer locations.
Source: *Airlines Reporting Corporation.*

Travel agents will also be the 'agent' for the sale of airline tickets, cruises, rail tickets, coach tickets and theatre tickets, earning commission on sales, and very often today the level of commission will depend on the level of sales achieved by the agent. Originally they were the agents of the railways and steamship companies and they remain very dependent on transport commission. This has forced some independent agents to form themselves into co-operatives so that they can benefit from the higher margin commissions that are paid on 'bulk' sales.

Tables 8.11 and 8.12 demonstrate the growth in the number of retail agents in the USA and the levels of dependence for business of tour operators and transportation companies.

Tour operators are sometimes manufacturers of the packages they sell and sometimes the wholesaler of another operator's land arrangements, adding the transportation arrangements between their home market and the country of consumption to complete the package. Tour operators, particularly the very large ones, are both manufacturers and wholesalers, and they will offer their products for sale through travel agencies to whom they pay a commission. Some tour operators will sell direct to the public; such

Table 8.12   Suppliers' dependence on US travel agents

	Estimated percentage of volume booked by agents
Airlines	80 (domestic)
	85 (international)
Lodging	25 (domestic)
	85 (international)
Cruise lines	95
Rail	40
Bus	Less than 10
Rental cars	50
Packaged tours	90

Source: *Travel Industry World Yearbook – The Big Picture,* 1995–6.

operators will either specialize in certain market segments with which they have some form of inexpensive communication, such as special interest clubs or with newspapers, magazines and other media, or they will depend on a carefully developed direct mail data bank.

Coach operators will also act as tour operators, setting up their own touring programmes and selling them through travel agencies in their own country or region, or through wholesalers in other countries who are customer suppliers; for example, Australians purchasing a coach tour starting in the UK or the USA before leaving Australia, and having made their own intercontinental transport arrangements.

Thomas Cook is a name synonymous with tourism. Although no longer a British company and now owned by a German banking and financial services company, it was the first travel agency/tour operator to operate worldwide. Until recently only American Express has managed to achieve a similar worldwide brand acknowledgement and coverage, but liberalization is developing other networks.

Today, small independent travel agencies can no longer afford to expand in a similar way, the cost of renting shop front premises in key locations in major cities is no longer viable, and once a travel agency entrepreneur has achieved a number of branches they tend to be bought out by the existing large travel agency chains. In their place there has been a growth of franchise operators such as the US-based Carlson Travel, who are also an international hotel chain operator. The company joined with Wagon Lits to form a worldwide chain. Other large travel companies have working arrangements with agencies to provide international operations.

Vertical integration of wholesaler with retailer

In the UK a number of major tour operators have adopted a strategy of vertical integration as a means to control and profit from the market for package holidays. Companies such as Thomson and Airtours are tour operators who also own substantial chains of travel agents which give them in depth selling benefits and national coverage. They also own and operate air charter companies which ensures that they have the capacity to meet the demand generated and to control the price of a substantial ingredient in the

Table 8.13   Cost structure of a typical Mediterranean package holiday from the UK

Item	% Total selling price
Air transport	40
Hotel accommodation/food	35
Services – transfer	3
Office and promotion costs	9
Travel agents' commission	10
Profit	3
Total	100

Source: Richards, W., *Tourism Research and Marketing*.

Table 8.14   Passengers carried under the largest air travel organizers' licences (twelve months to March)

Company	1995	1994	% Change
1 Thomson Tour Operators	4 m	3.5 m	17
2 Airtours	2.5 m	1.9 m	34
3 First Choice Holidays and Flights	1.5 m	1.5 m	−3
4 Avro	903 915	777 578	16
5 Iberotravel	671 444	466 172	44
6 Unijet	588 583	483 681	22
7 Cosmoair	563 580	382 954	47
8 First Choice Eclipse	290 359	271 488	7
9 Sunset	253 758	148 759	71
10 Kuoni	183 766	175 160	5
11 Inspirations	176 869	136 594	29
12 Virgin Holidays	166 115	159 842	4
13 Thomas Cook Group	165 511	86 108	92
14 British Airways Holidays	141 168	131 553	7
15 Hotelplan (Inghams)	119 990	111 764	7

Source: *Civil Aviation Authority*, 1995.

package. In addition, they also own a small proportion of the hotel accommodation they use at their best-selling resorts, again to give them a degree of stability in price and guarantee of capacity.

Based on industry research, Table 8.13 identifies the components of a typical Mediterranean holiday package from the UK, indicating the critical ingredients in terms of price sensitivity and why vertical integration and bulk-buying benefits help to stabilize the costs and give competitive advantage. This is especially important when the selling price has to be established many months and sometimes a year in advance of the sale/consumption, and when rises in fuel cost, currency fluctuations, government taxation moves and other political and natural disasters can seriously affect the price at the time of consumption.

The way in which holiday packages are constructed and the form in which they compete or cooperate with the market for independent travel is often influenced, or even dictated by government rules and regulations governing transport services. At one time, legislation decreed that transatlantic charter flights could only be organized by recognized non-profit organizations. Similarly, charter flights to European holiday destinations were only allowed to carry passengers who had also purchased hotel accommodation and a transfer with their air ticket.

The Civil Aviation Authority's Report for 1994/95 (to March) showed that more than 17 million people took package holidays by air, 13 per cent more than for the same period of 1994 (Table 8.14). They paid an average of £358 per holiday, a £6 per head increase on the previous year, but less than the rate of inflation over the same period. United Kingdom government departure taxes introduced in 1994, a weakening Sterling, rising costs of paper for brochures, and the introduction of the Tour Operators Margin Scheme (VAT), bit deeply into profits for the 1995/96 period.

For many years the larger UK tour operators have fought for market share, using heavy discounting to maintain the numbers. This has resulted in a public that books their holidays later and later in the year in the hope (often realized) of buying holidays at bargain prices. Such policies have weakened the profit margins of all UK tour operators. The CAA's market overview in 1995 demonstrates a slowing down of industry growth. For the year ended December 1994, net profit of the top 30 operators was £85.6 m, just 1.9 per cent of total turnover.

IATA rules, which in the past have determined the air fares that could be charged by their members over specific routes and distances, have eased under government liberalization policies to allow member airlines to sell their surplus capacity through 'wholesaler' outlets, once known as 'bucket shops' from where such 'illegally' reduced rate tickets were sold directly to the public. These reduced rate tickets are now available to virtually any travel trade outlet that can guarantee a certain volume of sales, and has done much in recent times to encourage the growing market for individual travel, especially to long-haul destinations.

Under pressure from consumer groups, the tour operator has had to take considerably more responsibility for delivering the actual holiday product that has been described and promoted in the brochure and advertisements, even though the operator may have no control over the actions of the hotel, coach operator or other contracted element in the package. These consumer pressures have been enacted in EU law in the form of the Directive on Package Tourism, which defines the responsibilities of the tour operator and the travel agent to the customer, and in other regulations that define and limit the forms of advertising that may be used to promote packages and destinations.

A growing affluence in the European market has generated a growth in long-haul traffic, primarily to the USA and also to destinations in the Far East. As this traffic has grown in volume, transportation and hotel prices have correspondingly fallen. Traffic to the Far East has been influenced by a search for the new and exotic, which has been supported by charter flights, new hotel developments and value for money quality, whereas the growth of traffic to the USA has been more dependent upon the level of air fares offered by scheduled carriers and the relative value of the US$.

Tourist boards – national/regional

Tourist boards are important coordinators and promoters of the product. National tourist offices have a catalytic role in bringing together all the complementary and competing products in their country and presenting them in simple-to-buy formats and packages for tour operators, travel agents and the general public in the target market countries. They will feed back from the marketplace information on the market profiles and specific product demands. This enables the travel trade to adapt and create easy-to-buy products for the individual markets and market segments and relate these to the customer delivery or transport systems.

Tourist boards, national and regional, will create and implement advertising campaigns, design, publish and distribute promotional literature and most importantly make available information literature and systems to ensure that visitors have the maximum knowledge about the destination, so that their visit is secure and enjoyable.

Tourist boards will usually organize training courses for information staff and register tourist guides to ensure that the quality of hosting and the accuracy of the historical and other information given by such guides, no matter in what language, is of the highest standard. Tourist guides and tour managers have a special role in tourism in so far as they are directly responsible for overall consumer satisfaction, and will be the first to know about matters which cause unnecessary problems and difficulties to the tourist.

In the UK domestic tourists rarely purchase a package. They tend to make their own arrangements direct with the transport company and accommodation provider. They will, however, make heavy use of the tourist information centre (TIC) operated by or in cooperation with the municipality which gives them assurance and fairly detailed information on what can be enjoyed in the area and when. TICs often provide reservation services for accommodation and entertainment and maintain supplies of relevant guidebooks and maps for sale.

In overseas destinations, it will be the private sector tour operator who trains and supervises the resort representative – the human face of the tour operator and catalyst and sometimes referee between the resort hotels and the holidaymaker.

There also exist regional organizations for promotion and cooperation in tourism, such as the Pacific Area Tourism Association and the European Travel Commission, comprising mainly national tourist boards working together to promote their regional destination to other major world markets.

There are also the suppliers of the sightseeing packages to the nearby tourist attractions and key tourist destinations that can be purchased from a variety of agents in most major towns and cities. Today, as well as being the principal counsellors and guides to the individual traveller, more and more tourist information offices, such as the UK TICs and the Netherlands VVVs, the network of official tourist information centres are becoming involved in the commercial service operations of tourism, selling sightseeing tours, accommodation booking services as well as guidebooks, maps and souvenirs.

Other travel service suppliers

There are several forms in which the suppliers of travel services direct to the consumer fulfil an important role, from theatre ticket agents to the foreign exchange bureau, and in this context the banks have made several attempts to enter the market as sellers of holidays, associated insurance services and foreign exchange.

A significant amount of tourism is generated by clubs and organizations either for the simple pleasure of visiting interesting places, or because the group has a serious interest in a particular subject. The 'group travel organizer' quite often in a completely non-commercial role has become an important catalyst in the organization of group visits to attractions and entertainment, as well as an organizer of overseas visits and holidays.

In addition, there are those that supply specialist services to the trade itself, most particularly the 'incoming tour handling agent' who will organize all the land arrangements for the overseas tour operator at the destination. Even within this area there are those that will specialize in handling incentive travel groups and, for example, will only handle visiting youth bands and choirs or visiting sports groups.

A further group of specialists are the professional conference organizers, who will process the conference and hotel reservations of delegates arriving individually from many different countries, and organize their pre- and post-conference tour programme.

Advance of technology

In the UK, Thomas Cook has introduced the selling of package holidays by machine, British Airways and British Rail sell tickets from machines. These are attempts to cut down queues and customer waiting times and have been developed as the growth of credit card ownership has eased the need for costly accounting processing and administration.

It is already possible to purchase package holidays from the home through cable television shopping channels throughout the USA and in several European countries.

The promotion of tourist products through closed circuit television in hotels is long established. However, the commercial promotion of telephone tourist information systems has failed to achieve satisfactory results, except where they can cater for a range of language demands.

More information about advances in reservation technology is given in Chapter 9.

Accommodation and catering

Whereas hotels are often viewed as the main providers of tourist accommodation, in developed countries they often only account for a third of the total tourist accommodation used by European residents on holiday, as is demonstrated in Table 8.15.

The World Tourism Organization estimated that there were 11.3 million hotel, motel and other international tourist accommodation rooms world-wide in 1991, and the world's inventory of rooms increased by an average annual rate of 2.5 per cent between 1987 and 1991 (Table 8.16).

However, whereas the actual number of rooms world-wide have been increasing, the levels of occupancy and room rates (relative to inflationary trends) have been decreasing see (Table 8.17). Part of the reason for the fall in average room rates may be attributed to the bargaining power of the large tour operators as they become increasingly important movers of large numbers. But the effects of world economic recession and other external forces must also be taken into account.

In recent times it has been the objective of the major hotel groups to grow even bigger. Brian Langton, Chief Executive of Holiday Inn World-wide said that 'Hotel companies must be like sharks, they have to move forward to survive. For the big the future is rosy'. In 1993, worldwide some 200 hotel groups accounted for 3 610 151 rooms and 25 150 hotels. Hospitality Franchise Systems (HFS) is the world's largest hotel marketing group, operating 384 452 rooms in 3790 hotels, followed by Holiday Inn World-wide with 340 881 rooms and 1795 hotels, and Best Western International with 272 743 rooms and 3308 hotels.

Table 8.15   Utilization of tourist accommodation in Europe – survey 1985

What sort of accommodation did you stay in?	All 12 EEC Members on 100 holiday-makers %
Hotel, boarding house, motel	32
Rented villa, bungalow, chalet etc.	17
Own weekend or holiday home	7
Parents or friends	21
Paying guest in private house	5
Camping, caravanning	16
Holiday village	2
Youth hostel	1
Boat, cruise	1
Other	2
	104*
How did you book this holiday?	
Through a travel agency as a packaged tour or organized trip	13
Through a travel agency only for travel arrangements	4
Through a club or association you belong to	4
By yourself or by family without using a travel agency	75
Not specified	4
	100

* Total greater than 100 because of multiple replies.

Source: *European Commission, Brussels,*1985.

Table 8.16   Summary of worldwide statistics for the hotel industry by global region

	Total revenues ($US)	No. of hotels	No. of rooms	No. of beds	No. of employees
Africa	6 299 852 778	10 769	343 347	675 960	1 259 019
Caribbean	7 917 081 463	5 290	155 253	300 097	277 614
Central America	1 199 700 716	1 160	41 221	83 862	232 180
North America	62 133 000 000	66 943	3 738 977	6 725 390	2 268 256
South America	9 844 502 435	14 576	487 787	1 005 972	1 283 917
Northeast Asia	23 732 570 935	10 192	719 480	1 470 857	1 120 339
Southeast Asia	12 841 018 075	13 211	453 657	898 212	730 585
South Asia	3 083 091 216	3 663	159 417	223 519	472 092
Australasia	6 602 490 053	10 082	229 319	567 346	539 286
Middle East	9 237 518 883	4 735	162 178	326 131	455 432
European Economic Area	87 490 841 936	151 945	4 242 193	8 108 983	1 873 772
Rest of Europe	17 397 271 566	15 117	600 370	1 153 939	681 926
Totals	247 778 940 056	307 683	11 333 199	21 540 267	11 194 418

Source: *International Hotel Association* (1994).

Table 8.17 International and US hotel trends, 1985–91

	Percentage of occupancy				
	1985	1986	1989	1990	1991
USA	66.9	65.6	67.2	66.2	65.2
All international hotels	70.0	67.1	69.0	67.2	63.0
Canada	70.7	68.2	67.6	66.3	60.2
Mexico	n.a.	65.9	60.1	61.7	63.7
Latin America	63.5	66.9	61.6	62.9	63.9
Caribbean region	70.9	69.6	71.7	71.3	70.1
Europe	72.4	66.8	70.8	68.7	62.3
Africa	68.0	64.5	69.0	66.6	60.7
Middle East	56.3	53.0	55.7	60.6	58.1
Pacific Basin	74.9	73.7	77.0	71.4	67.1
	Average daily rate per occupied room (US$)				
	1985	1986	1989	1990	1991
USA	62.60	66.56	73.23	78.76	75.14
All international hotels	59.57	64.53	81.54	94.45	96.83
Canada	48.56	53.97	73.07	77.95	78.37
Mexico	n.a.	n.a.	59.66	64.78	26.66
Latin America	44.35	34.07	61.75	66.76	69.56
Caribbean region	86.46	100.81	88.03	146.20	114.30
Europe	60.48	73.61	93.52	116.79	116.46
Africa	41.70	51.22	57.69	65.05	74.38
Middle East	72.69	79.19	74.97	83.02	92.06
Pacific Basin	66.06	69.81	87.91	97.02	103.60

Source: Pannell Kerr Forster Associates. *Trends in the Hotel Industry – International Edition.*

These three groups illustrate the different ways in which hotel chains have grown, HFS is the world's biggest franchiser of hotel brands. Holiday Inn is generally viewed by the consumer as a single brand, but it is a chain of mixed international investments in company-owned, managed, and franchised hotels, while Best Western is a consortium of privately owned hotels subscribing to what is primarily a reservation and marketing system.

Best Western represents one of the most efficient ways in which a single privately owned hotel can compete on equal terms with hotels owned by a large corporate group. It provides to its members a worldwide reservation system, bulk-buying efficiencies, and a corporate marketing brand image guaranteeing a level of quality to the tourist who otherwise might have no measure of an individual hotel's standards.

Crispin Tarrant, a business consultant, claims:

More business travellers attach importance to brands than to star ratings; 66 per cent of business travellers say that recognition of a hotel brand either has a great deal or fair amount of influence on their decision to use a hotel. The brand promises to the customer certain things they can expect. (*British Hotel Guest Survey*, 1994).

The contemporary appreciation of branding was recognized early by the French Accor Group, with their Novotels for business and family guests, and Ibis Hotels for the budget traveller. Forte Hotels had branded their properties in much the same way. The well-established Holiday Inn brand is trying to grow into product segmentation by introducing new types of hotels that appeal to different customers, such as the Crowne Plaza brand for business travellers and the Holiday Inn Express for the budget market.

Independent hotels have formed themselves into marketing consortia as a means of overcoming the competition from established hotel groups. They tend to brand themselves by confining the membership to certain types or categories of hotel, such as 'country hotels' or 'prestige hotels'. The main advantage to be gained from joining an independent hotel consortium is the ability of the single hotel to benefit from a more powerful marketing effort than any individual hotel could afford, to benefit from promotions mounted in international markets, and to be included within international reservations systems only normally available to the large hotel groups.

Hotel grading is an emotive subject, since apart from the star rating system forged by the motoring and motoring-associated organizations such as the Automobile Association in the UK and Michelin in France in times gone by, mandatory grading is generally carried out by the public sector. This is sometimes seen as a covert method of assessing suitable levels of taxation even when not actually applied. In some countries virtually all forms of accommodation are mandatorily graded. But it is by no means a common practice. Leading tourism countries manage very well without such a practice, e.g. Germany, UK, USA and Switzerland. The increasing segmentation of the market and new information technology makes such government intervention obsolescent or unnecessary.

In every country the private sector plays an important part in identifying, recording and promoting the good and not so good providers of accommodation and meals. Every year many guides are published listing the accommodation available in countries, regions and cities. Many of them adopt some form of grading or comment to guide the traveller in what individual establishments offer. Such guides range from the commercially produced *$5 Dollar a Day, Rough Guides* and *Badaeker*, which cover most parts of the world, to guides produced by tourist boards for countries, regions and individual cities.

Accommodation provision can be broadly divided into three sectors: (a) serviced accommodation; (b) self-service accommodation; and (c) visiting friends and relatives.

Serviced accommodation

Serviced accommodation, which includes hotels, motels, inns and guest houses, tends to cater for specific markets; for example, city centre hotels for businessmen and conferences, hotels for coach groups, hotels for different social and income sectors. But not all markets are necessarily specific to a location. Businessmen hold conferences in country and seaside hotels, coach groups are accommodated in industrial towns, and city hotels as well as hotels in distinctive tourist areas. Airport hotels have become important in catering for the air traveller, but often because of their strategic location attract business meetings and conferences.

Pressures to maximize occupancy have encouraged city hotels in locations not necessarily immediately recognized as tourist destinations, into manufacturing 'weekend break' offers to the second holiday market. The growth of independent car touring has led to many special offers for the motorist who is touring or planning a short break during low-occupancy periods.

Seaside resort hotels have learned to become flexible about arrival days and lengths of stay as the market has rapidly changed from the rigid weekend start and the one-week or two-week holiday allowance of the earlier industrial era.

Youth hostels have played a very important role in developing and supporting the youth travel and adventure holiday markets. The members of the European Federation of Youth Hostel Associations operate some 1500 youth hostels offering 150 000 beds every night and account for some 15 million bed nights each year.

In recent years, universities and educational establishments have entered the market. They only cater to young people during term time, but actually design their student accommodation to be suitable for the adult conference and course markets in the vacation periods. They utilize their built-in recreation facilities to offer sports holidays and many other special-interest products.

In Europe, as agriculture has continued to play a less important role in the economy of the countryside, farm tourism has become popular as a means to diversify and supplement farm incomes, giving an immediate financial injection into under-utilized accommodation and labour resources.

Holiday travellers are much more likely to use guest houses, holiday apartments and a variety of self-catering accommodation, which is why in a growing market, hotel groups have been investing in budget accommodation that provides only low levels of catering service, but simple well-equipped bedrooms at very competitive prices.

Serviced accommodation is also provided by cruise ships and this is dealt with under shipping in the transport section.

The trends given in Table 8.18, reported by Eurostat, indicate a slowing down or contraction in Europe, but some countries, especially in emerging markets, are buoyant. Future development of international accommodation may be limited in certain cities and regions, except in the budget sector, due to high costs of city centre sites and rationing of capital. Many hotels are situated in the middle of high-value land and may well be converted to other uses that generate a better return on capital.

Self-service accommodation

There are many varieties of self-service accommodation which includes self-service holiday camps, static caravan centres, caravans owned by caravanners themselves, and campsites.

Center Parcs is an example of 'added value' self-catering, where a permanent semi-tropical climate is provided within a transparent dome and sports activities are available to visitors year round while they are staying in their own self-catering chalets. An extension of this 'added value' is being

Table 8.18   Number of tourist accommodation establishments, 1989–93

Country	1989	1993	% (+/–)	Country	1989	1993	% (+/–)
Belgium	3 485	3 375	+3.0	Norway[4]	1 897	1 957	+3.1
Denmark	1 022	1 097	+7.3	Austria	22 921	21 656	–5.5
Germany	47 985	50 958	+6.2	Switzerland	100 797	100 118	–0.7
Greece[1]	6 868	7 840	+14.1	Finland	1 394	1 609	+15.0
Spain[2]	110 598	133 913	+21.0	Sweden	3 054	3 300	+8.0
France	88 049	85 233	–3.2	Iceland	361	448	+24.0
Ireland	864[3]	2 826	nc[5]	EFTA	130 424	129 088	–1.9
Italy	67 295	52 440[4]	–22.0				
Luxembourg	538	526	–2.2				
Netherlands	3 633	3 641	+0.1				
Portugal	1 908	2 005	+5.1				
UK	62 336	62 222	–0.1				
EUR-12	394 581	406 076	+3.0				

1 Excluding holiday dwellings and group tourism accommodation.
2 Excluding tourist villages, group tourism and special accommodation.
3 Hotels and similar establishments only.
4 Concerning supplementary accommodation figures refer to camping.
5 The analysis of the available data suggests that it could have a different criterion for data collection over the period.

Source: *Eurostat*, 1996.

developed by the Disney Corporation, with their Disneyland Institutes, enabling family visitors to enjoy a wide range of educational pursuits on site.

There are many agencies that specialize in letting holiday accommodation in the form of cottages, houses and apartments, made available to them by private owners. This is so popular that there have developed specialist agencies who for very reasonable fees introduce holidaymakers to home-swapping opportunities all over the world.

It is quite fashionable to purchase a second home in an attractive area, coastal or country, and although local shops will complain that these visitors very often bring everything with them, there is nevertheless money spent by such visitors in the area that is not being spent elsewhere, and it is often these second-home owners who make their property available to holiday-makers during the high-season periods.

Time share is another form in which people achieve 'second homes' and subscribe only for the purchase of a fixed-time week or two weeks in every year for a period of years, usually between 20 or 30 years. The 'owner' is entitled to use the property during that period, or rent it to somebody else, or in some cases swap with an owner in another resort.

Other forms of self-catering accommodation are to be found afloat, with boats for hire on inland waterways and yacht hire, the extensive marinas along the length of the Côte d'Azur are a good example of 'added value' self-catering. Camping and caravanning represent one of the larger forms of self-catering. Eurostat estimate that in the EC in 1991, the total capacity of camping sites, caravans sites and chalets was 7.1 million places in 18 898 camp sites, compared with 7.1 million hotel beds.

Large caravan sites, many with stationary 'vans', have many of the facilities of a large resort in sports, entertainment, shopping, and food and drink. In the UK, camping and more particularly touring and static caravan accommodation plays a major role in domestic holidays, especially by the sea. The British National Travel Survey estimates that camping is 5 per cent and caravan accommodation 22 per cent of the accommodation used for domestic main holidays of four nights or more.

Visiting friends and relatives

This is an extremely important sector of the tourist market, since the spending on transport, shopping and eating out tends to be as high, if not higher, than the average tourist spends. The presence of guests and hosts in these holiday or reunion circumstances tends to generate very high levels of 'out-of-home' eating and entertaining.

It is a very large proportion of the second-holiday and of the increasing short-holiday markets, estimated by the British National Travel Survey to be 21 per cent of total holidays of four nights or more. Of overseas visitors to London, 20 per cent are estimated to be visiting friends and relatives according to the BTA, London Visitor Survey 1995.

Hotel reservation systems

The 'information superhighway ' is having a significant influence upon who in the future will control the sale of the inventories of hotel rooms, airline seats, car rentals, tickets to attractions, etc. The owners and operators of these assets in the past have been in control of their distribution, but increasingly the control of this capacity is falling into the hands of those who own and manage regional and global reservation systems and/or negotiate for large buying groups.

The most significant driver of this change is the development of the telecommunications industry. Increasingly individuals, through their personal communications systems – cable TV, fax, personal telephone, Internet, personal computer device – can be directly in touch with reservation centres and/or transport companies and accommodation services.

American Express has announced that it will form a strategic alliance with American Online (a major player organizing information flow on the Internet) in order to allow travellers to make reservations anywhere in the world from their personal computers, including laptops. This is the first evidence that the race to dominate the market has begun.

Food and catering

While many people will claim that one of the pleasures of travelling is the opportunity to seek out and taste new types of food, the reality, certainly for the mass market and the popular destinations, is that most people after a short while seek the security of their own familiar types of food. The Spanish resorts are full of restaurants that serve dishes and drinks that are part of the everyday diets of the German, British and Scandinavian tourists who represent their largest markets.

Japanese visitors to Europe are certainly unused to the Western way of eating, and for some the Chinese restaurant is not an especially good substitute. However, food is rapidly becoming 'international'. The rapid spread of McDonald's and its ubiquitous hamburger, and the chicken, pizza and pancake chains usually franchised by American operators, are examples. The now common 'coffee shop' of most international hotels where local dishes are internationalized by the addition of 'chips' or European-style bread products, ensure that the menu is acceptable to the large majority of their customers.

Tourist attractions, recreation – activity at the destination

Apart from the conventional city and seaside resort tourist destination, there is a wide range of purpose-built destinations in the form of holiday camps and villages, which themselves cater for a wide range of market segments, e.g. the young person and family market served by Butlins. They have consistently developed their product to meet ever-changing needs and expectations of their market segments – most recently introducing theme park type rides and water park attractions, along with many new indoor activities that attract the older age groups and special interest markets during the 'low season'.

For the more discerning singles and older age group family market there are Center Parcs, built in countryside settings in Britain, the Netherlands and Belgium, serving a year-round market with a wide range of indoor sport and leisure facilities.

Throughout the world there are other purpose-built destinations such as the Club Méditerranée, attracting the young and not so young, but young at heart, to some of the more exotic, warm and tropical climate destinations. There are casinos and casino hotels such as can be found in Las Vegas, Atlantic City, the Bahamas, and Sun City in South Africa, attracting a round-the-clock visitor virtually throughout the year, adding high-profile entertainment features to attract the non-gambling visitor.

Spa towns are another form of tourist destination, today, geared-up as much to satisfy the relaxing tourist as they are to provide medical services for the invalid guest.

In an attempt to improve their overall revenue from tourist activity, theme parks are now beginning to develop themselves as resort destinations by adding accommodation, golf courses and other activities that will keep the visitor spending with them for longer periods than in the past. Disneyland Paris, formerly EuroDisney, was built as a resort destination with a number of hotels in place before the doors opened, and Orlando, Florida has innumerable competing theme parks and other attractions that help to maintain hotel occupancy and increase the average length of stay. In the past 20 years, Orlando has grown from a small resort community to a vast vacation and convention Mecca, where the hospitality industry is centred on

Table 8.19   Estimated theme park admissions and spending, 1994

	Attendance (millions)	% Change (1993/94)	Spend (£m)	% Change (1993/94)
UK	12.6	+ 5	170	+ 20
Other Europe	46.5	+ 1	910	+ 8
USA	94.0	+ 2	1795	+ 5
SE Asia	12.0	+ 20	107	+ 18
Japan	31.0	+ 7	860	+ 7
China	4	+ 25	9	+ 20
Australia	3.5	+ 17	36	+ 19
South America	3		9	
TOTAL 1994	206.6	+ 6%	3896.0	+ 7%
TOTAL 1993	195.0	ı 10%	3 628.5	+ 4%
TOTAL 1992	177.0		3 484.0	

Source: *Theme Parks – UK and International Markets*, Tourism Research and Marketing, 1995.

the Disney World complex. Today according to the Florida Tourist Commission, the area has 60 000 bedrooms and 350 000 ft^2 (32 515 m^2) of meeting space.

Theme parks have been a rapidly growing tourist attraction. They now feature in all parts of the world (Table 8.19). Originally catering to domestic markets, the example of the Disney developments in the USA encouraged many theme park operators to invest in 'unique' rides, with the objective of developing 'overseas' markets.

Centres of religious pilgrimage have always been, in effect, tourist destinations and they have developed over time to meet the overnight accommodation, parking and other needs of the visitors.

There are many specialist motives for tourism, encompassing theatre, opera, musical performances and a wide range of festivals. Sporting events such as motor racing, international football and rugby matches are also motivators for travel.

The destination develops as it adds facilities and attractions either to improve quality or make itself more attractive to a wider number of market segments, and in many cases for both reasons. Thus, UK seaside resorts have been improving the quality of their leisure centre facilities, and building or improving the conference facilities to broaden their market base and help to overcome seasonality. Also, importantly, they have begun to develop programmes and activities that have a special appeal to various market segments – seniors, families, special-interest groups, unique events – carefully programmed to respond to seasonal demand fluctuations.

Tourist destinations that are medieval towns, such as Chester and Salzburg, have seen their visitor numbers grow substantially over the last 50 years. This has required the provision of peripheral car parks, pedestrianized areas and control and management of coach tour arrivals, in order to preserve the heritage and to some extent enable the town to function in anything like a normal way for the residents. Such management systems can also have a deterrent effect on the spend potential of the visitors, as they have longer distances to walk to view the heritage sites. However, the itinerary schedules often cannot be changed, thus less time may be spent at the site and in the associated shopping areas.

To try to meet these challenges The Walled Town Friendship Circle was established as part of the European Year of Tourism in 1990 and currently represents 123 walled towns and cities in Europe. Together they host over 25 million tourists a year. For similar purposes, over 90 European towns and cities are signatories to a charter prepared by the European Cities and Towns towards Sustainability movement. The key plank of the charter is the need to move towards sustainability through partnerships with the local community, particularly local business people and industrialists.

Seaside resorts in the UK, and the more popular Mediterranean resorts, have to invest in maintenance and renewal in order to sustain visitor volumes. It is normally the public sector that is responsible for providing the swimming pools, sports facilities and theatres that are an integral part of the entertainment and recreational features of the destination. This will include ensuring that there are attractive flowerbeds, the roads and beaches are kept clean, and that catering establishments are regularly inspected to ensure they meet with high health and safety standards.

Some destinations are almost defined by their key activity, ski centres for example, which cater for a range of levels of proficiency, but where skilled consumption requires frequent participation to maintain and increase skill levels. Figures on 'regular' ski participation from the General Household Survey in the UK suggest that the core of people skiing regularly has also grown over time. A survey conducted throughout the UK during 1993 among regular holiday skiers indicated that over 90 per cent of respondents took at least one ski holiday a year, and over 40 per cent took more than one ski holiday a year.

Advance level skiers are almost twice as likely as intermediate level skiers to take multiple ski holidays annually (Table 8.20). The average advanced skier reported taking three long holidays (four or more nights) a year, compared with a mean 2.5 holidays for intermediate skiers, and 2.3 holidays a year for beginners. Frequency will however vary significantly with age group for activity holidays. In the case of ski holidays, the proportion of multiple annual ski holidays increases with

Table 8.20 Frequency of ski holidays by skill level

Frequency of ski holiday	Level of skier		
	Advanced	*Intermediate*	*Beginner*
More than 1 a year	65.0	36.1	10.5
1 a year	33.2	56.0	52.6
Once in 2/3 years	1.8	7.2	13.7
Less often	0	0.7	4.3

Source: *The US Ski Holiday Market.* Dr G. Richards, 1994.

age since those who keep skiing beyond the age of 45 tend to be those who participate frequently, and thus the average frequency of participation rises among older skiers.

The search for new challenges and stimulation among active holiday seekers has a direct influence on the destinations they visit. The choice of destination country for skiers differs significantly by skill level. Beginners and intermediate skiers are more likely to visit such countries as Austria and Bulgaria, which generally provide less sophisticated ski facilities and offer lower prices. Advanced skiers tend to favour France and Switzerland, or long-haul destinations such as Canada and the USA.

Business travel

Most tourism for business purposes is not at the discretion of the traveller. However, there are three important business travel market segments where choice plays an important role in selecting the destination – these are exhibition, conference and incentive tourism.

These market segments are important because they represent, on average, the highest spending of all tourists. However, they are also one of the most difficult sectors to quantify; for example, the largest sector of the conference market is the corporate sector, where many meetings take place on private premises. It is very difficult to research and to make assessments of the actual volume of this activity.

Conference and exhibition tourism are dependent to a large extent on the facilities provided for the activity. Throughout the world there are recognized 'conference towns' that have sufficiently large facilities to attract national and international conferences. Equally there are key exhibition centres that host large international exhibitions which attract substantial numbers of overseas visitors (Table 8.21).

Table 8.21 Exhibition centres in Europe, 1994

	Gross exhibition area (m^2)	No. visitors	No. exhibitors
Basel	147 800	1 067 519	9 487
Barcelona	116 000	1 683 951	16 048
Birmingham	158 000	2 976 191	38 855
Bologna	125 000	2 052 434	14 958
Brussels	114 362	2 579 125	11 072
Frankfurt	273 708	1 571 550	42 730
Leipzig	145 146	661 162	10 741
London	104 500	2 514 600	17 500
Lyon	92 657	953 470	5 228
Madrid	102 600	2 445 626	17 676
Milan	304 339	2 087 658	35 464
Paris	212 140	3 652 000	34 287
Paris – Nord	164 058	1 261 539	25 429
Utrecht	108 050	1 474 356	15 038

Source: *EMECA*, 1995.

Table 8.22   International congresses – top 10 countries, 1991

Country	No. of events
1 USA	880
2 France	761
3 UK	660
4 Germany	546
5 Netherlands	385
6 Switzerland	313
7 Italy	304
8 Austria	294
9 Belgium	289
10 Spain	264

Source: *Union of International Associations*, 1992.

There was an enormous expansion of conference centres during the 1970s and 1980s, as towns and cities throughout the world began to discover the important role that such centres could play in increasing the international profile of the city or even the country when they hosted international conferences, as well as generating high levels of tourism expenditure (Table 8.22).

According to the Convention Liaison Council based in Washington, in the United States by the 1980s, 145 cities had conference centres accommodating 20 000 or more. Over the same period the number of association conventions alone had grown from about 12 000 in 1975 to more than 21 000 in the mid-1980s.

The first benefit of a convention centre lies in the direct spending by the delegates and those organizing the event, the second direct benefit is the increased levels of local employment for skilled and unskilled sectors of the community.

In the USA, conventioneers represent a particularly important source of tax revenues. A study of the market potential for a conference centre in

Table 8.23   Average revenue per conference delegate by venue type, in the UK, 1994

	Residential (£)	Non-residential (£)
Purpose built centre		46.84
Multi-purpose centres		20.00
Residential conference centres	249.17	27.62
Universities	154.83	24.70
Unusual venues	115.25	18.24
Hotels – city	147.82	25.84
Hotels – country	152.81	24.84

Source: British Conference Market Survey 1994, *Tourism Research and Marketing*.

Madison, Wisconsin, by Pannell Kerr Forster in 1987, projected a total of US $1.2 m in sales, income and hotel tax revenues for 1991, based on an average tax of 5 per cent.

In 1992, in the UK, the Bournemouth International Conference Centre hosted 186 000 delegates and has estimated that the average daily spend per delegate in the town was £106.25, generating a total delegate expenditure of £19.8 m. In addition they estimate that exhibitions at the centre brought £4.2 m to the town over the same period. The estimated income generated by other conference venues in the town amounted to £13.9 m, making a total revenue generated by exhibitions and conferences during 1992 of £37.9 m. Table 8.23 gives the UK average revenue for conference delegates, by type of venue, for 1994.

Incentive travel

Incentive travel is often claimed as the fastest growing segment of the business travel market. In the USA, for example, a third of incentive travel awards are individual packages as opposed to group travel arrangements. It is almost certainly the highest spending sector, since the whole objective of the phenomenon is the rewarding of sales people, or people who achieve targets of varying kinds, with a unique vacation occasion. To develop this business, tour operators and handling agents have had to exercise their creative imaginations and persuade museums, historic houses, palaces, and many other 'unusual venues' to open to incentive groups for exclusive meals and entertainment, to create unique 'theatrical' occasions that are not generally available to the normal tourist.

Table 8.23 values the global incentive travel market by geographic generators of demand (i.e. the value of demand generated by geographical region, not the value received by the region). Estimated valuation incorporates transportation, accommodation, food and beverage, excursion and entertainment spending.

Of all business travel and tourism expenditure in North America, 6 per cent is incentive travel oriented. The comparative figures for incentive travel business generated are 2 per cent in Europe and around 1 per cent in other parts of the world. An overall growth rate of around 13 per cent per annum over the next decade is predicted in a report 'The European Incentive Travel

Table 8.24 Value of incentive travel market

Generating market	Total (US$bn)	Domestic (US$bn)	Outside country of residence (US$bn)
North America	8.8	5.3	3.5
Europe	6.4	2.0	4.4
Rest of the World	1.7	1.0	0.7
Total	16.9	8.3	8.6

Source: European Travel Commission, *European Incentive Travel Survey*, 1990.

Survey 1990', produced by Touche Ross, and published by the European Travel Commission with the International Hotel Association and the European Commission.

Shopping, craft centres

As Table 8.1 clearly demonstrates, shopping accounts for more than 25 per cent of all international tourist spend in the UK. For many, shopping is reason enough for visiting a destination. With the growth and spread of the shopping mall, complete with restaurants and many minor and major entertainment facilities, it can be the destination and attraction all rolled into one.

Money spent on shopping tends to circulate more immediately into the local economy in which it is spent than most other forms of tourist expenditure. There are several categories of shopping. First, general shopping, where visitors buy the products available in the major shopping centres because of their quality and pricing; there are, for example, many domestic and overseas visitors to London during the January sales period. Secondly, crafts and artefacts shopping, concentrated on the visitor purchases of unique souvenirs as reminders of the visit or because of the high quality of craftsmanship. Third, duty free shopping, mostly undertaken at airports and consisting primarily of alcoholic liquor, tobacco and other goods which normally attract high duty in the home market.

Developing destinations can fail to benefit from this high-expenditure opportunity if they do not make attractive ranges of quality craft and souvenir products easily available to the tourist, and ensure that the product range meets the tourist needs and expectations.

Retail shopping is heavily concentrated in the prime visitor sites and centres. Airports also play their part in mopping up the final amounts of spending money with their attractive arcades and duty-free incentives. BAA now leases over 400 retail sites at its seven UK airports and is rapidly expanding as an operator/contractor at a number of overseas airports.

Spending in this sector most often has an immediate economic impact on the local population through the large amount of cash spent, resulting in wages and profits for the retailers and other suppliers, purchases of locally made products and goods that would not sell so easily further afield. Only the advent of credit cards has slowed down cash flow, although this is being overcome through debit card systems and the widening ability to use cash cards to withdraw cash from automatic dispensers wherever travellers may be.

The growth of out-of-town shopping centres in Europe and in North America has had a serious effect on the quality, choice and attractiveness of city centre shopping facilities. Most tourists are attracted to the town centre, since this is most often the area in which the major heritage attractions are to be found, along with catering and accommodation.

Secondary and tertiary trades

The secondary tourism trades are those that benefit directly from tourism spend on arrival at the destination. These primarily tend to be shops, followed closely by entertainment and leisure activities and personal services, hairdressing, laundry, insurance, banks, etc.

But there is a further wide and important range of tertiary tourism trades. These supply the tourism industry in all its integral parts; for example, the wholesaler and manufacturer, of bathing costumes, or photographic equipment and supplies, are major beneficiaries, although indirectly, of the tourism spend.

Also benefiting indirectly are local governments, who are responsible for ensuring that health and safety legislation is enacted, that the best environmental conditions are sustained, and for the provision of leisure and recreation facilities. The public sector achieves its revenue from admission and other charges, from the local taxes on business, including restaurants and shops, and in some cases from levying sales and other taxes on visitors.

In some countries, towns and cities apply sales taxes to generate revenue. In the USA, many large cities finance their tourist promotion and services through the application of bed taxes which are directly applied to the running and operation of a convention and visitor bureau. This is not a common practice worldwide; most cities finance these activities from public resources and only draw revenue from the private sector through joint marketing schemes.

Local authorities provide both 'free' and charged-for attractions in the form of parks and esplanades, theatres and sports facilities. These facilities help to attract tourists, sustain and support their enjoyment, and make their own contribution to generating a positive economy for the town, city or region. As with shopping, they also improve the range of facilities for the local residents. The local authority also provides basic public services. The increased levels of commercial activity generated by tourists through the development and success of hotels and shops provides revenue to the local authority in the form of rates and taxes.

Another significant benefactor of indirect tourist spend are the investors, designers and contractors for the capital developments of tourist hotels, airports, golf courses and many other destinations, tourism activity and support infrastructure developments.

The tourism multiplier measures the impact of tourism spending on the economy of a country or region. After the initial injection of money into the economy as a result of direct spending on such items as accommodation and meals, the income derived is multiplied as the money circulates in the local economy. The payment of the hotel and restaurant account will be used by the hotel to pay staff and local suppliers. The total income generated in the local economy, therefore, will often be greater than the initial injection of tourist spending (see Chapter 5).

Banks are ubiquitous benefactors of tourism, originally through the issuance of travellers' cheques and exchanging foreign currency, making a charge on every transaction. Today there is an almost universal use of credit cards, with the benefit in developed countries of being able to draw local currency from bank machines at any hour of the day. Thus the banks play an important role in facilitating travel and in relieving some of the insecurities often suffered by those travelling in strange countries.

Where there are tourists there is a need for 'excursions' – carefully organized visits to places of interest, usually with a guide, so that the visitor can easily appreciate important historical and other sites and win the best enjoyment from such visits. Such excursions are often organized by public service and school bus operators benefiting from the availability of their coaches during holiday and slack periods.

London theatre would certainly not be as diverse in its offerings, nor would so many theatres be in daily operation, were it not for the overseas tourist market. This is another example where the residents of London benefit from the volume of and revenue generated by the tourist. The wide range of classical music and opera programmes on offer similarly benefit and would barely exist were it not for the tourist revenue.

References

International Hotel Association (1994) *White Paper: Into the New Millennium,* IHA, Paris

Kleinwort Benson (1995) *Quoted Hotel Companies,*

OECD (1994) *Tourism and Employment,* OECD, Paris

Waters Somerset, R. (1995–6) *Travel Industry World Year Book,* Child and Waters Inc., Rye, New York

Wheatcroft, S. (1994) *Aviation and Tourism Policies: Balancing the Benefits,* WTO/Routledge International Business Press, London

Further reading

Association of European Airlines, *Annual Forecasts,* AEA, Brussels

Civil Aviation Authority, *Annual Reports,* CVA, London

Eurostat, *DGXXIII: Services and Transport – Series A: Year Book* and *Annual Statistics*

Eurostat (1995) *Tourism in Europe*

Pannell Kerr Forster Associates (1987) *Trends in the Hotel Industry – International Edition,* London

Syratt, G. (1995) *Manual of Travel Agency Practice,* 2nd edn, Butterworth-Heinemann, Oxford, UK

The British Road Federation, *Road Facts* (annual), BRF, London

World Travel and Tourism Council (1995) *European Union Travel and Tourism,* April, WTTC, Brussels

9 Marketing

Introduction

To appreciate the marketing role in tourism, one should first consider the definition of marketing as an art or management practice and then the concept of marketing in tourism. There are special characteristics, since tourism is itself a demand force and the total 'product' is made up of a range of different components. This provides a basis for examining marketing planning – the tactical and strategic implications.

The next stage leads to market research, demand and supply determinants, price and the importance of segmentation and motivation in analysis of demand. The counterpart on the supply side is the strength and weakness analysis of the product (SWOT).

These essential planning tasks lead to the preparation of the action plan, taking into account product market fit studies and the marketing campaigns themselves. These are made up of the marketing mix, the selection of marketing tools (controls and media) and the budget implications.

The marketing mix embraces details of promotion, distribution and after-sales service. All these elements are examined in turn, following a logical order of tasks from the provision of the product to the final sale.

Definition

The term 'marketing' is comparatively recent. Traditionally selling, the salesman and his art described the practical aspect of the key commercial task of finding customers for the organization's products. In the contemporary world of big business, world-scale operation and high technology, the marketing oriented organization ensures that marketing is involved in its main activities from the evolution and manufacture of the product to the sale to the customer.

There are a number of definitions. One of the best known is that by Philip Kotler (1967, p.12), Professor of Marketing at the North Western University in the USA. He writes that

Marketing is the analysing, organizing, planning and controlling of the firm's customer impinging resources, policies and activities with a view to satisfying the needs and wants of chosen customer groups at a profit.

The task of marketing is essentially to provide the right product at the right price and the right time. Kotler comments further that:

The marketing concepts hold the key to achieving organizational goals, consists in determining the needs and wants of target markets, and delivering the desired satisfactions more effectively and efficiently than competitors.

Two more useful definitions come from practitioners in the tourism field. Gerry Draper, Marketing Director of British Airways for some years, describes the activity concisely as

ascertaining customer needs, tailoring the product as closely as possible to meet those needs, persuading the customer to satisfy his needs, and finally, ensuring that the product is easily accessible when the customer wishes to purchase it.

This latter point is especially important in tourism when major purchases are infrequent and the customer often lacking in knowledge and experience, so that 'making it easy to buy' can be a crucial factor in commercial success.

Melvyn Greene (1982, p. 6), with great experience in the hotel industry, writes:

Marketing is basically seeking out a demand first and then making the product or supplying the service to satisfy that demand. Selling is rather the other way round – creating a product or service and then trying to find a market for it.

There is much common ground, as there should be. Summing up a commentary on definitions and concepts, Alan Jefferson, Marketing Director of the British Tourist Authority for some years, wrote:

Marketing is....common sense applied to a coordinating function. Marketing is concerned with research which is the foundation for organized planning. Marketing is concerned with production and pricing and promotion, and not least 'profits'.

The marketing concept

The emphasis on the coordinating function rightly indicates the significance of the marketing role in all aspects of the organization's activity. This is particularly important because tourism is essentially a movement of people – a market and as noted in Chapter 1 not a single industry. Thus the marketing concept embraces product development at the start of the production cycle in policy formulation and the preparation of strategies to achieve corporate objectives. There are many case histories of serious failure when the marketing element was separated from or overlooked in product development.

A number of functions and disciplines must be brought together in a coordinated and professional way. The Marketing Action Plan embraces the resources available to influence and encourage the consumers of the target audience, and their behaviour towards specific goods, services or other desired objectives. Government, for example, may use marketing techniques to deal with political or social aims, such as campaigns to improve public health and safety or for environmental improvement. Many public authorities use such approaches in the tourism field to enhance host–guest relations or visitor amenities and satisfaction.

The combination of marketing resources as a vital part of the total commercial activity is sometimes described as the 'marketing mix'. Kotler (1984, p. 68) defines this as 'the mixture of controllable marketing variables that the firm uses to pursue the sought level of sales in the target marketing'. Clearly this relates to a commercial operations and is to some extent a simplification of the process in tourism or indeed in the public sector generally. Travel and tourism have some unique characteristics which makes the organizing and selling task a complex one.

Some components of the final product are intangible and cannot be stored. If a hotelier does not sell his rooms every night, his product – the overnight stay – is gone forever.

The product may be fixed in place and in capacity so that the output cannot be varied to match changing demand over a season or period. Like farmers, hoteliers and other tourist businesses have long-term fixed capital investment in building and plant, and are subject to seasonal and other external factors which they cannot control.

For a large part of the market the consumer must be brought to the product, which in many cases will be bought 'at a distance and unseen', unlike the normal retail sales of goods in the shops.

However, the principles of the marketing mix remains valid. The main 'variables' which the business can control, at least in part, are product, price, promotion and place of sales. The businesses can shape and alter the product: in some cases of service quality quite rapidly. Industry has always been an innovator in price and discrimination between the various segments. A good example of this is the extension of differing prices and discounts in air travel. For the same journey in the same plane, fares may vary by 100 per cent or more.

In practice the cycle starts much earlier, at the fundamental stage of setting objectives, policies and strategies. There are many options and many markets. In today's world the markets are increasingly highly segmented, not one homogeneous population. For example, changing demographics must be considered; more richer, mobile older people and fewer young people in the developed economies where mass tourism markets are to be found. There is increasing specialization in purpose of trip. Business travel subdivides into business visits for conferences, for trade fairs, on incentive trips or on individual company or organization tasks. Private or non-business travel subdivides to an even greater degree, for example, pleasure, health, education, to stay with friends or relatives and for many other reasons. Furthermore these 'behaviour groups' or market segments, as they may become, will act very differently and many will have unique characteristics.

There will be external factors which the organization cannot control, the economic tides on which as it were the marketing manager must navigate. These include:

1 Economic growth rates, which imply an understanding of cyclical forces leading to boom or recession.

2 Inflation, often linked to growth rates.
3 Fiscal regulations.
4 Exchange rates.
5 Political stability.
6 Price changes and value for money.
7 Competition, including consideration of subsidy or free market forces.
8 'Consumerism', including state intervention in constraints for consumer protection.

Marketing principles, of course, apply to the whole economy and all economic activity, but there are differences and unique elements in dealing with the public service in contrast to the private sector, especially in the case of competitive commercial operation in a free marketplace.

There are elements and requirements unique to each particular trade or industry. It is a golden rule in marketing, for example, to know what business you are in. The fate of Britain's spas and some of the seaside resorts demonstrates what Theodore Levitt (1964, p. 35) called 'marketing myopia'. He claimed that every major industry was once a growth industry, but may decline through failure to satisfy the wants and needs of the customer and to recognize what business they are in. He cites a number of examples – the American railroads and the Hollywood film industry are but two. The railroads did not stop growing because the need for passenger and freight transport declined. That grew. The railroads are in trouble not because the need was filled by others (cars, trucks, planes) but because it was not filled by the railroads themselves. They assumed themselves to be in the railroad business rather than in the transportation industry. They were product oriented instead of customer oriented.

Similarly, Levitt demonstrates how Hollywood was nearly killed off because it defined its business incorrectly. It thought it was in the movie business when it was actually in the entertainment business.

In Britain after the Second World War, the railways were nationalized. At that time they owned the largest hotel chain in the country, the main tour operators and travel agents (Thomas Cook, Dean and Dawson and Pickfords) as well as the principal sea ferry passenger fleet. The hotel chain was the only one which did not expand in the boom of the 1970s. The travel group did not participate in the package tour explosion. They, the hotels and the shipping fleet, privatized, have all gone their separate and successful ways. The failure to develop was the result of the public sector's inability to develop the business they were in – tourism on a large and dynamically expanding scale, not rail transport.

Understanding the business means an appreciation of its unique features, its strengths and weaknesses and in the case of the specific product its unique advantages. The marketer turns these into unique selling propositions in the approach to the clientele.

Tourism a demand force and the tourism product

The unique features of tourism are, first, its character as a demand force, and a market. Thus the consumer is king. Secondly, its nature as a service trade embraces a wide range of components or services. In addition there is a large range of related purchases or goods such as food, drink, leisure and sports equipment.

The true tourist product, as explained in Chapter 8, is made up of two elements: (a) the destination, e.g. a resort; and (b) the satisfaction provided at the chosen destination, such as relaxation on a beach, health facilities at a spa, educational or cultural experiences at a concert or theatre. For the business visitor, accounting for perhaps 25 per cent of total tourism revenue in some countries such as Britain, specific attractions of a conference or a trade fair as well as pursuit of commerce, may represent the appeal and the satisfaction.

This duality gives rise to problems as well as opportunities. The destination, usually represented as an entity by the municipality, has a responsibility as the host for maintenance of the environment, public services, information and reception. Furthermore, as the guardian of the image, local government must take responsibility for the broad strategy and supervision of development. The municipality may also be a major operator in providing infrastructure and basic services in transport, attractions and facilities such as concert halls, exhibition sites and cultural and sporting amenities.

The municipality has a key responsibility in providing the focal point for an essential public–private sector partnership, as the private sector will normally be responsible for providing a wide range of services, catering for visitors' needs to ensure that they can enjoy the destination's attractions. The service trades provide the means to the end. Thus the delivery of the true product requires a major effort in coordination and partnership between the public and private sectors. Many resorts have failed in the past in marketing and production, e.g. the spas in Britain. Indeed in recent years some major resorts in the Mediterranean have suffered. Where this necessary cooperation does not work, there can be a damaging decline in tourism revenues.

The tourist service trades in general cannot store their products. Thus 'occupancy' and 'load factors' in transport are vital considerations. In order to maximize, the commercial yield operators use a variety of marketing devices, including packaging, inclusive offers and discounted prices, since profitability lies in the marginal sales. Seasonality, previously regarded as an insoluble problem, is now more of a marketing challenge than an inbuilt characteristic of the trade. Many 'cold' cities and resorts in northern Europe, including Britain, have extended their season and developed new markets for what was formerly considered only a peak summer product. Weekend breaks in the cultural capital cities of Europe, for example, have become one of the fastest growing new traffic trends in the former 'off-season' months. Resorts have discovered conference and trade fair business which with cultural, sporting and other specialist appeals offer year round trade. The expansion of the senior citizen travel movement has been very beneficial in extending seasonal flows. However, all these new and successful innovations required new marketing skills and approaches. They did not occur 'naturally'.

Another feature of much of the tourist trade is the capital-intensive nature of the plant. Hotels need substantial long-term capital investment in buildings and equipment. Markets demand increasing quality of service on an internationally competitive scale and a range of additional services such as swimming pools, health facilities, gymnasia and saunas, tennis courts and access to other sports. Resorts similarly have been forced to update their attractions to include, golf courses, marinas, congress and sports centres, theatres, theme parks, etc. This heavy fixed capital investment cannot be moved, so there is the continuing imperative of bringing the market, the customers, to the product or 'factory'. Transport likewise requires vast capital investment and in supporting infrastructure for roads, sea and air-ports, the latter is usually the responsibility of the public sector. There is an important difference in the case of road, air and sea transport, in that the equipment has great mobility and to an extent can move to accommodate changing demand trends. Aeroplanes and ships can be allocated to new routes to cater for changing traffic flows, although much travel, especially air transport, is still regulated by government. There is still, except in the USA, a controlled not a liberalized free market for air travel.

Manufacturers of travel goods, and to a large extent the travel trade providing package tours and inclusive services, enjoy a high degree of free trade and can move their production or products with ease in major world markets. The expansion of free trade in travel and the freedom of the customer – the traveller – to choose from the vast range of travel services in the world marketplace makes the need to remain competitive and to offer value for money an ever more pressing imperative. In recent years, for example, Europe has lost world market share to a major extent as the competitive edge is eroded.

All these factors have their place in the formulation of strategies, business and marketing plans and promotion programmes.

There are some further important general considerations. First, a tourist product as with all products may have its own life-cycle, changing from growth, to a period of stability and then decline. In most cases the marketing task will not start from the beginning or the product launch. It will be important to build in some stability from a diversity of markets. It is unusual for all markets to decline at the same time. Some will be growing and some will be declining.

Second, any destination or service should avoid overdependence on one or two large powerful markets, or on a few powerful buyers whom they cannot control. For example, for some years Malta was dependent on the British market and a small number of British tour operators and their air transport. For a number of reasons, some political and some economic, the British market declined. Tour operators and their planes moved out with little advance notice, leaving tourism in Malta in a very difficult situation. Malta's Tourist Organization took action to restore fortunes with skill and success, but the weakness required a major redevelopment plan and there were casualties. Heavy state expenditure and investment in such circum-stances may be needed to restore prosperity.

Marketing planning

The research and planning task leading to the formulation of policy and corporate objectives will require an intensive strengths and weaknesses analysis both for the destination, normally by the tourist board, and for the product, the responsibility of the company concerned.

Formulation of policy and strategies, based on good research and market intelligence and the preparation of plans for the development and marketing of the products concerned, must go hand in hand. These functions cannot be separated. Moreover, there must be a high degree of cooperation and coordination between the public and the private sectors, for example, the country, the region or the resort and the providers of the destination services, transport, accommodation etc. These providers catering for the visitor, make the journey and the visit possible. But the destination as a whole provides the ambience and the scene setting which ensures satisfaction and enjoyment, making the dream come true, and delivering the theatrical appeal of travel.

Such cooperation is necessary for success but unfortunately the public–private sector partnership is often lacking. Coordination of activity in

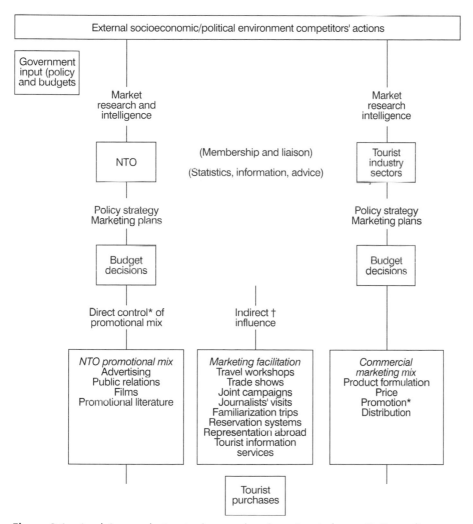

Figure 9.1 Applying marketing in the travel and tourism industry. (*, Expenditure mainly in the countries of origin from which international tourists are drawn; †, expenditure in countries of origin and the destination). (From Middleton, 1988, by permission)

planning, investment and operation and also in collective marketing can be weak. There has been a tendency in recent years in the industrialized countries for governments to withdraw from intervention in tourism, and to treat the industry as a private sector or marketing responsibility. Yet if the state and the municipality do not play their part effectively the tourist trade in the region concerned cannot flourish in the longer term.

Middleton (1988) explains the complex activity of tourism planning and marketing in Figure 9.1. This illustrates the role of the destination authority or National Tourist Office (NTO) and the collective interest with the trade in providing destination services.

Melvyn Greene (1982) describes the continuous nature of marketing in a simple diagram (Figure 9.2) which reflects the marketing process, beginning with research and ending with the marketing or sales operation. At the end, research takes over again with the all-important task of appraisal. This last job is too often treated lightly, indeed sometimes not carried out at all or performed very inadequately. This can occur through failure or indeed inability to foresee major changes in demand determinants or even the more usual short-term changes in external factors. Product failures, choice of wrong market segment, and sales approach to the chosen clientele, are more serious.

The marketing cycle is a continuous process, beginning with market research and market analysis, proceeding to the formulation of the marketing or corporate strategy, then the marketing and operational plan – the programme of action – and ending with the essential appraisal or performance against objectives examination. There the process starts again. However, as with most trades, it is rare to start at the grass roots, from a

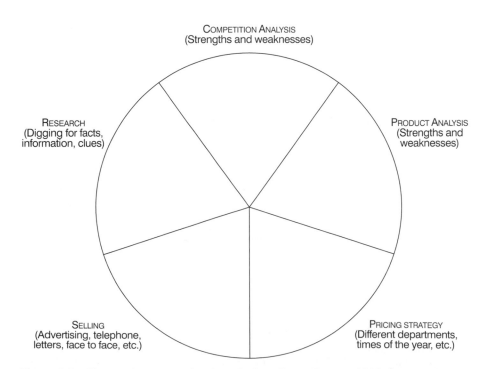

Figure 9.2   The continuous circle of marketing. (From Greene, 1982, by permission)

green field site, or with entirely new products. There is a history, an established base both in terms of market and production.

Strategic and tactical planning

Middleton (1988, pp. 120–121) distinguishes between strategic and tactical market planning.

Strategic planning

1 *Goals and objectives.* The place in its market which an organization seeks to occupy in a future period, usually broadly in terms of target segments, volume of sales, product range, market shares and profitability.
2 *Images and positioning.* Where the organization seeks to be, in terms of customers' and retailers' perceptions of its products and its corporate image.
3 *Budget.* What resources are needed to achieve its goals.
4 *Programmes.* Broadly what actions, including development, are required to achieve the goals and objectives, expressed in terms of buildings, equipment or plant, personnel, administration, organization structure and marketing.

Tactical planning

1 *Objectives.* Quantified, volume and sales revenue targets and other specific marketing objectives.
2 *Mix and budget.* Marketing mix and marketing budget decisions.
3 *Action programmes.* The implementation of marketing programmes and coordination of promotional activity.
4 *Evaluation and control.* Monitoring marketing results on a regular or continuous basis with regular evaluation.

In Figure 9.3, Middleton indicates the process in marketing planning moving from the longer term strategic considerations to the shorter term tactical marketing plans and the marketing programmes.

As an example, the strategic planning process by the British Tourist Authority (BTA) identified the following objectives for 1992/93:

Marketing Objectives 1992/93 (BTA Marketing Plan 1992/93)

For 1992–93, BTA's Marketing Objectives are, in conjunction with the industry, to

1 Re-establish confidence in travel to Britain disrupted by worldwide recession and changing political attitudes.
2 Generate an increase in overseas visitor spend in 1993 in Britain of 10 per cent over 1992.
3 Increase, in pursuit of the above, visits to Britain from abroad in 1993 by 5 per cent over 1992 without increasing congestion.

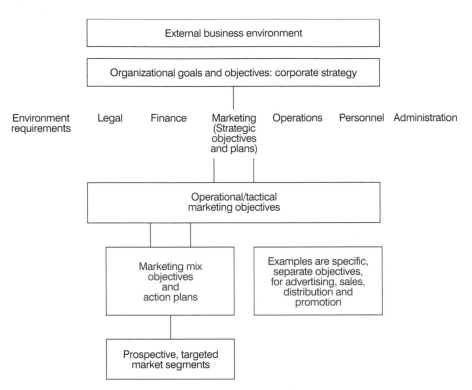

Figure 9.3   Elements involved in a corporate business strategy and hierarchy of objectives. (From Middleton, 1988, by permission)

4 Secure a good spread of markets throughout the world with earnings in 1993 of: 20 per cent from North America; 49 per cent from Europe; 31 per cent from the rest of the world.
5 Maintain out-of-London overseas visitor nights at 60 per cent of total, encouraging the use of regional gateways while continuing to promote London as a major international gateway and Britain's major visitor attraction.
6 Promote tourism to Britain in off-peak periods to obviate potential congestion; encourage more off-peak packaging and more facilities and attractions to open out of season.
7 Encourage the industry to continue to raise standards, improve ease of purchase and improve welcome.
8 Improve the quality, timeliness and dissemination of market intelligence and research about market opportunities and visitor needs.

The marketing mix

BTA needed to address eight key tasks in 1992–93:

1 To undertake 'reassurance' campaigns to nullify the negative impact on tourism flows of the recession and changing political circumstances.
2 To maintain Britain's broad spread of markets to mitigate any sudden drop in traffic from individual markets as a result of external factors.

3 To emphasize value-for-money products in Britain in light of the continued strength of sterling against the currencies of many key markets. To encourage value-added offers.
4 To arrest the decline in traffic from North America, Australia, New Zealand and Japan and increase traffic from European and other long-haul markets.
5 In European markets, encourage regional spread and gateways, but not neglecting the promotion of London and the South East as our principal international gateways – marketing will be increasingly geared to the opportunities offered by the opening of the Channel Tunnel and Single Europe in 1993.
6 To increase share of Japanese visits to Europe.
7 To address seasonality, seeking to fill troughs wherever and whenever they occur; to encourage better utilization of tourism infrastructure and so greater full-time employment; to obviate potential areas of congestion due to tourism.
8 To increase non-government funding in support of BTA marketing activity.

In seeking to fulfil those tasks, specific segments offering the greatest potential were identified for each market. These were classified, for example, into senior citizens, youth, 'special interest' and business travel segments.

Primary, Secondary and Pioneering Markets and specific segments therein were identified by geographical areas.

Moving focus from national to commercial marketing, Middleton gives some examples of application of marketing planning in the business sector, which like all organizations in the growth trade of tourism needs to review regularly the opportunities to expand profitably (Middleton, 1988, p. 125). The four numbered items in Table 9.1 may be illustrated with typical travel and tourism examples as follows:

1 The case where a hotel group, already servicing the corporate meetings sector as its principal products, decides that it is well positioned to expand in this market. With its existing portfolio, any expansion above natural market growth would represent an increased market share, which is known as 'penetration'.
2 The case where a British tour operator, already operating a portfolio of European inclusive tours, decides to expand its operations by developing long-haul tours to the USA, aiming at the existing British inclusive tour market. This decision represents an addition to the portfolio and is known as 'product development'.

Table 9.1 Product market growth strategies (four basic options)

	Present products	New products
Product markets	(1) Market penetration	(2) Product development
New markets	(3) Market development	(4) Diversification

Source: Based on Ansoff, *Corporate Strategy*, 1968, p. 99.

3 The case where an international resort operator, such as Club Méditerranée with a largely European clientele, decides to market its European villages in the USA in order to extend its sales potential. This represents 'market development'.
4 Finally, if an airline company decided to buy a hotel company, through an acquisition, it would be stepping completely outside its existing product/market portfolio and effectively diversifying its business activities, thus representing 'diversification'.

Market research

Market research involves the systematic collection of information about the supply and demand for the industry. In tourism this is an essential task because the trade sectors involved are market oriented. The research will be needed to help formulate policy and strategy as the basis for operational plans, for the marketing programme but also for development tasks. Thus a measuring activity both in market and product aspects should provide a guide for long-term action, especially to plan for growth and related investment.

Four general categories identified for statistical work in tourism apply equally to research in tourism in general:

1 *Measurements of demand*, notably volume (traffic flows) and value (expenditures). These records will be the basis for forecasts and studies of the impacts of external factors, forces generally outside the control of the tourism industry or tourist destinations.
2 *Market analysis, segmentation and motivation*. Competition and demand changes, e.g. in varying 'lifestyles', need constant monitoring.
3 *Product studies.* These embrace infrastructure, plant, equipment and the wide range of facilities and services. Occupancy and load factor records are important in estimating capacity as a basis for marketing operations.
4 *Performance.* Appraisal of marketing and production and performance against objectives tests.

Market research is vital for survival. The organization must track changing trends or competitive influences. The world travel market is becoming increasingly volatile and short term. But capital investment in infrastructure, facilities and equipment requires larger units and global approaches which involve major long-term expenditure. The task starts with measuring traffic flows, forecasts, and research into changing trends in both well-established and emerging markets. A wide variety of information and statistics will be available from official and industry sources. Reports from the marketplace, especially directly or indirectly from those in contact with the tourists will supplement the information from economic reports. Information is available at the international, national and local level. However, much industry information may not be accessible or may be expensive, thus placing the small business at a disadvantage. Government agencies, notably tourist boards and trade and professional associations, can help. Also market research agencies can provide much assistance.

Essential information on traffic flows (volume), e.g. number of visits or overnight stays and expenditure, comes from government, and is produced on a national basis. Unfortunately, as mentioned earlier, the national systems vary and results are not fully compatible. Some are late in reporting. Some of the information is not reliable. The gradual introduction of survey systems, the increasing role of institutions and the private sector provision of industry records helps to fill some of the gaps.

Determinants of demand

As building materials in formulating corporate policy, the determinants of demand must be carefully examined (Chapter 4). These will apply to world, national and local markets. Together with the effects of government intervention they establish the conditions of trading and the state of competition. These factors shape the market. They influence the ability of the population of a country to buy goods and services. Clearly the trades supplying basic travel services will not be able to control these influences.

The supply determinants

There are supply determinants, ranging from absolutes such as under- or overcapacity to infrastructure weakness, e.g. transport bottlenecks and health and security dangers or political instability. Such factors can seriously limit or even destroy for a time a tourist destination's reception capacity. The marketing plan will take such factors into account.

External factors

There are another range of forces which can be described as external factors, usually shorter term in their effect unlike the more permanent determinants of demand. Again they are not easily influenced by the producer of tourism services. When short term in effect, however, they leave the producer some room for manoeuvre to benefit from favourable conditions – exchange rate changes for example – and thus gain competitive advantage.

External factors include those listed on pages 137–8.

There are a number of determinants on both the supply and demand side which, unlike external factors, are partly or wholly within the control of the buyer or seller. These are the forces that interact in the marketplace and in effect make the market.

On the demand side, three determinants are all important: time, money and preference. They decide the extent to which the consumer enters the market and in which way the market will dictate results.

These three demand forces act not only in a general way, but specifically in relation to each product or tourist service. In transport, for example, travellers' choice will depend on the time of the journey, the cost and a combination of factors contributing to preference such as convenience, fashion, image. In this trinity of forces any one mode of transport with an advantage over the competition in two of the three forces is likely to win the competitive battle. Travellers may, for example, sacrifice comfort for price. Many holiday flights start late at night or early morning. Businessmen may pay a premium for speed and comfort. The traveller taking a package holiday lasting a week or two can afford a longer journey. The businessman making a short trip, must save time.

Price

While time and price are self-explanatory, pricing is an art in itself and requires careful study as part of corporate policy. Price is the most powerful single variable in the marketing mix. But it does not operate in isolation. Value for money, albeit at different levels, is imperative. The product must be in demand or fashionable. It may be in short supply. Competition can be weak or strong, affecting achievable rates. The wide variety of airline and hotel rates for basically the same product at different times and conditions of sale reflect these characteristics. The market may be very price sensitive, as in the case of traffic from Northern European urban areas to Mediterranean beaches where there is a strong competition and a wide choice. There are also resorts and their establishments offering exclusive attractions, justifying a premium price.

Price discounting and discrimination, and segmentation, in the market has always been a feature in travel services. The historic rule is to charge what the market will bear. The product is highly perishable and cannot be stored. It is necessary normally to appeal to a number of different segments. The railways invented first-, second- and third-class travel on 'scheduled services'. When capacity exceeded demand, excursions and package tours were invented, the purpose being to sell to capacity and maximize the yield or return. Prices can be lowered segment by segment. But the marketing task is to ensure that cheap traffic does not drive out or invade the higher price and regular clientele. Airlines, for example, offer Saturday night stopover fares at half or less than full fare, on the assumption that full fare paying travellers, notably business travellers, will not stay over the weekend.

In times of crisis or recession, special rates apply. In fact, recession has always been the mother of invention in tourism, giving rise to new initiatives that created new movement. Packages, cruises, specialist tours are all examples. Indeed many hotels have created events to attract business.

Tactical plans must be highly flexible, short term and changing to meet the varying 'tides' in demand, especially seasonal change. Economic and political 'perturbations' usually unexpected, can alter trade suddenly and sometimes with great force. Currency devaluation, the Gulf War and the severe recession of 1991 in world markets are examples.

The strategic plan with its long-term marketing implications needs consideration with the development plan. As marketing has a key role in product formulation the plan must select market segments. For example, it may give priority to quality and higher priced services, which will affect the investment in equipment to provide luxury items. It will be important to select segments that fit together. At a later stage in preparing the marketing plan, a detailed product/market match exercise will be necessary.

The early resort promoters understood the selective approach very well. There were from their inception select resorts, usually quiet, small and patronized by the 'upper classes' and higher spenders, and large, gregarious resorts which were popular centres for 'lower class' visitors.

Segmentation and motivation

Two key aspects of the third demand determinant – consumer preference – need careful study. Indeed the success of the whole marketing operation depends on this. They are segmentation and motivation.

Tourism's mass expansion takes many different forms. It is a heterogeneous not a homogeneous movement, made up of many different types of traveller, seeking a wide range of tourism products. Thus the mass movement divides up into a number of segments, each differing from the others and needing a separate approach in sales, servicing and product provision.

There are many possible divisions and subdivisions which can be made usefully in planning, but essentially the segmentation task is to identify specific groups in the travelling population interested in the same type of facility and service. The group identified must be large enough to warrant separate marketing or production attention, to make a specialist approach profitable. It must also be possible and practical to reach this section of the population in an effective way. This means that the group should not be too dispersed, and that there should be efficient media and distribution channels enabling the producer to reach the customer at a reasonable marketing cost.

There are a number of criteria and categories in segmenting the total market. First, geographic selection; most travel markets are country based. The conditions of trade, legislation, regulation, fiscal and economic conditions are set by each national government. Even in Europe, despite the efforts of the EU, national trading standards and conditions prevail in the travel trade for both tour operators and retail travel agents. Language, fashion, travel behaviour patterns and the organization of the travel trade preserve national markets for travel, including international travel. There are exceptions, notably the growth of hotel chains, but they differ from the more general pattern of industry organization in tourism.

While changing at a faster rate than previously, the geographic influence in marketing lies in the national structure. Thus the marketing plan assesses each main geographic market separately and provides a basis for a programme of action, varying according to potential, country by country.

It will be important to ensure diversification among the geographic markets, avoiding 'too many eggs in one basket'. Several times in recent years weakness in the US travel movement to Europe has been compensated by a growth in intra-European travel by Europeans. This was indeed the case in the year of the Gulf War. Places and services, such as hotels overdependent on American visitors, suffered.

Recession affects countries differently and with some time variation. Currencies may be devalued, but not all of them and not at the same time.

There is continuing choice between strengthening and weakening geographic markets. In 1993, Britain and a number of other European countries devalued their currencies on leaving the European monetary system, offering their visitors cheaper tourist facilities by 15 per cent or more. Chapter 4 explains the importance of exchange rate variations in travel. The US dollar, for example, weakened considerably in 1991–92, stimulating a large outward flow westbound from Europe to America. But a rapid revival in dollar value followed which reversed the relative change in a short time. Thus these movements can be volatile and substantial in volume.

Significant forms of segmentation deal with the more permanent divisions by age, education and purpose of journey. Currently longer term demographic change points to a growing number of elderly travellers, relatively affluent and active, and thus with the time and the means to spend more on tourism and international trips. However, for a variety of reasons youth travel has been declining in Europe even if still substantial in numbers. In general, international travel still appeals more to the better educated urban residents with above-average incomes.

As tourism grows in size so the movement becomes more specialized. There are many differing motivations and purposes in taking a trip away from home. A broad approach to segmentation will embrace the following: demographic characteristics (age, sex, family); economic (income); education; occupation; region of residence; social aspects or lifestyles (including religion).

Populations can be divided by socioeconomic groups, commonly referred to as A, B, C, D. A being higher incomes, D low incomes. The groups can be further subdivided, such as C1 and C2, to show finer gradations. This subdivision is widely used especially in describing the media audience, or newspaper circulation, indicating type of readership or television viewers. However industrialized countries have become more and more specialized in their interest and lifestyles, so that this first attempt at socioeconomic segmentation has become less efficient in identifying separate markets.

Travel motivations

These powerful influences are a mixture of interests (hobbies, leisure pursuits) and temperament. Classifications are complex because each traveller as an individual will have a number of preferences. Nevertheless it is usually possible to classify 'behaviour' groups to indicate main interests and indicate likely product demands and the marketing approach.

Behaviour linked to purpose of visit determines travel patterns, where visitors go and their expenditures, thus shaping the evolution of the market, travel 'packages' and ultimately the destinations themselves. There is an important difference between the organized package traveller and the individual tourist. However, increasingly mass tourism creates a very large body of sophisticated international tourists able to make their own arrangements. To meet their needs a form of 'do-it-yourself' packaging has developed, offering packaged components or services such as fly-drive offers, combining air transport and car hire at the destination airport. Such offers are especially appealing to the motorist, since cars are the majority form of transport. In Europe, 'individual' travellers have been increasing, even in recession years when much package travel decreased. Such travellers outnumber the package tourist by a substantial margin.

A motivation study for American Express Europe Ltd (1983) provided an example of travel behaviour and motivation patterns as a basis for segmentation. Although the study was directed to the identification of American attitudes to European travel, there is an increasing uniformity in travel attitudes in the Western urban society. This is especially likely with the relatively wealthy whose needs are broadly satisfied. They look for new interests, often in non-material fields.

This research revealed some significant changes in Americans' approach to travel. In general, Americans believe that vacations are no longer a 'luxury' but a right and no longer a 'once in a lifetime' thrill. Moreover, they perceive travel as 'needed to enhance my life' and use their travel experiences as a type of status badge. More specifically, the research reveals that vacations are really a reflection of a traveller's own beliefs and values. Attitudinally, individuals typically act on vacation with one of three frames of mind:

'1 "Survey Tourists'" who want to cover as much ground and see as many sites as they can. These people need support, a buffer between themselves and the foreign or unfamiliar.
2 "Aspiring Explorers" who want to be independent, yet privately admit to a desire for some kind of framework or umbilical cord to support them in case of emergencies or difficulties when travelling.
3 "Seasoned Travellers" who have the experience and confidence to be truly independent.

European travel marketing must respond to the needs of a number of distinct segments within American society. At one level, American society broadly splits between individuals who have "traditional" values versus those who have "contemporary" values. Within the "traditional" value category, two further segments exist, and while Europe can, and does, attract them, this research suggests that Europeans should be less interested in them. These two segments can be broadly described as:

1 "Stay at Home Americans" whose fear of "foreignness" outweighs all else. (This group talks of political unrest, terrorism, language barriers and foreign exchange confusion.)
2 "Play it Safe Travellers" to whose values Europeans are unresponsive.

The most attractive segments are those holding "contemporary" values, namely:

1 "Special Interest Travellers" who go on tours to get the most out of their travel experiences, and tend to choose tours linked to some particular interest they may have.
2 "Adventurers" who are young, "up-and-coming", travel frequently and look for immersion in new cultures, experiences and exotica.

3 "Elitists" who are very frequent European visitors and who are very affluent, travel throughout the year, and visit the less traditional European tourist markets.

4 "Grey Panthers" (i.e. the affluent retired) who have the time, money and inclination to take long European vacations.

5 "Extenders", i.e. those business travellers who frequently extend their business trips by taking a few days holiday at the same time.

6 "Elite", invariably high income, who visit very remote places such as the Galapagos Islands or Alaska or alternatively travel to the "in" places made fashionable by royals or the "jet set". These are the status seekers.

7 "Adventurers", often loners, who are prepared to rough it to an extent in the interests of seeing the new place – Tibet and parts of India are good examples. The explorers.

8 "Quality Seekers" – perhaps the largest group – seeking comfort and security, good-quality hotels, guides for excursions and visits to cultural or historic sites. Packaged and independent.

9 "Pursuers" – the "special interest" traveller – who pursues his hobby or a vocation even on holiday, ranging from railway buffs to painters and potters.

10 "Action Man", who pursues a sport and takes activity holidays – cycling to canoeing, golfing to tennis and, of course, skiing.

11 "Economy Seekers", the bargain hunters who will go to wherever is cheapest, invariably packaged.'

At least two of these segments – the 'Pursuers' and 'Action Man' – can be sub-segmented almost infinitely.

As the marketer pursues segmentation analysis it becomes clear that while demographic variables are useful in guiding the allocation of marketing resources, they should be used as a supplementary rather than a primary basis for determining target groups. Senior citizens do not represent a homogeneous group. They are heterogeneous, ranging from 60-year-old passive entertainment types to the 70-year-old active tourist who goes trekking in the Himalayas.

Greene (1982, p. 101) suggests a number of motivational factors that make people buy or spend their money (Table 9.2). Although identified for hotel services, they have a more general tourism application.

Part of the segmentation exercise is relatively straightforward, although involving substantial and professional desk work in economic analysis. The motivational or human part is complex and more difficult. Customers may not fit neatly into just one segment. Much will depend on reliable market research and survey material, and the skill of the operator in the marketplace with an intuitive feel for the customers" interests. The end result must be the identification of practical, valid market segments, in other words real "markets", using the motivation and "behaviour" information as criteria for establishing the separate categories.

The segments must be described in terms of quantity, i.e. volume and value. Each must represent a discrete or distinct group of people likely to behave in a similar way regarding desires and expectations. The segments identified must be responsive to cost-effective marketing. This means that it

Table 9.2 Motivational factors inducing people to buy

1. Fear	– insurance
2. Security	– burglar alarms, spy holes, new door
3. Loneliness	– televisions
4. Curiosity	– televisions, historical buildings
5. Status – 'keeping up with the Joneses'	– videotape recorders to a Rolls-Royce
6. Ego	– this seemed to relate to Status
7. Possession/envy	– this seemed to be related to items under Status
8. Basic needs	– water, salt, bread and a blanket for warmth
9. Religion	– money spent on christenings, etc.
10. Mental relaxation/ physical health	– hobbies – sports – relaxation
11. Price	– buying something reduced in price
12. Value for money	– not necessarily related completely to price
13. Investment	– shares, stocks
14. Personal comfort	– central heating, air conditioning
15. Guilt	– present for wife!
16. Shortages	– in some countries with import controls
17. Educational/research	– correspondence courses, evening classes
18. Sentiment	– photographs

Source: Greene, M., *Marketing Hotels into the 90s*, 1982, p. 101.

must be possible to reach the group through available and affordable sales techniques, implying a concentration of likely clients in certain cities and towns.

Motivations cannot be measured precisely. Several may interact. Individuals are motivated in different ways. Research attempts to find the common dominators. The marketing task is to identify segments where a large enough number of people have similar needs and to satisfy these needs at a profit. Figure 9.4 sums up the approach to the segmentation exercise.

The promotion activity itself aims to influence expectations, to build on or in some cases to create a favourable image. Sales may depend on the brand or brand image. This is often true in tourism where the product is sold from the promotion material, the brochure or poster, at a distance, unseen and unsampled at least for the first visit. Then the promotion can be the package or the product.

However, it is essential that the promise offered in the promotion is delivered. The penalty for failure is high in business terms. Loss of goodwill and credibility when the glamorous image fades can be fatal. Some severe decline in traffic to the Mediterranean and other hot sun resorts including the Caribbean, at the beginning of the decade, resulted in much loss of tourism revenues. Package travel out of Britain, for example, largely to certain Mediterranean and especially Spanish resort areas decreased by 20 per cent or more in two years. Package trips declined from over 12 to 9 million in that short time; a sudden drop large enough to cause financial dislocation in many areas. This new volatility in some forms of mass travel creates new economic problems for both public and private sector interests. However, during this period individual travel and total outward travel from Britain continued to increase, albeit at a slower rate due to recession and other factors.

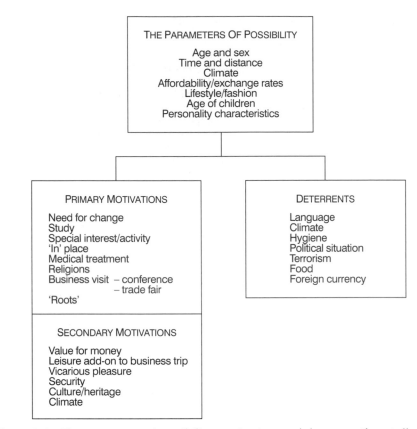

Figure 9.4   The parameters of possibility: motivations and deterrents (from Jefferson and Lickerish, 1991 by permission)

Product strength and weakness analysis

Market product analysis and market appraisal in terms of strengths and weaknesses, sometimes called a SWOT (strengths, weaknesses, opportunities and threats) analysis is as fundamental as the basic market investigation.

Marketing action must have a strong product responsibility, and ensure that periodic testing is carried out with precision. All organizations concerned with the tourist trade, whether public or private sector, must be market not product oriented. It is not good enough, nor likely to be successful, to make a product simply because it suits the destination residents" interests or the resource owners. Product evaluation and new product formulation starts as an essential part of the development plan, just as marketing strategy must itself be related to the development plan and the organization"s business strategy.

The following examples indicate the approach to strength and weakness analysis as a basis for product formulation.

The British Tourist Authority has carried out from time to time a thorough SWOT analysis, taking into account visitor surveys. The study also deals with matters to be addressed, and reports of action taken or planned with government, local authorities, tourist boards and industry (BTA, 1989; BTA, 1991, 1992).

The SWOT analysis can play an essential part in the marketing planning process. Such techniques were instrumental, for example, in overcoming off-season troughs. London hotels with a low winter week-end occupancy 25 years ago created city weekend breaks which transformed their trade by attracting new clientele for a new product. The words "off season" were banished. City attractions in the theatre, entertainment, shopping and sports (football) were promoted, featuring as city highlights in the "lively months" and attracting a substantial clientele from home and abroad.

Once clearly identified, the strengths will be strongly promoted and the weaknesses in many cases can be corrected. Indeed many of them may in fact prove to be unjustified perceptions, such as "it always rains there", or "restaurants are not good". Generalizations are rarely true, but criticism can be very constructive in sharpening the competitive edge.

The SWOT analysis must be a strictly objective assessment. This is essential in a competitive situation when switching brands or products is a real possibility. Factors such as food, hygiene, safety and government controls must be measured as accurately as possible.

Britain: Strengths and Weaknesses As Seen in the Early 1990s (BTA *Strategy for Growth* publications)

Strengths:

1 Product strengths:
   (a) politically stable
   (b) internationally recognized
   (c) wide touristic appeal
   (d) many year-round attractions
   (e) international communication centre
   (f) English is the main international business language
   (g) London Heathrow – international gateway for Europe and the world
   (h) links of kinship with many countries
   (i) unique appeal of British countryside
   (j) scenic diversity.
   (k) London's worldwide reputation
   (l) centre of commerce/business and communications
   (m) entertainment capital of the world
   (n) heritage, culture and the arts
   (o) long history
   (p) tradition and pageantry
   (q) the Royal Family
   (r) entertainment
   (s) sporting events
   (t) other spectacles
   (u) wide range of accommodation from international luxury hotels to bed and breakfast guest houses

(v) good universities/colleges and English language schools
(w) good information services in Britain and abroad
(x) ease of movement around Britain by a variety of transport

2 Market strengths:
(a) worldwide; EEC and rest of Europe, North America, Australasia, Middle East and Africa, New Markets, e.g. Far East – a better spread than other European competitor countries
(b) product market segments
(c) business, business-related, especially conference/trade fair/incentive travel
(d) youth (including education)
(e) senior citizen
(f) ethnic
(g) visits to friends and relatives
(h) specialist appeals in sports, hobbies and other leisure pursuits, offering stable and resilient traffic with great worldwide potential.

3 Weaknesses:
(a) service quality: more attention to improvement needed in view of high and increasing international standards
(b) litter and environmental protection: clean beaches, rivers etc.
(c) unfavourable perceptions: Britain abroad, e.g. climate and value for money in certain markets
(d) the travel trade not committed to British tourism products – information and reservation systems need improvement, especially for the independent travellers
(e) more investment needed in capital projects, especially in resort amenities
(f) more budget-priced accommodation needed in London and certain other urban centres
(g) inadequate investment in transport infrastructure, e.g. port facilities, airports and air traffic control, rail travel, roads and parking, especially for coaches
(h) better reception and entry formalities required
(i) improved training and better language abilities needed in key tourism trades
(j) longer opening hours required for attractions, out-of-peak periods and shops in certain tourism areas.

Greene (1982, p. 28) comments:

It is essential to decide what the strengths and weaknesses of your product are, bearing in mind the demands and requirements of the different sources of business and the strengths and weaknesses of your main competitors.

He emphasizes two key points. First, there will almost certainly be several types of business or several market segments, e.g. business travellers on weekdays and pleasure travellers at weekends. In fact, the variation in the segments is likely to be much greater. The second important point is the competition. In a free market this must be matched. The competitive edge must not be eroded. Currently in Europe there are serious weaknesses: world market share is declining substantially, and the competitive edge is in practice suffering erosion, especially from North America, Asia and the Pacific. Transatlantic traffic, for so long dominated by American visitors to Europe, now depends for a majority of passengers on Europeans visiting north America.

The object of the SWOT analysis must be to select those segments and products where the organization"s advantages are greatest, whether the marketing objective is a particular hotel, an airline, a resort or a country as the destination.

Greene points out that even for the hotel the product can be changed, and some of the changes can be made quickly, e.g. new decor, special themes, new designs and staff uniforms. The business can grade up in price and service, or grade down, moving towards the bargain basement. But this requires careful market study, as in some cases it will be difficult to change back.

The action plan

The SWOT analysis will lead to policy formulation, and plans for product improvement, with the marketing plan following the product/market match studies. These must be the basis for the operational and business plan.

Clearly the "action plan" must be a combination of marketing and product improvement as the two are so directly related, with marketing orientation the leading force. Sometimes product improvement will follow naturally from a definition of the offer or repositioning the product in the marketplace. The opening of a modern hotel in a town or resort may threaten an old-fashioned hostelry. The new establishment is bound to attract business. The result will depend to some extent on external factors, such as whether the total market is growing. However, the traditional hotel may be able to concentrate on its unique differences: historic connections, old-fashioned charm, and appeal to new market segments, e.g. overseas visitors. Marketing initiatives could feature packages for short stays (breaks) with tours based on local features of interest, and changes in price and services.

There is sometimes a temptation for a product-dominated approach to be chosen by the destination authority, usually the local authority. They will be keen to maximize the use of existing facilities, even if are they not up to date, or improved to meet changing demand. There is no justification for such a policy even if, in a largely non-commercial operation, the discipline of profit and loss may not operate.

Cost benefit guidelines, and appraisals of performance against objectives are much more difficult but no less necessary. The principle of operation must be the same; the most effective use of inevitably limited resources in meeting agreed objectives for the business. This is as compelling for the destination – the resort – as for the individual business.

It is not the tourists themselves who need or indeed should be managed, but rather the tourist resources, often the responsibility of the public sector. Tourist resources are an essential item in the planning and marketing process. There should be an agreed strategy for their management, clearly expressed in the business and marketing plans. Of course, special skills are required in organizing, guiding and catering for large groups of visitors, and controlling traffic flows, especially at peak times, by road and in congested areas. Such needs, together with other aspects of the supply of services necessary to cater for tourist traffic, must be in development and marketing plans.

The host region has an obligation to welcome, care for and serve the visitors, their paying guests. The regional or local authority on behalf of the population must decide how they wish to develop their tourism trade, that is if they wish to welcome visitors and benefit from their company and expenditure. The decision must involve the preparation and agreement of a strategy and plan as the basis for the invitation, the promotion and the product supervision and delivery.

Market research and analysis, listing of options, careful examination of product provision, and the product market match, provide the basis for the formulation of overall policy and the related strategies for both marketing and product development. The two are interdependent and indeed the time scale for planning and operation is similar. The main difference is that the product may require long-term fixed capital investment with limited means of rapid change, whereas markets may become increasingly volatile with short-term variations.

Product/market fit

There are a number of ways of preparing product/market fit strategies. The following charts taken from the British Tourist Authority's Market Plan, show how the process can work for a destination authority. Allowance has to be made for the fact that usually the destination marketing organization, such as a national or local tourist board, has no direct control or responsibility for most of the services and facilities making up their 'product'. Of course, such a body can and should have a powerful influence, especially if the marketing operations are carried out in consultation and cooperation with the operating sectors. In this way the destination promotion will carry commercial messages and often specific sales offers from the chosen commercial partners.

Combining destinations and product publicity can be very effective. It is rather like a two-stage rocket. Destination selling attracts attention for the whole area – the first and vital task. The second and later stage when the potential traveller has clarified intentions and moved closer to the point of sale, involves much greater precision as to cost, brand and specific services to be chosen. This is inevitably a more competitive activity.

It will be noted that BTA segments traffic first into holidays, centred and touring, and business travel. These main segments are then subdivided into much more detail, examining specialist activity and varying behaviour groups which can be separately identified.

Table 9.3 Nordic markets: product demand – Sweden

Product	Lon.	S. Engl.	M. Engl.	N. Engl.	Wales	Scot.	N. Ire.
			Demand (region)				
Coach tours, origin in Britain	L	L	N	L	N	L	N
Coach tours, origin overseas	M	M	L	L	L	M	L
Car touring, preplanned/booked	N	L	L	L	L	L	L
Car touring no accommodation booked	N	H	M	M	M	H	L
Coach independent	L	L	L	L	L	L	N
Rail independent	M	M	M	M	M	M	N
Camping and caravanning	N	L	L	L	L	L	N
Motor homes	N	L	L	L	L	L	N
Centre holidays	H	M	L	L	L	L	N
Short breaks	H	L	L	N	N	N	N
Waterway holidays	N	N	M	M	M	M	N
Self-catering	M	M	M	L	L	M	N
English language study	H	H	N	N	N	L	N
Youth activity centres	M	M	L	L	L	L	N
Association conferences	H	H	L	M	L	M	N
Corporate conferences	H	H	L	M	L	M	N
Incentive travel	H	M	L	M	L	M	N
Visits to trade fairs/ exhibitions	M	N	M	L	L	L	N

Key: N, Nil; L, Low; M, Medium; H, High demand.
Region: Lon., London; S. Engl., Southern England; M. Engl., Midlands; N. Engl.,
   Northern England; Scot., Scotland; N. Ire., Northern Ireland.

Source: *BTA Marketing Plan, 1992–93*.

A product/market fit chart is given also for a hotel to indicate the difference, more of detail than principle, applying to any commercial service or undertaking.

The charts can be much more complex, dependent upon the marketing task. Since tourism is becoming much more specialized, there are an increasing number of smaller markets, some mini mass markets and what are often termed 'niche' markets which specialist operators can develop. Furthermore, a wide range of non-commercial operators – associations, clubs, institutions, such as schools, church groups and societies offering travel and recreation as a membership benefit – are together responsible for a substantial part of total movement. In practice, each category of product in such cases is likely to appeal to a specialist market segment. The organizations should ensure cost-effective marketing, especially if promotional funds are very limited which is usually the case. The likely clientele must be targeted narrowly, concentrating on priority groups which may be limited in numbers (Table 9.3). The product list (Table 9.4) is capable of much expansion to isolate the hotel's special advantages and the locality's attractions as the setting for special events or amenities and tours, etc.

In planning promotion, priority should be given to yields. Some forms of traffic will be more profitable or fill empty beds in the slack periods. Some may be regular, others dependent on intermediaries. Groups and marginal trade may require substantially discounted rates.

Origins of traffic may need a more detailed analysis, such as domestic business by distance, e.g. up and beyond 100 miles (160 km) travel. Overseas business is likely to be concentrated in a few markets; for example France, Belgium and North America and perhaps in a small number of cities in each country. Clearly this information is vital in directing sales efforts.

Marketing campaigns

When the planning stages are completed, the final and most testing marketing task is to implement the action plan through the specific marketing campaigns. These must be directed to the selected segments, and will use a variety of media, or means of reaching the potential client with the message about the product for sale and its availability. The campaigns represent the sales effort, crucial to the success of the organization.

Table 9.4 Product/market fit: table for a hotel

	Domestic			Overseas*						
	Local	(Up to 100 miles)	(Up to 200 miles)	Rest	A	B	C	D	E	F
Meeting/hobby/groups				1						
Weddings/banquets	5									
Lunches/dinners	4									
Association lunches/dinners	4									
Independent leisure			1		1	1	1	1	1	1
Car touring leisure			2		2					
Leisure learning weekend		1	1	1	1		1			
Off-peak break			3	3				1		
Coach touring				2	2	2	2	2	2	2
Independent business	1	1	1							
Corporate meetings		2	2							
Trade fairs										
Incentive travel				1						

* A, B, C, D, E, F denote countries of residence of visitors, e.g. A for USA, B for Germany, C for France, D for the Netherlands, in order of priority. Boxes would be completed on a scale of 1–5 or 10 as preferred, to denote relative importance or size, depending on the hotel's record of visits. Day visits should be indicated for important segments. Some examples are given.

Source: Based on Lickorish *et al.*, *Developing Tourism Destinations*.

The marketer will use a variety of media or sales tools, dependent on the segment to be targeted.

Choice depends on judgements as to cost effectiveness. Media, especially advertising, can be relatively expensive. However, tourism promotion has some special advantages if properly planned. The supplier is interdependent on many other interests, some competitive but some complementary. Most to a greater or lesser extent share a common interest in the destination. Thus there is a strong cooperative factor. Usually the tourist board or local authority will provide the focal point or platform for selling the destination. For a small hotel with very limited promotion resources this cooperative opportunity can be crucial. Many of its visitors will come in response to advertising in the local guide or from the local information centres, many of which provide a reservation service specializing in inexpensive accommodation or last-minute bookings which the commercial agencies cannot handle profitably.

Campaigns will evidently vary according to the product or objective, but all will have certain elements in common. The aim must be clear and should be measurable; for example to reach existing markets, or to create identifiable new markets, or both, and to make it 'easy to buy'. This factor, realized through effective distribution of the product and efficient reservation systems, is vital to success and indeed can be the most important single element.

The marketing mix and marketing campaigns

The marketing plan requires selection from a number of variables and promotional media and resources. Table 9.5 summarizes the principal variables.

In this age of communication and related revolution in marketing practices new methods, resources and tools are available to bring the product to the notice of the customers and to make it easy to buy. Figure 9.6 describes the promotional techniques used in tourism in more detail.

The marketing variables and promotion tools are not equal in their effects. Table 9.7 sets out a suggested weighting of marketing tools for a hotel and

Table 9.5 Marketing and promotion techniques

Marketing variable	*Application to tourism*
Price	Policy, margins, discounts and special offers seasonal rates
Product	Quality, range, packages, group offers
Place (of sale)	Shop (travel agent or principal, e.g. airline). Home (other intermediary such as an institution, e.g. club, school, church). Home via direct mail, phone, video, television systems, computer reservation systems.
Promotion	Advertising, public relations, literature, trade promotion, merchandising.

Source: Based on Lickorish *et al.*, *Developing Tourism Destinations*.

Table 9.6 Promotion options and tools

Promotion and sales media	Application to tourism
A Persuading and informing the prospective clientele:	
Advertising	Press, magazines, radio, TV, posters, and other-paid for media.
Literature	Brochures, guidebooks, maps and other print and photographic material.
Display material and sales	Exhibitions, workshops, road shows, etc., and distribution of display material to agents. Intermediaries, shops, libraries; in general material for use at point of sale.
Films	Widely used on the TV, video cassettes in special promotion by trade and intermediaries and in the home.
Direct sales	Usually by direct mail to the prospective client, but by many forms of distribution often linked to public relations action, direct contract with the principal airlines or hotel.
Public relations	Information and material, (films, photos), provided for inclusion in the press, radio, TV and other media. Sponsorship, journalists' visits, press conferences, seminars, etc.
B Persuading and informing the trade (travel agent or other intermediary):	
Trade promotions	Advertising, display market, literature, trade shows.
Educational visitors and courses	The aim is to ensure that the trade can present the product in an attractive way and make it easy to buy.
Commission	The agent is not normally paid by the client (except as wholesaler or tour operators), so payment by the principal as commission, incentives rewards, display and other technical support is compelling.
Distribution networks	Sales and reservations links between the producer (the principals and their agents or sales point). For example, computer reservation systems, marketing franchises, hotel consortia, 'book a bed ahead' schemes, in local information bureau such as the VVV network in the Netherlands. Networks are increasingly linked to direct selling operations in the home.

for a national tourist office (NTO) as an illustration. Although this shows the NTO as having no role in product policy or pricing, this ignores the strong indirect influence of the official government tourist organization. Some have powers to monitor or control prices, in hotels for example. There may be subsidies or tax remission schemes to encourage certain types of tourism, and other institutions. The NTO may initiate new products or packages through the trade and at the local centres, etc. Nevertheless its role as a producer or trader is normally marginal, although the indirect influence can be marked.

Table 9.7   Relative weighting of marketing tools

Hotel		NTO
3	New product policy	
1	Pricing and margins	
2	Branding	3
2	Promotions/themes	4
4	Channels of distribution	3
1	Personal selling	6
6	Public relations	3
5	Advertising	2
3	Packaging/product marketing	5
5	Exhibitions	3
	Display and posters	6
	Information services	1
6	Print	2
7	Films and video	4

Source: Jefferson and Lickorish, *Marketing Tourism*, 1991, p.169.

Distribution

The marketing task consists of two basic functions. First, to ensure that the consumer likely to be interested in the product knows about its existence and values, and secondly, how to buy it through efficient supply channels. The two functions are of course interrelated and need to be coordinated in practice.

The special characteristics of tourism referred to earlier need to be taken into account: the wide range of products and the interdependence of the components (e.g. transport and accommodation). Methods of promotion and distribution will vary in each of the main travel trades concerned and by market segment.

For a large part of the total market the traveller will go to the product and not as customary in trade the product brought to the consumer, displayed for example in the retailer's shop for inspection and even trial. Most tourists, especially in the case of international travel, will buy 'at a distance' 'sight unseen', e.g. package holiday abroad at a strange destination.

The promotion media and the distribution channels accordingly will be many and varied. The linked systems and the distribution process in particular are best studied by examining the ways in which the varying segments or types of traveller buy their services, and more precisely the place or points where the sale is concluded. These include:

1 *The travel trade*: wholesalers (tour operators who are also principals) and retail (travel agents). It is not always appreciated that the travel agent acts for his principal, the supplier of key services, transport and accommodation, etc. However, the tour operator is not only a distributor, but a manufacturer of a complete tourist product, and is a principal.

2 *Travel shops*, normally the retail travel agent's premises. Increasingly the large tour operators in a process of vertical integration own or control retail outlets, as well as charter airlines, and computerized reservation systems. A proportion of their clients will book directly by phone or through new technology, as well as by mail.

3 *The principals*, transport organizations especially airlines, hotels, theatres (box offices) and other entertainment, and event organizers.

Many customers will buy at a distance, using computer reservations systems, described further in more detail, by credit card and in some cases by personal calls at the principals' premises or travel shop.

Many principals clearly encourage direct selling to cut out the expenses of the middleman by offering benefits. Airlines set great store by their loyalty schemes, e.g. the British Airways Executive Club offering airport lounges and other services.

Airlines have a special position in their control of reservations systems which cover other journey-related services such as accommodation. This, together with globalization of big business and mulitnational operation, gives rise to fears of monopoly positions.

The development of information technology in many forms is occurring so fast that it is difficult to forecast impacts on the total distribution system. Information systems, such as Minitel in France, have succeeded in attracting a noticeable market share and substantial use by consumers. Similar attempts in Britain failed. Home buying by computer or television is not yet popular. But for some segments there is clearly potential. Credit card booking and video sales promotion facilitates buying.

The tourism movement is now so vast and so highly segmented that there is room for many distribution systems. The frequent traveller and the more sophisticated tourist is more likely to buy directly from the principal (the airline, hotel, car hire company, etc.). The travel trade is most important in the international field, but in Europe it has only a minority share in international leisure travel. Of domestic travel it accounts for less than 5 per cent in many countries.

Thus the majority of tourists in Europe do not use the middlemen, but make their own arrangements with the principals. In fact, most domestic tourists are self-motivated, self-organized and 'self-transported' in their own cars. Finally over 50 per cent stay in non-commercial or supplementary accommodation: with friends and relatives, camping and caravanning, hostels, second homes, etc.

4 *Other (auxiliary) travel organizers.* A large force of non-commercial or specialist operators have always been a force in tourism and appear to be increasing as the travel trade proper concentrates on selling a limited range of 'mass products'. These outlets are found in clubs, institutions, societies and organizers in the educational, social (youth) cultural and religious fields. The American Society for Retired People, for example, is a powerful force. Many act as principals, organizing complete packages for day, weekend and longer outings at home and abroad.

Thus the marketplace is enormous and varied. The principals accordingly must operate in the marketplace in a number of different ways. In general, the higher the price and the longer the distances travelled, the more likely the professional agent or tour operator will handle the sales. This is also true in the case of a mass market for a standard product which can be mass produced, such as a holiday for Northern Europeans in the sun. The tour operators will be able to offer acceptable quality and competitive prices and by so doing will need to control the distribution and sales points for their product.

The importance of coordinating key travel services and their distribution over the years of massive expansion in international movement led to much vertical integration: airlines owning hotels, tour operators owning charter airlines and latterly chains of retail travel agents and now computer reservation systems (CRSs). Vertical integration, stimulated by the need to ensure the supply of essential services, has diminished. However, the pressures to safeguard market access has increased.

Each business, however modest, needs to develop its own marketing plan and related distribution strategy. Techniques and marketing tools change constantly and more rapidly in the modern world. However in tourism the travel guide, article and brochure – the printed word – continues to play a leading role in the marketing system, particularly for the independent and usually sophisticated traveller interested in new places to visit and new experiences. For many in the mass market, television, video cassettes and other developments in information technology become more important. Yet selling by such methods in the past has not made much progress. Advice and guidance through the travel trade outlets has become more difficult, as in many cases they concentrate on the sale of a limited number of package tour programmes. The official local information offices in resorts and tourism centres, usually the responsibility of the local authority, have become an important provider of sales information for the individual traveller. Many offer sales services e.g. accommodation booking, essential for the provision of low-cost accommodation such as bed and breakfast facilities. They play a key role in welcoming the independent domestic and foreign visitor. However, many are underfunded and without resources and new technology. They have a great potential and are often the key to the provision of a satisfactory 'after-sales service'.

The greatest change in recent years in the marketing mix and promotion tools can be seen in the advance of information technology and reservations services. An increasing proportion of sales is being made direct from the home or client's office by phone and credit card. New technology continues to advance; the Internet for example. These developments have important implications for tourism at a time when the proportion of repeat and sophisticated travellers increases much faster than the total market, encouraging the growth of independent travel. The limited services of many retail travel outlets encourages this change in the sales process.

Computer reservation systems

A computer reservation system (CRS) is a computer distribution system for displaying available services and facilities, making bookings and ticketing by tourism producers (e.g. airlines and other transport modes, hotels, car hire, inclusive tours, cruises etc.). The principal systems have a major advantage by securing payment for the producer and providing management information and capability of last minute changes.

In addition to benefits of rapid service and making it 'easy to buy', the resulting increased productivity in the sales chain leads to lower distribution costs.

The main systems were developed rapidly in the 1980s by the major airlines. They, and other large companies such as hotel chains, have their own in-house or house systems which stock availabilities of capacity of inventory. There are other distribution services reviewed in this chapter which might be more suitable for smaller businesses. Different systems may interface. Multi-access links specific market segments or regions. Mass distribution through retail stores or electronic media (Minitel) are examples of a wide field which is developing rapidly as tourism expands.

In the late 1980s Global Distribution Systems (GDS) developed by the airlines, the main customers of the systems and paying the costs, installed terminals in agencies worldwide. By 1996 most travel agencies in the USA were connected (over 90 per cent) and the majority in major European countries (over 60 per cent), but some parts of the world, e.g. Africa lag behind.

To avoid unfair or monopoly trading it is essential that the systems are neutral and objective in information provision. Governments have introduced mandatory codes of practice to ensure this.

By 1996 following mergers there are six major systems: Abacus, Amadeus, Gallileo International, Sabre, System One and Wordspan. This remains a field of fast-moving technology but the costs are massive.

After-sales services

A tourist product, i.e. the provision of services and facilities for a complete visit whether for business or leisure, is a relatively expensive 'mass' purchase. A package holiday or even a short business trip abroad may cost £300 or more, the price of a relatively large purchase of consumer goods. The manufacturers of such goods, however, will provide after-sales service to ensure satisfactory use or enjoyment. This is often lacking in tourism, partly because of the range of services and suppliers involved. The after-sales service is just as important in tourism to safeguard future business and recommendation, and by increasing satisfaction to generate repeat custom and greater length of stay. This is one of the necessary cooperative tasks in tourism, and an essential responsibility of the destination interests, the local or state tourism office. They need to research visitor behaviour and recreation. Action can then be taken to improve services and deal with deficiencies.

Tourist information offices can play a key role in this task and supplement or extend their services by recorded telephone messages, radio and television programmes, and the distribution of literature in hotels and other tourism centres. 'What's on' reports are very important in increasing satisfaction with the visit and stimulating sales, and delivering the product to the customer.

Budgeting

The cost of the different techniques or media varies greatly. Advertising, especially on television, requires a large budget but is most used for the mass products (airlines, tour operators). It is, however, possible to mount very effective campaigns by smaller destinations and businesses, at modest cost using literature, public relations methods and distribution and sales networks.

The budget allocation will determine in part the selection of media. Some may be inexpensive such as public relations activities: persuading journalists and travel writers to feature the establishment or service, but in such cases there is a 'price to pay'. The seller has no control over timing, the audience reaction or the message itself. While this can provide a useful background medium for tourist boards, or when opening up new markets, the effects are likely to be uncertain. Good news about good tourism services travels fast. The product is popular and can be of great interest. However, the reverse is true. Bad news can circulate rapidly and failures can be costly to rectify or mitigate damage in crisis reporting.

The search for new markets can be expensive, but some investment is necessary as tourism movement becomes more volatile. Most businesses have a mix of clientele, where some forms of trade complement others. A hotel, for example, may have a local clientele, important for catering, a business clientele, and a tourism trade providing weekend and holiday season visitors when business travel declines.

Budgeting marketing campaigns is never easy. Clearly the total investment must be related to the business and revenue to be generated. A simple rule is to estimate the cost of reaching potential clients identified and the expected response in sales. This is more practical if regular appraisals of past promotions have been carried out, so that there is some guidance from practical experience of likely response to media selected, such as replies from advertising in the local guides or in tourist board publications. This gives an estimated promotion cost per sale, important in planning promotion for new business.

There will be special situations, such as crisis periods, when for example trade may be diverted as a result of new attractions, recession or political instability. Great efforts may be necessary to mitigate damage, or to seek new trade, but it is important to plan even more carefully and to use basic market research or intelligence. In past years, for example when transatlantic traffic to Europe has faced sudden disruptions through crises such as the Gulf War, some destinations spent substantial amounts on promotion to no good effect. If markets collapse in such circumstances, neither the will nor the money to buy may be available. The only practical action will be to wait for stability to return and seek alternative trade if possible. In fact in the Gulf War period intra-European and domestic traffic increased for a number of successful European resort areas, as the European residents themselves cancelled their long-distance trips and chose tourism services nearer to home.

Thus it is important to ensure that promotion is directed accurately to the segment representing people who have incomes and interests suited to the product to be offered for sale. Tourism may be an enormous and growing mass market, but it is very heterogeneous. Segmentation study must identify precisely clients interested in the specific destination or service. Demand becomes increasingly specialized. One man's idea of heaven on earth is no paradise for another. At any one time there are both expanding and declining market segments. Even in the boom years of the past, some resorts declined.

There will be a variety of approaches, according to destination, location, trade and business objectives. Assessment of results is essential, with continuing effort to measure performance against objectives, using market research as a basis for future market planning and related product development. The trade must remain market oriented.

References

American Express Europe Ltd (1983) *1985 European Travel – The Way Ahead*, London

British Tourist Authority (1989) *Strategy for Growth*, BTA, London

British Tourist Authority (1991, 1992) *Guidelines for Tourism to Britain*, BTA, London

Greene, M. (1982) *Marketing Hotels into the 90s*, Heinemann, London

Jefferson, A. and Lickorish, L. (1991) *Marketing Tourism*, Longman, Harlow, Essex, UK

Kotler, P. (1967) *Marketing Management*, Prentice Hall, London

Kotler, P. (1984) *Marketing Management: Analysis Planning and Control*, Prentice Hall International, London

Levitt, T. (1964) *Modern Marketing Strategy*, edited by Bursk and Chapman, New English Library, London

Lickorish, L. *et al.* (1991) *Developing Tourism Destinations*, Pitman, London

Middleton, V. C. T. (1988) *Marketing in Travel and Tourism*, Butterworth-Heinemann, Oxford

Further reading

Davidson, R. (1994) *Business Travel*, Longman, Harlow, Essex, UK

Holloway C. (1995) *Marketing for Tourism*, 3rd edn, Longman, Harlow, Essex, UK

Seaton, A. V. and Bennett, M. (1996) *Marketing Tourism Products*, Chapman & Hall, London

World Tourism Organization (1993) *Recommendations on Tourism Statistics*, WTO, Madrid

10 Tourism policy, planning and development

Introduction

Planning for tourism development can take place at various levels. Some countries have national tourism development plans and it is not unusual within this national structure to find similar planning exercises having been made for subnational regions, towns, cities, etc. The concept of planning is very wide. Planning is essentially about the utilization of tourism assets and their development into a marketable state. So before the planning exercise begins it is necessary to set out tourism development objectives, i.e. what the development plan seeks to achieve.

These planning objectives are often formulated into a tourism policy statement which sets out parameters or guidelines which steer development planning into the future. A tourism policy is not a tourism plan, but rather the reference point against which planning decisions should be related. Once the tourism policy has been agreed and established, usually by government, then a tourism planning exercise seeks to achieve the objectives which have been incorporated into the policy. The planning exercise must incorporate considerations of implementation i.e. how the plan is to be achieved. Following from implementation there is a need to establish a monitoring mechanism which constantly reviews the implementation of the plan against the set objectives. Very often monitoring might be highly specific, e.g. relating to number of forecast tourist arrivals or earnings from tourism; or sometimes it will be much less formalized e.g. in relation to cultural impacts of tourism. The monitoring of tourism development is important because it is likely that not all policy objectives can be achieved and therefore there is a need to refine and probably reformulate the plan.

There are six stages in tourism development planning:

1 The establishment of objectives.
2 The incorporation of these objectives into a policy statement.
3 The formulation of policy guidelines to establish planning parameters.
4 An implementation programme to achieve what is set out in the plan.
5 A monitoring mechanism to assess whether the tourism development plan is meeting its objectives.
6 A review process to revise and refine objectives and policies as necessary.

This sequence is ongoing and should be used as a flexible rather than a rigid approach to tourism development.

Tourism objectives

Because tourism impacts on a country in relation to its economy and society there are many issues to be considered. For example, it is not only the economic advantages which tourism might generate, but also it is well known that tourism is likely to have impacts in environmental, cultural and social terms which will require very careful evaluation. Depending on the level of the planning exercise, the formulation of objectives for tourism will be the responsibility of governments, with local governments and other representative bodies. It is now fairly common that part of the establishment of objectives for tourism involves discussions between government and private sector partners. Traditionally, policy and planning has been undertaken by government alone, but this is a practice which is changing in many countries. As tourism is recognized as a market-driven activity, increasingly the private sector expects to be included in the policy formulation process.

In most developed countries there is the expectation that tourism will be facilitated by government at the national and regional levels, but the main commercial services for tourists will be provided by the private sector. This is not always the case, as examples in Chapter 11 illustrate. However, government now tends towards providing a so-called 'enabling environment', that is, providing the legislative and infrastructural framework to encourage commercial activities to flourish. The Indonesian government's and international agency investment in the preparation of the Nusa Dua site in Bali is one example. In recent years there has been a considerable shift in governments' attitudes to the tourism sector. In the UK, the government has progressively reduced its direct financial support to the national tourist boards; in Sweden, the national tourism board was suspended; the US government has closed the United States Travel and Tourism Agency.

Despite these examples, most tourist-receiving countries recognize a need to establish a national and international presence in the tourism market. All significant tourism countries except the USA have representative tourism organizations. Tourism is an important activity for many countries, and governments usually want to have some control over the type and direction of the sectors' development. In countries such as France, Italy and the Republic of Ireland, governments have and continue to play a major role in the tourism sector. Their most important intervention is to provide political approval for the type and direction of development objectives.

Tourism objectives are often unrealistic because they are statements of ambition rather than of reality. For this reason it is necessary to look carefully at what might be possible and how to achieve those possibilities. This is an essential starting point for sound and sensible planning. It is, of course, possible to undertake tourism planning without either having considered objectives or determining policies; that is, the objectives are created by the planning exercise. It is interesting to note that in the UK and the USA and in some other well-developed tourism countries there is often

no formal statement of tourism planning or evidence of a tourism policy
ever having been determined. There is no tourism policy in the EU, nor is
any priority given to the industry in the Union's programmes. In the
developing countries, on the other hand, the scarcity of resources and the
need to utilize these resources carefully and to allocate them between
competing demands makes planning an essential input to the development
process.

Without objectives it is very difficult to formulate a realistic policy for
tourism. The starting point is to look at what objectives may be appropriate
in developing tourism. This task must be related to national development
objectives. The tourism sector is one sector in the economy; it may be the
dominant sector or a minor sector. In considering future development and
support for the sector there has to be a clear vision of how tourism fits into
the overall economy. In some oil-rich countries it may be that the foreign
exchange earnings potential of tourism is less significant than its ability to
generate employment; some of the Gulf States fall into this category. In other
countries, e.g. India, the main importance of tourism in economic terms is
the earnings of foreign exchange. A further consideration is that the
importance of tourism's ability to contribute to national objectives is not
necessarily the same priority at subnational level. In Zambia, for example,
the potential to earn foreign exchange from tourism is seen as the main
means of substituting for falling earnings of foreign exchange from copper
exports. However, in that country most tourism activity is based on wildlife
viewing in the bush areas, and tourism is accorded a high priority to
increase rural employment and income and to stimulate the multiplier effect
in some of the poorest areas of the country.

Even in developed countries where there is no formal national development plan, there will be extensive planning undertaken at subnational
levels. Where tourism is important, e.g. the Lake District in England, the
Alpine regions in Austria and Switzerland, the Mediterranean basin in
Europe, considerable attention has been given to what objectives should be
set for tourism development. As noted in Chapter 7, environmental factors
are becoming global concerns and tourism depends on a high-quality
environment for its future sustainability.

Tourism policy

Not every tourism-receiving country has formulated a tourism policy. In
some cases we find that written tourism policies exist, e.g. in the Republic of
South Africa, Namibia and the South Pacific states; in other cases one can
assume that a tourism policy is implied rather than having been made
explicit, e.g. that the UK government supports tourism. Although this has
often been stated there is no actual policy as such which guides the
development of tourism in the UK.

There are many definitions of policy, but perhaps a good working
definition is 'a policy is a reasoned consideration of alternatives'. This short
definition implies that all resources for most countries are scarce – capital,
land, manpower, etc. Where there is resource scarcity one of the policy
issues must be how best to allocate these scarce resources. The second

implication from the definition is that there are opportunity costs involved in using resources in one way rather than in another. For example, tourism development might require the use of land, whereas land might have alternative uses in terms of agriculture, building, forestry, etc. So in most countries there are always alternative uses for the scarce resources which are available for development. Therefore, policy is necessary to consider what the alternatives may be and what the benefits of one alternative use against another could be. The latter evaluation, of course, probably requires technical studies.

There are a number of basic questions, considered below, which exemplify the need to develop a tourism policy.

What type of tourism product can be supplied?

In examining this particular question as part of a planning exercise, it will be necessary to evaluate tourism assets. From a policy point of view, what can be offered to tourists may attract a market which the country concerned does not wish to encourage. For some countries, certain types of tourism would not be desirable development options. For example in Indonesia and Pakistan gambling is not permitted, whereas in many of the Caribbean islands gambling is one of the major aspects of the tourism industry. So in some countries there will be moral objections to the use of gambling as a type of tourism. In other countries, particularly Islamic nations, beach tourism might be regarded with some scepticism, particularly if it attracts a type of tourist whose immodest dress can cause local consternation and objection.

The need to determine what type of tourism should be supplied is discussed below. To a major extent the question is evaluated through market studies – will tourists be prepared to buy what we want to offer? But there is a further issue. Government is the guardian of society and it essentially has to decide what type of development is acceptable. It is now fashionable, perhaps, to reduce the role of government in development planning, but in tourism with its capacity to generate a demonstration effect, government still has a role to play as the final arbiter of taste and acceptability. Acceptability is not only a moral and religious issue, but can also have political implications; for example, the United States government's embargoes on Cuba and, until recently, Vietnam; its decision to prohibit tourists to visit North Korea.

What type of tourism product should be supplied?

Again this question is very important because the marketing of tourism is essentially based on segmentation in an attempt to match supply and demand according to market characteristics. The type of tourist attracted and tourists from particular countries might be more acceptable than others. It may also be that certain parts of the countries might be earmarked for specific types of development. For example, in Spain the major thrust of tourism is on beaches where the attraction and the market segment is mainly budget package tourists, whereas in other parts of Spain attempts have been made to develop the regional hinterlands and attract tourists interested in the cultural appeal of the country.

The questions related to subnational development again focus on the issue of development objectives. Although tourism can provide economic and social benefits, a decision might be taken not to allow any development in a region or location. In many countries, national parks are established for recreational and conservation purposes, with no type of development permitted. This is one example where a national objective, i.e. to conserve recreational space, is given a higher priority than the economic benefits which could have derived from development.

How should tourism be marketed?

The marketing of tourism raises a number of issues which are discussed in Chapter 9. The sales distribution network is largely determined by relationships between tour operators, travel agents and the host countries. This is an important area and one which often increases or limits the success of the marketing effort. However, a major policy issue in tourism marketing relates not to consideration of the distribution channels, but rather to the image that the country and its tourism sector wishes to project.

Image is perhaps of prime importance to underpin the marketing effort. A country has to create an image which is attractive, realistic and attempts to differentiate the country from other destinations. As the proposed image reflects the status and identity of a country, government would usually want to satisfy itself on the acceptability of the proposal. It is a very sensitive area and has to balance two sometimes conflicting objectives – what image will attract tourists to visit the country against the image which the country is comfortable with. The case of Jamaica is instructive. As primarily a beach destination it sought to differentiate itself from neighbouring Caribbean countries by its marketing campaign. 'We are more than a beach – we are a country!'

The question of image creation is particularly difficult in many developing countries where potential visitors have little or no knowledge of the destination, or have a distorted image which needs to be corrected and changed. Government should be quite clear in its objectives for the tourism sector, including the type of destination image it wants to project. The image, of course, has to be realistic and workable for the travel trade. However, to leave the travel trade to create the image it wants to boost sales, may give rise to problems in the long term.

Which type of tourists might be attracted?

The type of tourists to be attracted will in part be determined by the tourism assets available and the support facilities of accommodation, transport and services. Marketing studies will be carried out based on an inventory of supply, i.e. what the country has to offer, and the relative stage of development of the supply assets. Most countries will have a range of attractions which could be used in a marketing strategy. Sometimes there is an abundance of attractions, as encapsulated in the marketing slogan of South Africa: 'A World in One Country'. It is important to identify options for development and marketing and to consider the consequences of pursuing one option rather than another. These choices are usually determined at the planning rather than the policy stage. However, clear government guidance on the non-acceptability of certain options, e.g. casino tourism, will enable planners to discount such options from their deliberations.

In the same way that governments may not approve certain development operations, it cannot dictate to the market. Eventually and essentially it will be market forces which determine whether tourism will develop or not.

What are the likely impacts arising from policy choices?

The development of tourism is a long-term process which requires substantial and continuing investment in infrastructure and related facilities. For these and other reasons most governments are concerned with the economic benefits which tourism can generate. However, as noted in Chapter 6 tourism can also create impacts of a social, cultural and environmental nature (Chapter 7). Although experience allows us to have some understanding of the likely consequences of encouraging one type of tourism rather than another, unanticipated problems may arise in the future. There are also market uncertainties which can dislocate the best-laid strategies. For these reasons, tourism policy has to be flexible to react to changes in circumstances and to reorder priorities as necessary. Fortunately, tourism has a long history and many of these considerations can be evaluated against the historic experience of tourism in other countries.

Evaluation of tourism policy

In considering the role of tourism in any destination there are many policy areas which have to be evaluated. It should also be remembered that as tourism develops the economic impacts are immediate. The social and cultural changes emerge over a much longer term and are difficult to recognize.

There are a number of examples which show the importance of policy. For example, to what extent will a country rely on the government as opposed to the private sector to develop the tourism business? Traditionally, and particularly in developing countries, it has been the government which has undertaken the entrepreneurial role. In many of the developed countries the reverse is true, with government providing an enabling environment but with market initiatives and provision of tourism investment and services coming from the private sector. Developing countries' tourism initially, and probably into the secondary stages of development, will rely on international tourist arrivals, with domestic visitors being given very low priority. There are political as well as economic considerations in determining what priorities should be. In some countries it might be recommended that tourism is developed in an enclave rather than in an integrated way. This means that tourism is developed with the idea of segregating visitors and the host community. Although this is now a relatively unfashionable approach, it was used in Tanzania in the 1970s and was a common feature of tourism in the former Soviet Union. Island countries like the Maldives can easily implement such a strategy.

There may be good economic and social reasons why an enclave policy is adopted. It does permit the concentration of infrastructure into a location, with consequent benefits arising from economies of scale. It may use land resources effectively and efficiently, and it may permit the segregation of visitors and residents. In countries where there are religious and cultural sensitivities, a concentrated development might be a preferred option.

Land ownership is often a problem associated with tourism development. One of the policy issues here is whether or not foreigners should be allowed to buy land or to lease it. The question of human resource training and development is an emotive issue in tourism, the commonly heard complaint being that indigenous people never rise to the senior levels of the industry. The question of funding tourism development and the role of international as opposed to domestic capital also is very important. Before tourism is planned it is good practice to set out policy guidelines for future development. It is a process which has to be based on a realistic assessment of what government wants to achieve from its tourism sector and how this achievement can be attained. The process will require coordination between the public and private sectors, with the latter being the main implementing force. As the main implementing force, the private sector should be a party to the decisions taken on future options. This cooperation can be cemented in the planning process.

Tourism planning

With reference to planning for tourism, it is useful to make a distinction between the developed and the developing countries. In most developed countries there is no formal tourism planning mechanism and whatever planning is done is usually incorporated into regional rather than national plans. Planning at national level is usually a function of the size of the country, so it would be virtually impossible to plan for tourism development in the USA and even in the UK. This does not mean, of course, that at subnational level tourism plans do not exist or that specific considerations of tourism have not been taken into account.

In the developing countries, on the other hand, development planning is a well-established practice, normally based on five-year development plan periods. Where tourism is important in a country, then it is usual to find a chapter devoted to the tourism sector in the national plan. In some cases, e.g. India, Indonesia, Malaysia, specific national tourism development planning exercises have taken place. In most countries there is an abundance of tourism assets and therefore tourism development possibilities. What is required is a careful evaluation of the assets and matching them to a potential market. Therefore tourism development planning has a number of well-defined steps, as discussed below.

Analysis of demand

This exercise looks at the international trends of tourist travel patterns, particularly patterns relating to a region or to a specific country. The purpose of the analysis is to make some estimate of future demand of tourism for a particular country or region of the country. This demand is usually expressed in terms of visitor arrivals and of visitor characteristics. Estimating demand is a problematic exercise, but it is the foundation of tourism development planning. The analysis will seek to provide as much detail as possible on volume of demand, visitor characteristic, possible expenditure targets, and main source countries of origin. The detailed analysis is only usually constrained by cost and time considerations.

Analysis of demand will usually involve three stages: historic demand patterns relative to the country; current demand patterns; and future potential. Each of the first two phases should provide some indications of trends and permit identification and analysis of significant market changes. This information then becomes the framework to consider future development options. Should the present market mix be continued? Is there scope and need for changed emphasis in future market development? Can part of competing countries' markets be diverted? Are there problems identified in the analysis of demand which need to be actioned? There are many questions which are incorporated in the analysis of demand which must be related to the analysis of tourism supply assets.

There is usually some debate as to whether the analysis of demand should take place before or after a similar analysis of supply. For most countries there is an existing tourism demand for tourist attractions and facilities. Very few countries begin tourism planning from a zero base. Therefore, in a planning exercise analysis of demand and supply is usually a contemporaneous activity. Once the analyses have been completed, relevant consideration can then be given to future product and market development which may be dependent on investment in tourism infrastructure and development of attractions. Such development will have financial implications which are discussed below.

Analysis of supply

Most countries have a wide range of potential tourism attractions and assets which include natural attractions, e.g. climate; historic attractions, e.g. museums; cultural attractions, e.g. festivals; and service attractions, e.g. shopping. As a general principle, the larger the country the greater the number and variety of attractions. For tourism development purposes the list of potential attractions is the starting point. These attractions have to be identified and integrated into a tourism inventory. In large countries such a task will have to be done in subnational regions, often in designated tourism development zones. Once the inventory has been completed it is necessary to prioritize the assets listed: which are more attractive and accessible than others? Are there any assets which are unique and might provide the region or country with a unique selling proposition (USP) which would confer a comparative marketing advantage on a region or country relative to competitors?

In itself a unique asset may not be marketable if it is difficult to access, or requires substantial development, or is little known. Decisions have to be taken on what constitutes a marketable inventory. Some of these decisions will relate to the following:

1 *Access*. Can the location be visited easily or are there particular difficulties which will inhibit tourists from visiting? Examples might be long and arduous road journeys; long hikes to the location; dangers from natural hazards.
2 *Support services*. Are there facilities at the location for rest and lodging? Are there medical facilities available in the area? Is personal security a problem?
3 *Intrinsic attraction*. Is the tourist attraction sufficient to justify the visit? Are there other things to do in the area – can the location be combined with other visits?

Where there is a large inventory it is necessary to prioritize the attractions – what is the most famous historic site in a location may have limited national significance and perhaps no international appeal. Many domestic and international tourists visit Stonehenge on Salisbury Plain; but except for special interest visitors, Stonehenge is not ranked as a priority destination for most visitors to the UK. A similar site, the Standing Stones of Callenish on the Isle of Lewis in Scotland, receives much fewer visitors. So obviously location is an important aspect of inventory evaluation. One approach to evaluation is to establish a small working group or committee to carry out this task.

Group members will require local knowledge to identify the tourism sites and to provide specific inputs. The travel trade should be represented to assess the marketability of the attractions. Special expertise may also be incorporated to consider issues relating to sociocultural dimensions of the locations. Group membership should be as representative as meets the needs of the exercise. Eventually, probably using a weighting criterion, the group will establish a ranking for each of the identified assets. The assets themselves can be plotted on a map to determine whether a geographic clustering is available which may facilitate marketing by providing a range of activities or attractions to sustain a visit to the area. Once this exercise is completed it can then be related to the market analysis to suggest what development options may be available.

Forecast of demand

From the matching of supply and demand the tourist planners will attempt to forecast demand over a period of time, usually a medium term of five years and a long term of ten years. The demand target is a central aspect of the tourism development plan; demand drives other sectors of the plan. For example, the demand targets will be used to forecast necessary accommodation developments. They will also relate to developments in infrastructure, and specific amenities. These demand forecasts essentially provide the financial estimates for implementing the plan. As the forecast determines what has to be done to achieve the plan, then it has implications for manpower, training and funding. It will also have relevance to land use and possibly locational development decisions.

It may not always be possible to accept the demand targets. In some cases a target which is ambitious cannot be funded because of the cost or non-availability of capital. In other cases there may be a situation, as happened in the Bahamas in the early 1980s, where to meet the forecast market demand would have meant importing labour with major effects on social conditions, particularly relating to schools, housing and overcrowding.

The demand forecast will be made using three general scenarios: low demand, medium demand and high demand. Each forecast will have certain conditions attached to it, e.g. external trends in visitor arrivals, transport links and price expectations, competitors' actions. These externalities will be further conditioned by internal factors, e.g. ability of the existing infrastructure and facilities to absorb the expected inflow of tourists; possibilities of introducing extra capacity or developing new products and areas. Forecasting is not just a mechanical exercise; to be useful it has to attempt to quantify options to allow planners to evaluate the consequences of choosing the particular options. It may be at a certain time and location that increases in demand can be satisfied by the existing facilities, but there will come a point where new investment will have to be considered. Investment in new facilities will take time to come on stream; this is a further factor to take into account.

Costing and financing the plan

Once the demand options have been forecast it will be necessary to cost the plan – how much will it be to implement it? Costing does not only apply to physical facilities and infrastructure but also, for example, to provide training facilities and perhaps recruitment of new workers to the sector. A comprehensive costing of the plan on a proposal by proposal basis must be made. At the completion of this exercise it may be found that the total is too high and the proposal will have to be scaled down. Whether this action is taken will depend not only on the amount of funding required but also on who is providing the funding and on what terms.

Funding for tourism development can come from many sources: from the private and public sectors, from banks and international agencies. Infrastructure is still largely provided by government, although that is changing with more investment coming from the private sector. The second Severn Road Bridge linking England to Wales and the Skye Road Bridge are recent examples of privately financed infrastructure. Turkey has also been successful in private sector infrastructure funding to support tourism. In developed and increasingly in developing countries, the private sector is providing funding for tourist accommodation and related facilities. These investment decisions are based on commercial criteria and many governments provide favourable conditions by offering tourism investment incentives to stimulate private sector involvement.

Tourism planning has to be flexible to accommodate the prospect that only part of the plan might be implemented for whatever reason.

Implementation

In many developing countries, planning exercises have remained as monuments to the expertise of consultants. A very high proportion of tourism development plans have never been implemented, either because of non-availability of funding or non-availability of the expertise to undertake the implementation process. It is essential that as part of the planning exercise implementation is costed and accounted for.

As implementation takes place it is important that the plan is followed and that the sequence of planned events is adhered to. However, as noted above, one of the problems associated with tourism development planning is the absence of qualified people, particularly in the developing countries, to manage this implementation process. Implementation strategies must be considered at the very early stage of tourism development planning.

One way of dealing with the need to create expertise to implement plans is to use a counterpart training initiative. This means that at the early stages of the planning exercise each expert is assigned a local counterpart. The counterpart works alongside the expert and is involved in specific tasks, e.g. forecasting, marketing, training. The purpose of counterpart training is that the local person will gather sufficient knowledge and expertise to continue the implementation process after the specialist consultant has left. In practice this does not always work as planned, perhaps because the counterpart is transferred to other duties or that he has not acquired sufficient experience or skills. For these reasons, in many developing countries consultants are retained to manage the implementation process.

Monitoring

It is important that, as the plan is implemented, the targets set are monitored. There are a number of ways of doing this. Perhaps the best is to use a steering committee, which is a representative body bringing together members of government and the private sector. They should look carefully at the way in which the plan is being implemented and to react to any problems arising.

Targets should wherever possible be specific, e.g. number of tourist arrivals, length of stay, average per visit spend. In relation to human resource development, targets might refer to number of people trained, levels and type of training. The monitoring process should include an achievement index, e.g. what has been achieved against the set targets.

The major problem area relates to qualitative assessments, particularly in tourism developments impact on social and cultural norms. As noted previously, this is a very difficult area to assess as many of the changes will be slow and evolutionary rather than instantaneous. Perhaps the only way to monitor such changes is through community participation and representation where the community can voice its opinions.

Evaluation

The monitoring process provides both quantitative and qualitative information. Evaluation is the stage where remedial action can be taken to counteract any of the problems encountered. For example, there may be difficulties relating to the scale of operation, or with the availability of manpower in certain areas. There are many problems which can arise from tourism development. It is important that the evaluation process is thorough. It is then possible to re-examine objectives and policy.

As tourism is essentially a 'people industry', policy and planning should be coordinated. It is well known that tourism is multi-sectoral, involving both government and the private sector in its development. It has economic, social and environmental impacts, many of which may prove in the long term injurious to the political environment. There are many possible conflicts, for example in relation to land use; should people who traditionally have grazing rights in an area be dispossessed in order to develop a game reserve? Should foreigners be allowed to buy land as opposed to leasing it? Should large-scale developments in tourism be encouraged or is a more selective approach preferred? In each of these areas there might be potential conflicts which in the long term would make tourism unsustainable.

Sustainability

It is now fashionable to look at tourism development in the context of sustainability and it is common to note terms such as 'alternative', 'green' and 'eco-tourism', which all have particular meanings to particular adherents.

A general interpretation of these terms would be to encourage tourism developments which are sensitive and sympathetic in the use of finite resources. Unfortunately many of these labels have been interpreted to refer only to small-scale tourism, as low volumes of visitors are more easily managed than large volumes and do less damage to sensitive environments. This is true, but global tourism reflects the movement of large numbers of people which cannot be scaled down. The principles of sustainability must apply to both high- and low-volume movements of tourists. There is also another dimension to sustainability.

Sustainability does not only apply to finite and environmentally fragile resources; it should also be related to communities. As tourism develops there is a need to consider the question of carrying capacity at a location or site. Many factors are considered in estimating carrying capacities, but often the capacity of the host community to accept tourism is ill-considered or not considered at all. A community which is overwhelmed by tourists is likely to develop antipathy and possibly antagonism towards the visitors, thereby threatening the long-term sustainability of tourism in that particular location.

Summary

For different countries it is not possible to specify a single model of tourism development. Development must reflect the circumstances of the country, the stages of development and obviously the market opportunities available. The preferred style and scale of tourism is the basis of a planning exercise. But because of the nature of tourism and the way in which it impacts on societies, it is important that planning does not take place in the absence of policy guidelines. As a concept it is useful to consider that 'policies precede planning'.

This concept indicates the primacy of policy overplanning. It suggests that policies will provide the framework within which planning takes place. This sequence should ensure that market forces alone do not dictate tourism development.

Further reading

Edgell, D. (1990) *International Tourism Policy*, Van Nostrand Reinhold, New York

Gartner, W. C. (1996) *Tourism Development: Principles, Processes and Policies*, Van Nostrand Reinhold, New York

Gunn, C. (1988) *Tourism Planning*, 2nd edn, Taylor and Francis, New York

Hall, C. M. (1995) *Tourism and Public Policy*, Routledge, London

Hall, C. M. (1996) *Tourism and Politics*, John Wiley, Chichester, UK

Inskeep, E. (1991) *Tourism Planning: An Integrated and Sustainable Planning Approach*, Van Nostrand Reinhold, New York

Lickorish, L. J., Jefferson, A., Bodlender, J. and Jenkins, C. L. (1991) *Developing Tourism Destinations: Policies and Perspectives*, Longman, Harlow, Essex

Medlik, S. (ed.) (1991) *Managing Tourism*, Butterworth-Heinemann, Oxford

World Tourism Organization (1994) *National and Regional Tourism Planning: Methodologies and Case Studies*, WTO, Madrid, Spain

11 The role of government

Introduction

The role of government is an important and complex aspect of tourism, involving policies and political philosophies. State intervention in the trade is a relatively recent practice for central government. State participation increased as tourism became a mass phenomenon, reaching a peak shortly after the Second World War in 1939–45. A slow withdrawal began in the boom years of the 1980s with the shift to the market-oriented economy.

These trends are noted in this chapter, together with an examination of the principal aspects of state intervention:

1 Areas for state action.
2 Definitions of the role of the state.
3 Principal state functions.
4 Tasks of the destination authority.
5 Government tourism policies.
6 International intergovernmental bodies concerned.
7 International trade organizations with an advisory role.
8 International regional organizations.

The importance of many international organizations depends to some degree on the extent to which national governments have delegated their powers to intergovernmental bodies. This is the case with the European Union (EU), where many functions in taxation, regional and infrastructure development, and policy matters in transport, social and environmental regulation, are now within the competence of the administration in Brussels

For the most part, intergovernmental bodies' activities are advisory or technical in character. There have been few intergovernmental initiatives outside the EU leading to action in the travel field, but there has been a slow movement towards liberalization of movement.

The ways in which governments administer their tourism programmes vary considerably as the OECD reports have indicated, from Ministries of Tourism usually with a low political profile, to a small coordinating or supervisory unit in a major government department. Action may be devolved to a specialist agency or further to a cooperative system with the trade and sometimes in part to commercial contractors.

In practice, close cooperation with the operating sectors in commercially related functions such as marketing works best, but governments cannot abdicate their responsibilities. Tourism development cannot be left to market forces alone if national benefits are to be secured.

Tourism has grown rapidly in relatively free market conditions. This new and powerful trend reflected the new wealth of the industrial age. New forms of more efficient, safe and speedy transport, notably the development of railways, stimulated mass traffic flows. New resorts, some large towns, established themselves in a short space of time, and developed an effective public–private sector partnership to ensure the prosperity of the resort or tourism regions. Early pioneers seem to have had an instinctive understanding of the development and marketing tasks required and the sharing of responsibilities between the public sector – the municipal council – and the tourist sector trades.

Thus modern tourism grew up largely through a system of market enterprise and municipal patronage, with the individual resorts competing actively for trade. Indeed, often the fiercest competition was between neighbouring centres, even if there was a common interest in the region they served together. However, in the early days the visitors, depending on public transport, were not mobile; they stayed in the resort of their choice. It was much later, with mobility and increased frequency of trips, that a regional as well as a local and indeed a national approach became practical and necessary.

In those early days, central government played little or no part. It was not until after the great depression of the early 1930s that the state began to realize the size and importance of the tourism movement as an economic and social force which impacted substantially on the national and local economy. The reason for intervention was an economic one. There was an urgent need in the post-Depression years, at least in the European countries, to stimulate foreign currency earnings, when most of the main industries were suffering badly.

Intervention in general took the form of marketing support for promotion abroad, an activity which the diverse trade sectors find difficulty in undertaking without a collective destination platform. There were, however, examples of industry assistance. In Switzerland support for the hotel industry, crippled by the First World War, was provided to keep the hotel stock in good repair. In Britain the government gave a small subvention to the British Travel Association. This was a marketing cooperative to promote Britain abroad. The Association had been established by the industry sectors, notably shipping companies, especially those engaged in transatlantic passenger movement, railways, hotels and resort local government in 1929.

Most governments in Europe seemed convinced that intervention, principally in international promotion, was justified by results. In some countries, resorts were permitted to levy an overnight tax or *taxe de séjour*. More generally, extensive local authority activity was financed from local taxation. Tourism slowly recovered from recession in the 1930s and was beginning to reach new peaks when war started again in 1939.

In the interwar years there was a growing interest in social aspects, or in what is now sometimes termed social tourism. This took the form of assistance for specific groups of the population with some disadvantage, usually the poorer people, who were either unable to enjoy holidays or leisure pursuits or were not provided for by the commercial sector. Some of this non-commercial and non-profit-making intervention was charitable, institutional and even political, as explained in Chapter 2.

However, in general in the Western democracies state intervention was strictly limited, modest in size, and concentrated on promotion of tourism as a foreign trade and currency earner. There was, of course, much indirect intervention in transport through the state railways and cultural support for museums, the heritage and the arts, and for sports facilities. But the motivation was the benefits for the resident population not the visitor.

After the end of the Second World War in 1945, governments had to give priority to post-war reconstruction, especially for key industries. Europe, badly devastated and with international and much domestic tourism halted, had to begin again. Apart from mass destruction, tourism resources had been diverted or run down in the war years. Many hotels and other tourist accommodation had been destroyed or requisitioned for military use. In fact, a substantial part of the tourism and transport infrastructure had been turned to military use in the war effort.

Private travel had been discouraged. Government posters in Britain asked: 'Is your journey really necessary'? There was no currency allowance for foreign travel, and passports and visas constrained movement.

An intergovernmental agency, the Organization for European Economic Co-operation (OEEC) was established by Western European governments and with generous aid from the USA through the Marshall Plan set about restoring postwar Europe to prosperity. For the first time tourism was given a degree of priority as an important industry in the process of recovery, not least because of its dollar earning potential, and thus a means of repaying the massive dollar loans necessary to repair the economic ravages of war. An OEEC Tourism Committee was established and developed a tourism recovery programme removing constraints to travel in the form of currency restrictions, customs, passports and visas. A 'Come to Europe' campaign was launched in the USA with state funds, carried out through the newly formed European Travel Commission in 1949 by the state tourist offices in the Western European countries.

Most governments gave a high degree of priority to tourism in their national economic recovery programme at this time, intervening with fiscal, financial, planning and other forms of aid. It was, of course, a period of major state involvement in economic and industry affairs. To a large extent European countries, many with socialist governments, operated semi-planned economies rather than the market-oriented systems which did not then enjoy the support achieved subsequently.

However, as the memories of the war receded and economies recovered, governments' interest and support for tourism waned. Countries became richer. Balance of payments difficulties and shortages of strong foreign currencies such as the dollar lessened. Consequently, state priorities inevitably based on national needs, changed and interest turned more to regional development. It is common for tourism to flourish in poorer isolated regions, where political advantage lay in special support for important minorities.

This gradual change in government economic policies reflected a broader and less interventionist approach on the international scale and concentration of activity at a more restricted European level, eventually through the EC and devolution of economic support to regions. Governments' withdrawal from direct intervention was a gradual process, but quite early in the postwar years the priority accorded to tourism, as soon as major constraints were lifted, began to decline.

The OEEC had been expanded to include the richer industrialized countries, 24 in number, with the USA and Japan playing a prominent part in the reconstituted Organization for Economic Cooperation and Development (OECD). Although their tourism activity declined, the OECD published a remarkable report 'Tourism Development and Economic Growth in 1966', which for the first time at government level examined government's role in tourism and policy implications.

The report emphasized that governments have a number of options in formulating their tourism policies:

1 Deciding the appropriate rate of growth desired for the tourism sector: the encouragement of mass tourism or a preference for a slower and more selective growth.
2 The respective roles of the public and the private sectors in development.
3 The degree of priority to be given to tourism in national and regional development plans.
4 Whether to treat tourism in the same way as any other growth sector or whether the nature of the industry requires special administrative and credit arrangements.

This last option is the most important and critical. It is open to government to decide that tourism is not a key national interest or to regard the trade as part of the competitive private sector best dealt with by market forces without state interference. In past years the Soviet Union and the Burmese government among others decided after the war that free travel was not in the state's interest and that the dangers of social disruption outweighed any economic benefit.

Until recently a majority of countries worldwide practised policies of substantial intervention in their economies and in major industries in their attempts to regulate foreign trade, often through bilateral agreements.

Public transport, particularly railways and airlines, were largely state controlled. A large part of tourism and resort development depended on state planning and in many cases state subsidy or fiscal discrimination in the immediate postwar years. Tourism policy at the national level reflected a simple approach to maximize benefits through stimulating foreign trade and foreign currency receipts and increasingly as a support for schemes of regional development.

Although policies and practices were far from satisfactory and often inefficiently implemented, there was little debate on the proper government role in tourism or professional appreciation of the need or indeed results of state intervention where this was practised on any scale. OECD (1986, p.13) advised that

government's tourism programmes should be determined primarily by considerations of economic policy and the basis of benefits to the economy, which may be expected to follow, recognizing that tourism 'can represent one of the most hopeful economic resources of the country'.

OECD pointed out that there were non-economic considerations deserving state attention: cultural benefits in conserving the country's heritage and environment, and social gains in leisure and recreation for the resident population. There are of course many other considerations; for example, substantial secondary effects of tourism growth on transport expansion and employment. There can be major communication values in the promotion of the country's traditional goods and services and, if the tourism resources are properly managed, a build-up of international interest and goodwill which no amount of state propaganda could achieve.

However, OECD also observed that 'statutory tourism bodies were ill equipped to deal with the new problems posed by the boom in tourism'. Yet 'few major sectors have seen their resources and institutional frameworks challenged as often as tourism'.

Over the years, inevitably and properly, state policies and political organization change. In the postwar recovery period up to 1960, foreign exchange earnings were the main tourism objective, at least in Europe. In the 1970s development of poorer or decaying and declining regions became more important and, latterly, job creation was the dominant feature in many regions.

Social and environmental aims impacted more forcibly on tourism activity, not always favourably. The pursuit of social and cultural objectives began to take a political character, such as consumerism and the green movement, appealing to the resident not the visiting population, often with negative effects for the trade, such as in constraints, regulation and fiscal action. Changes in the structure of government, notably in trends towards decentralization, privatization and market orientation, further weakened government support for tourism by direct intervention.

These changes suited the evolutionary trends of the times. OECD observed that state withdrawal from necessary functions needed to be accompanied by regional planning and integration. Even greater efforts at systems of coordination and cooperation were required in such a diverse activity as tourism, involving interdependence of public and private sector activity. In practice, coordination of government functions impacting on tourism has always been a weakness at national as well as at international level.

Definitions of the role of tourism

In recent times a number of experts have attempted to define the role of the state in tourism. These vary, reflecting current thinking at the time. However, whatever the political system or the changing policies towards market orientation, the state's role is indispensable for successful tourism development. The case for government intervention needs continuing presentation, not least because governments continue to question the necessity of public sector tasks. As the OECD pointed out, the state must first decide whether to give tourism treatment different from that accorded to other major industries. The question is made more difficult to resolve because tourism is itself a market rather than a single industry. Traditionally the state supervises market forces but does not intervene directly; it is the referee not the player.

Pearce (1992, p. 6) points out that the public sector

becomes involved in tourism for a variety of reasons, the extent of government intervention varying from country to country, in large part as a function of broader political philosophies and policies. Economic factors are nevertheless usually to the fore. These include increasing foreign exchange earnings, state revenues (taxes) and employment, economic diversification, regional development and the stimulation of non-tourist investment. Social, cultural and environmental responsibilities may also lead to government involvement as may a range of political considerations. The state may also play a role as a landowner or resource manager.

According to a study by the Commission of the European Communities (EC) rationale for state intervention is based not only on the nature and extent of perceived economic and social benefits, but also on the impracticability or inability of the enterprises representing organizations and individuals to undertake certain necessary functions.

In one of the first definitive studies of tourism, Burkart and Medlik (1981, p. 256) emphasized that in any destination a variety of interests are involved in tourism. The government is concerned at all levels in protecting its citizens, providing essential services and in creating the conditions in which their institutions, including enterprise and trade, can operate favourably. They point out that

at the national level, tourism is in the first instance a government responsibility, to formulate a tourism policy, which may be translated into a plan'. Such policy clarifies how tourism is seen in the context of the national economy, what objectives are to be pursued, how tourism enters into national and regional planning. These objectives can then be translated into quantified targets and rates of growth. When the role of tourism is defined, the policy provides a statement of the means by which the objectives are to be attained; the means cover such matters as the administrative arrangements, the respective role of the public and private sectors and the fiscal arrangements.

The problem with such a concept is the nature of tourism, where the market not the state is largely in control. Few countries now have a national tourism plan.

There has been an increasing impact on tourism by government action to secure social and environmental aims not always favourable for travel. The pursuit of these objectives sometimes takes a political position, appealing to the resident not the visiting population, leading to constraints and regulations. Although the host community has an obligation to welcome and receive their paying guests in an appropriate manner, the visitor, the stranger, is not always well received.

In its annual report, the OECD (1991, p. 21) concluded that

The general climate today is towards privatization, but there are inherent risks in the privatization of national tourism promotion and marketing. Governments are responsible for national transportation policy and economic policy aimed at maximizing tourism's contribution to the nation's economy. It is also government's responsibility to deal with issues related to the workforce, training matters, consumer affairs and public awareness campaigns. The provision of specific public infrastructure and facilities for the tourism industry, as well as local planning and zoning arrangements, land use, environmental protection matters and national parks are other examples – even if some of these functions are delegated to the local or municipal levels of government.

If national tourism promotion and marketing were left entirely to the private sector, this could result in the unbalanced development of infrastructure and market expansion, with the risk of growing congestion and increased pressure on environmental resources.

Over the years the OECD has made more in-depth studies of state tourism policies than any other intergovernmental body and consistently has drawn attention to the economic importance of the industry. Tourism is a major contributor to national economies. It also helps promote regional development and more significantly the development of poorer regions (shown in Chapter 5).

It seems all the more paradoxical that the more significant the position of tourism in economic and social terms in the industrialized countries, the less interest the government appears to take in its necessary role of creating conditions for the trade's prosperity. As the OECD observes, governments, except in certain relatively short periods of economic crisis have had great difficulty in determining their role in the travel and leisure fields.

The World Travel and Tourism Council using more elaborate techniques of economic analysis, has demonstrated the vital role of tourism as the world's leading trade. The Council comments on governments' failure to come to terms with the industry's economic significance or to give it the priority in policies commensurate with its prominence. The WTTC (1992, (p. 3) report comments:

It's an industry which receives little acclamation, but which has created enormous wealth and jobs for those countries and businesses which have recognized its potential for economic growth and development.

The council explains why:

The primary reason travel and tourism has received so little attention has to do with the way governments report their economic activity. Traditionally governments have compiled their economic results in conformity with their national chart of accounts. In general this structure has failed to properly document the fast growing service industry and even worse has failed to identify travel and tourism as an industrial entity. Instead the industry's contribution is spread through the national accounts, diminishing its overall impact.

It admits that the problems are being tackled, as work to include tourism in systems of national accounting, as recommended by the WTO and the United Nations Statistical Commission is going ahead, and will help in the future to demonstrate the industry's dominant role in many economies.

However, there are other reasons for the lack of governmental priority; principally a lack of political will to include the trade in mainline policies, strategies and resultant operational programmes. Thus the impact of these mainline policies, uncoordinated in regard to travel and leisure, can be very negative. For example, there are at least 10 Directorates General in the Commission of the European Union dealing with major policy issues, such as transport, fiscal action, regional development, labour and social affairs, concerned to a greater or lesser degree with tourism. Where coordination is weak, consultation and cooperation with industry on implementation is inadequate or non-existent.

It is perhaps not surprising that the advent of the Single Market in 1993 increased constraints and burdens rather than removing them, eroding Europe's competitive edge in tourism, and in world tourism markets where Europe's share of traffic continues to fall. Even the promised borderless Europe had not emerged two years after the market had been legally inaugurated.

Another and perhaps more powerful reason for inattention lies in the fact that political power and thus government aims are based on the interests of the resident population and their votes. Tourists, the mobile population, have no votes, but only taxes, except indirectly in the recognition of their commercial interests by the business and trading community.

Furthermore, the tourism industry is wide ranging, diverse and highly fragmented. The individual trade sectors making up the whole – hotels, transport modes, etc. – are vocal and often very effective in presenting their own industry sector's case to government separately. But their efforts in establishing a strong collective voice for tourism is modest and often ineffective.

A seminar on tourism and transport policies at the World Travel Market in London, in 1993, showed clearly the relatively strong position of the transport industries, notably aviation. The insignificance of the tourism voice and the lack of consultation and coordination between the interests of the government departments responsible for tourism and transport were apparent. The weakness identified at the national level extends to the intergovernmental organizations, notably the Commission of the European Communities, the OECD and the UN.

Areas of state intervention

In general the state recognizes that the duties of the public sector must cover such matters as health, safety, fair trading and consumer interests and infrastructure in transport such as roads, railways and ports. These are all matters of direct concern to the resident population. There is a mixed record in the provision of leisure facilities, environmental protection and conservation which includes responsibility for the unique cultural heritage, an important part of Europe's visitor attractions.

When the state is active in these fields, usually by the extension of programmes designed for the resident community to the visiting 'population', there is often no coordinated approach in the visitor interest. Action may from time to time be taken reluctantly, inexpertly and without the necessary involvement of the visitor service providers.

At the regional and local level, especially in the resorts, the public sector usually provides key attractions such as parks, sporting facilities, conference, concert halls, exhibition centres and local transport services. Many of these operations are substantial and involve a high degree of commercial enterprise. In addition, the municipal and especially the resorts responsibilities for marketing, information, reception and product development are fundamental for the locality.

The state, the central government, has a key responsibility for setting fiscal and financial conditions for prosperous industry operation. Governments from time to time will provide special incentives for development in the form of subsidies or tax advantages. This is very common in the developing countries and in poorer regions with little other resources for growth. In past years in certain countries where increased visitor revenue was regarded as a key priority, the state extended its operations in investing in and operating certain tourism enterprises including hotels. There were, in fact, for a variety of reasons state hotel chains in industrialized countries, in Britain for example as a by-product of the state's nationalization of railways, in Spain and Portugal and in New Zealand. Except in special circumstance such as the pousadas in Portugal, the state was not a successful hotel operator. Many of these properties, as in Britain, have been privatized with good results. More recently, even in the former communist planned economies, the state may continue to own properties, but recognizes that operation, in varying forms of joint scheme, is best left to those skilled in the private sector and market economy.

Direct subsidies vary from systems of loans and grants to stimulate the provision of certain types of service and facility, especially in poorer or remote regions, to massive development schemes involving the creation of new resorts and regions. In the French Languedoc-Roussillon Scheme or Cancun in Mexico (and on a smaller scale Aviemore in Scotland), resort areas or resorts were created by state intervention and initiative.

The success of this form of intervention has varied and the record is patchy. It has always been more important in industrialized and market-oriented countries for the state to create the right conditions for prosperity, and to remove constraints, including discriminatory taxation on industry operation. This is a situation far from realization at present in many countries, including those in membership of the EC. Direct state management in market economies has too often proved to be inefficient and less profitable than private sector management.

Since the Depression years of the 1930s the government in many countries has accepted some responsibility for promoting the national destination in foreign countries. Operations have increasingly been devolved to a state agency or national tourist organization, a practice that has become more common where market-oriented policies are adopted.

Government intervention in infrastructure and tourism plant may similarly be devolved to specialist regional and local development agencies with skills in planning, and supervision, which the tourism department or organization would not have. Needless to say the tourism officials should be consulted, as product development is an essential element in marketing which is their principal concern. Local authorities have always been active in their own area in marketing, servicing, investment and sometimes subsidy. Both state and municipality may subsidize or even operate services and facilities considered to have an important public benefit which would not be provided through market forces. Transport services, cultural and sporting amenities, conference and exhibition halls are examples.

Strategy

Whatever form of organization or degree of devolution in the state's role, it is essential that the public authority, central or local government should agree an overall strategy. This should be reinforced by an outline plan or guidelines, to present a coordinated picture of the destination's future shape as a tourism area, both at national and local level. This may apply at regional level where the regional destination is in fact an accepted tourism entity, for example the Lake District or the Norfolk Broads in England.

The state tourism agency, tourist board or government department will have an important role to play in advising on the strategy, offering opportunities to consult and cooperate with a dispersed private sector, and preparing a destination marketing strategy based on an identification of the appropriate markets and their needs and wishes. This leads to a product market fit indicating products and services required to attract the preferred visitor traffic. This is a vital role. The market will determine the outcome and the marketers have the essential responsibility to ensure product development to suit the required visitor movement.

Thus the public authority, at both the national and local level, has a dual responsibility. In the first place it is the guardian of the public benefit and the regulator, setting the conditions for operation. It must accept responsibility for essential public concerns such as health and safety, consumer protection and the operation of a free and fair market economy, and help maximize national or local benefit. Secondly, as an operator, it must take the lead in the task of attracting and receiving the visitors.

Forms of state organization

The WTO (1992) researched the practice of its member governments, over 100 in all, in carrying out these tasks, and found no consistency in their approach, or in the forms of organization or agencies carrying out both direct and devolved functions. The more commercial the tasks, such as marketing activity or operating facilities and services, the more desirable it seems to devolve operations to a specialist agency or even a public–private sector cooperative. In the industrialized countries, the majority carry out state-financed promotion schemes through a specialized agency – National Tourist Office (NTO) or Tourist Board – with increasing efforts by government to encourage industry support. Development schemes are more usually handled by a separate state agency responsible for regional economies. In developing countries where the role of the state is much greater, Ministries of Tourism tend to have overall responsibilities, but not always for large-scale planning and investment.

In its early study the OECD (1986) reported the variety of practice in the richer countries and in the scope and structure of government tourist authorities, but concluded that provided policies and objectives were clear, the precise form of agency was not a vital issue. However, the trend towards the establishment of separate marketing agencies and marketing cooperatives seems clear, accompanied by a tendency for governments to withdraw, at least to an extent, from marketing operations.

Where this results in weak state action and a low priority for tourism, reflected in the absence of appropriate policies and strategies, the national interest is certainly at risk. It is essential that the state provides the platform or focal point for necessary collective action at national level and likewise municipal provision at the local level. Without this support base the separate interests in a competitive and market-oriented environment cannot cooperate successfully. Of course, it is important to distinguish the fine dividing lines between the necessary competitive and cooperative fields of action. Yet without collective action the many separate and diverse interests cannot compete successfully in the national and international marketplace.

Based on periodic surveys of the government role by the WTO, the OECD and individual countries, the principal functions of a Ministry of Tourism or of agencies under government control can be summarized as

1 Research, statistics and planning.
2 Marketing.
3 Development of tourism resources.
4 Regulation, including trade regulation.
5 Training and education.
6 Facilitation/liberalization.

The WTO reported that two-thirds of government tourist departments were ministries sometimes responsible for a number of functions, e.g. transport or foreign trade, but one-third were state agencies such as the British Tourist Authority with a degree of freedom of action. However, the majority of the WTO member governments are from the developing countries and operate through ministries. In many cases the private sector may be weak and unable to play a leading role in partnership with government. To an increasing extent tourism promotion in the industrialized countries is devolved to a specialist agency with strong trade links.

While foreign investors may prefer the security of working in cooperation with the government, the trend towards devolution to forms of marketing cooperatives seems to be growing.

The OECD observed in its 1968 report that there is no ideal form of organization. Separation of function may prove increasingly practical, and in principle the more commercial functions should be carried out at arm's length from the state. Government departments are, however, well equipped to regulate and to intervene in forms of fiscal incentives or taxation. Such functions are best left to government and not their agencies. Coordination of government functions is a key task, indeed one of the most important, because of the range of interests and responsibilities. The lack of coordination and consideration of the impact of main lines of policy can greatly constrain tourism growth.

In the EU, for example, directives on taxation, especially VAT, labour controls and regulations such as impractical consumer protection, introduced without examination of the total impact on the trade, threaten to erode Europe's competitive edge.

Principal state functions

Some governments, especially in the industrialized market-oriented economies, may have no explicit tourism policy. Their political philosophy will prevent any form of state planning, and even strategic action in the industrial or commercial fields may be strictly limited to urgent problem areas or to cases of 'market failure', itself a very limited concept. For reasons indicated by OECD and others, the immense economic and social importance of tourism, the wide-ranging but fragmented nature of the economic activity and considerations of regional development or foreign trade will oblige the state to look to its tourist duties. In the absence of policy and political will, action may be uncoordinated and reactive, with problems attached to this form of reluctant attention.

Principal functions of government can be summarized as follows (Lickorish *et al.*, 1991, p. 131):

1 Formulating policy and approving broad strategy for development.
2 Regulation, inspection and consumer protection where needed.
3 Provision of a consultative forum, as a basis for coordination both within government and between the public and the private sectors. Because the range of tourism interests and operators is so wide, this is an essential function for successful growth.
4 Fiscal action. Intervention to safeguard tourism interest will be needed to ensure that the impact of main line domestic fiscal policy does not impact unfairly on the mobile population of tourists. Inadvertently fiscal action may discriminate against the visitor as it will be designed with the resident population alone in mind.

    For example, the advent of the Single European Market brought a major endeavour to harmonize taxes, excise duties and other imposts. This in practice resulted in an increase in taxation in tourism, through higher rates of VAT, and abolition of favourable tax treatment at national level. There is also an attempt to abolish duty free shops. This, together with an increasing trend towards the taxation of individual travellers through port exit and other charges, can lead to higher trading costs and prices.
5 Financial assistance for development, notably through the provision of infrastructure, correcting 'market failure' and implementing main policy lines where tourism can contribute substantially, for example foreign currency earnings, job creation and regional prosperity, especially in poorer areas. Tourism may also provide a valuable stimulus in promoting trade and cultural wealth.

6 Establishing favourable conditions for growth for the private sector and small business in particular, in the market economy.
7 Provision of statistics, economic and other technical information and support to ensure effective management of national tourism resources by both public and private sectors.
8 Promotion of the national destinations in foreign countries and at the local level by the local or regional authorities.

It is the general practice for governments to accept a role in the promotion of the country abroad. The operating sectors, both public and private, are unable, because of the wide range and volume of small businesses, or unwilling because the necessary investment is not cost effective in an internationally competitive situation, to undertake the responsibility for the promotion of the national destination. Even in a competitive situation it has always been necessary in tourism to take collective action in destination marketing on a cooperative basis.

It is also common practice at the local level, e.g. tourist resorts, as already explained, for the local authority to play an important operating as well as a promotion role. The municipalities invest in and manage a range of tourism services and facilities.

In general such facilities are required to provide the basis for resort development and attraction. Each service of this kind will normally have an element of monopoly value. Many can at best operate at little more than at break even and on a non-profit basis. Thus municipal intervention of this kind has not only been accepted but welcomed and, in the case of best practice, well done. The justification must be that the facility is necessary for the prosperity of the destination and will not be provided unaided by the private sector.

However, the operation of tourism services, especially on a national basis, which could be run at a profit is not always successful in public sector hands. There have been a number of cases where the state-owned tourist businesses, e.g. hotel chains, were privatized and successfully developed by commercial companies. There are cases, especially in the infrastructure field, where public–private sector partnership deserves encouragement, in transport and provision of amenities for example. Unfortunately, government systems of administration cannot adapt well to commercial disciplines.

There is nevertheless a long history of subsidized private sector activity and public service trading in tourism. Under the Development of Tourism Act 1969, in the UK, a major part of the legislation was devoted to an open-ended subsidy for hotel construction. Generous capital grants were offered for new hotel bedrooms, owing to capacity shortages, without discretion or discrimination relating to quality or need. The number of good-quality hotel rooms in the country doubled in little more than four years after a period of nearly 50 years of little or no large hotel building. The subsidy required was very substantial, many times the government's estimate of cost. At the end of this period of massive investment, the first post-war economic halt and the oil crisis affected tourism and crippled the transatlantic movement on which many hotels depended. The industry at the height of its investment boom was plunged into a critical situation, an experience which has been repeated over the years.

Tasks of the destination public authority

Devolution of the state's functions to specialist agencies (National Tourist Offices, Tourist Boards, etc.) or to regional or local authorities does not diminish the state's responsibilities, chief of which must be to ensure that the public benefit is secured in an efficient and cost effective way. This should involve the provision of at least a national policy and strategy for tourist development, and the necessary coordinating and consultative machinery involving the key interests concerned. Usually the state will not be the provider of services. The commercial sector should operate or manufacture the necessary facilities and attractions which make tourism possible, and earn tourism revenues.

This may seem self-evident, but even in the industrialized countries many governments are not expert in supervising the management of national tourism resources; the task may not be well done. The coordinating role of the state is especially important, as so many of the service providers are interdependent. They need close links with the public sector which will not only be responsible for establishing fair and favourable conditions for prosperous trading, but will provide much of the infrastructure in transport and other key areas, and may indeed operate a number of essential services. A common and sometimes serious mistake is to separate tourism and transport policies and investment plans. Hotel expansion may run ahead of transport facilities, as happened in the recent rapid expansion of tourism in China, or a rapid growth in air transport may outpace a parallel expansion of destination services. This happened in Europe, including Britain in the late 1960s, with the advent of the large-bodied jet aircraft.

Prime task of the destination public authority

The prime task of the destination public authority, whether at the national or local level, must be to initiate destination policy formulation. The following stages indicate the scope of this task (Lickorish *et al.*, 1991, p. 124):

1 Review of present trade and its evolution; note stage in growth cycle and changing trends.
2 Strength and weakness (SWOT) analysis.
3 Product–market match: identify broad market opportunities and compare with resource and product capacity; note constraints and ability to overcome.
4 Select priorities and examine cost benefit, including options, if any.
5 Formulate policy options in consultation with trade sectors and communicate to
  (a) private and operating sectors
  (b) other agencies of government, local or national, concerned
  (c) public (residents).
6 Review policy with input from 5 (above), and set objectives and targets.
7 Prepare marketing and development plan and seek consultation on implementation, as at 5.

8 Establish monitoring process to measure performance against objectives.

Tourism policies

The following examples of tourism policy, explicit or implicit, will illustrate the different ways in which governments deal with their vital role.

The European Union

Under the Treaty establishing the European Union (EU), revised from time to time, substantial fiscal, financial and legislative powers have been transferred from national governments in member countries to the EU, and its executive arm, the Commission. The European parliament, an elected assembly, in turn has considerable powers in approving budgets and legislation.

However, with growing recognition of the importance of tourism and with some encouragement from the Parliament, the Community set out in 1986, albeit rather late in the day, objectives related to the trade, realizing that many mainline policies of the Community impacted on tourism to a major extent and that there were spin-off benefits that had to be recognized.

European Community objectives

1 To facilitate and promote tourism in the Community.
2 To improve its seasonal and geographic distribution.
3 To make better use of the Community financial instruments, e.g. the European Regional Development Fund (ERDF).
4 To provide better information and protection for visitors.
5 To improve the working conditions of persons employed in the tourism industry.
6 To provide more complete information on the sector and set up consultation and coordination between the Commission and Member States.

Impacts of EU mainline policies on tourism are very considerable. For member countries, it is by far the most important international organization. The inception of the Single Market in 1993 has so far proved to be of little benefit to tourism, which was already largely a free international trade. Fiscal intervention has been unfavourable, with VAT at high and varying rates (0–25 per cent) in member countries, and extended to additional services such as transport. This distorts trade and erodes Europe's competitive edge. Intervention in labour, social and environmental regulation has also burdened the industry with increased costs.

However, major investment in the poorer regions and in transport through the structural and social funding programme has assisted tourism developments, in some cases substantially.

Problems have arisen through the imposition of main-line policies suited to manufacturing or other key economic areas but inappropriate for tourism. The Community (now the European Union) has never had a tourism policy and no priority has been given to the trade which under the principle of subsidiarity is a matter for national governments. There is merely a passing reference in the Maastricht Treaty (Article 31).

This is clearly unsatisfactory, as increasingly business and professional organizations are developing on a European or indeed global scale.

The situation may change. In preparation for the 1996 revision of the Treaty the Commission of the Union has published a Green Paper to consult widely on the future role in tourism. This consultative document proposes four Options for Action, from virtually complete devolution of responsibilities to Member States to Option Four which would imply an active tourism policy and programme and a full 'competence' or authority in the Treaty.

Since tourism policy must take account of the administrative boundaries, a European tourism organization must eventually develop, recognizing the transfer of national powers to Brussels, e.g. in taxation, transport and industry regulations, if tourism is to develop in a satisfactory and prosperous way.

Switzerland

An explicit tourism policy for Switzerland was not adopted officially until 1979. Government considered the Swiss tourist industry as largely a matter

La Conception Suisse du Tourisme

Global objective

To guarantee optimal satisfaction of the needs of tourists and individuals from all walks of life in effectively grouped facilities and through conservation of the environment

Secondary objectives

SOCIAL	ECONOMIC	ENVIRONMENTAL
Create the best possible social conditions for locals and tourists	Encourage a tourist industry that is both competitive and efficient	Ensure the relaxing quality of both the countryside and man-made attractions

Intermediate and partial objectives

Ten more objectives, e.g. more participation from locals	Eleven more objectives, e.g. optimize the operation and structure of the industry	Eight more objectives, e.g. develop facilities in harmony with the environment

Figure 11.1 List of objectives of La Conception Suisse du Tourisme. Source: Horwath & Horwath, *Hotels of the Future* (a report for, and published by, the International Hotel Association)

for the private sector. State intervention was limited to help for seasonal hotels, some infrastructure financing and funding for promotion overseas by the Swiss National Tourist Office.

La Conception Suisse du Tourisme set objectives for society, the economy and the environment. The aim was to encourage a competitive and efficient tourism sector with the intention of both improving the position of the tourist in terms of choice and of the country and regions as a whole. The objectives can be summarized as in Figure 11.1.

United Kingdom

In Britain, the government has been reluctant to publish an overall tourism policy issuing guidelines to the statutory agencies (the British Tourist Authority and the Tourist Boards). However, in 1985 a senior cabinet Minister, Lord Young, took an active interest and instituted an annual report on tourism. The following extract from the 1985 report 'Pleasure, Leisure and Jobs – the Business of Tourism' illustrates the attitude to policy and is a clear statement of the government's role at that time (Department of Employment, 1985):

1 It may be asked why the government should involve itself directly in this topic, which is primarily a matter for private enterprise. Indeed, the government believes the best way it can help any sector of business flourish is not by intervening, but by providing a general economic framework which encourages growth and at the same time removing unnecessary restrictions or burdens.
2 Yet government has many interests in tourism and leisure. It is itself in the business, through ownership of national museums and galleries, the preservation of ancient buildings and monuments, support for the arts, sport and recreation, and the conservation of the countryside. It is involved in the way people get to and around this countryside – airports, seaports, railways, roads, waterways. Government departments set many of the rules which regulate the industry, such as liquor licensing, shops hours, advertising restrictions, and employment legislation. Government gives grant aid to the statutory tourist boards, which provide marketing and advisory services to the industry, and through the boards to a range of tourism development projects.
3 Finally, the government has a direct concern with the industry's great potential for growth, job creation and enterprise. As patterns in society and industry change, we need to encourage the new strong points of our economy, many of them in service sectors. Across the UK few industries offer as great a scope for new employment as tourism and leisure, much of it in self-employment or small firms, involving a far wider range of skills than most other growth sectors and a broad geographical spread.
4 That is above all why the government has taken a fresh look at whether there are obstacles it can remove in order to enable this important sector of industry to develop further and faster. Two main areas of improvement have been studied – ways in which business can be made easier for the industry itself; and ways in which people can get more out of their time off, which in turn must benefit business too.

The BTA publishes from time to time a Strategy Document based on marketing considerations, setting out forecasts of growth, strengths and weaknesses in the product, and action needed both in the marketing and product fields. The BTA has statutory duties, according to the legislation, although not all of them are carried out and its objectives as stated in its Annual Report for 1990 were as follows.

Statutory responsibilities

The BTA was, in common with the English, Scottish and Wales Tourist Boards, established under the Development of Tourism Act 1969. The Authority assumed the principal responsibilities of the British Travel Association which until then had been Britain's national tourist organization.

The BTA's responsibilities are to

1 Promote tourism to Britain from overseas.
2 Advise government on tourism matters affecting Britain as a whole.
3 Encourage the provision and improvement of tourist amenities and facilities in Britain.

The National Tourist Boards' (ETB, STB, WTB) responsibilities are to

1 Promote their own country as a tourist destination.
2 Encourage the provision and improvement of tourist facilities and amenities within their own country.

BTA objectives

To this end the BTA has set the following mission and key objectives.

Mission: To maximize the incremental inbound tourism spend generated by investment of the grant-in-aid plus private sector funding while beating the world average tourism growth rate.

Objectives: To provide leadership to the tourism industry.

To develop key market intelligence to inform BTA's planning and to communicate to trade partners in Britain and overseas.

To promote Britain in overseas markets to raise awareness among potential customers and generate optimal mix of incremental spend in the short and medium term.

Spain

One of the surprising new trends in tourism demand towards the end of the 1980s was the slowing down and in some cases a decline in traffic flows to the Mediterranean. An official enquiry (Economist Intelligence Unit, 1990) into the tourism situation in Spain tried to discover the reasons for this serious change and to advise on future action to correct the problems involved. The report identified the respective roles of the public and private sectors.

The main reasons identified for the loss in value for money were divided into those for which the state should take full responsibility, those which were due to deficiencies in both the public and private sectors and those which could be attributed solely to the private sector as follows.

Public sector

1 Spanish roads and traffic conditions (inferior).
2 Railway transport (not suited to mass transport).
3 Air transport (air traffic control delays, etc.).
4 Sea transport.
5 Post and telecommunications (described as chaotic).
6 Hygiene, environment, noise, ecology and beach cleanliness.

Other factors criticized as hindering development:

1 Urban security.
2 Taxes.
3 Lack of coordination, central and regional government.
4 Lack of clear legal framework for certain activities (e.g. time share).

Public and private sectors

1 Exchange rate.
2 Service and training.
3 Complementary facilities (activities in addition to accommodation and climate).

Private sector responsibility

1 Quality of product.
2 Marketing.
3 Traditional standards for hospitality for foreign visitors diminishing.

USA

Pearce (1992, p. 9) writes succinctly on the situation in the USA. Destination tourism responsibility and promotion is taken not by the central government but by cities, resorts and the states, especially in places where the convention trade is well established.

The budgets of city convention and visitors bureaux were in some cases much larger than the funds voted for the United States Travel and Tourism Administration (USTTA), the Federal Government Body. Many cities finance their tourism expenditure by special taxes. For example, sales taxes on hotels, catering, etc.

The USTTA, an agency of the US Department of Commerce headed by an Under Secretary of Commerce for Travel and Tourism, had as its objectives:

to develop travel to the United States from abroad as a stimulus to economic stability and to the growth of the US travel industry, to reduce the nation's travel deficit and to promote friendly understanding and appreciation of the United States.

and

to increase the US share of worldwide tourism receipts and to increase this nation's real earnings from tourism.

Its tourism offices abroad supplied information directly to prospective visitors and assisted tour operators and travel agents, by a variety of promotional activities.

The USTTA was never securely funded and eventually was closed down in 1996. However, as in the similar case of the Swedish National Tourist Organization, efforts by industry sectors and a realization by government that national benefits were at risk resulted in a cooperative solution to carry on promotion in foreign countries as a minimum and necessary national programme. It is instructive that business appreciated as government did not, that promotion abroad for the national tourist destination was a vital task in a competitive world market for travel. A platform for collective action is essential, as explained in Chapter 9.

Pearce comments that 'For its size, the USA had a very small national tourist organization with a limited range of functions'.

The USTTA had a base budget of $14.6 million and a staff of 95, of whom 51 were in overseas offices. The USTTA was established by the 1981 National Tourism Policy Act. The resulting administrative structure for tourism in the USA is the outcome of the interplay of various forces. In part it is the outcome of an administration which at best has seen a federal involvement in tourism being confined to the promotion of international tourism for balance of payments purposes and at worst has seen no explicit role for the federal government in tourism. In part it is the outcome of a Legislature who have seen a much stronger role for federal government in tourism and one which is more broadly based. At its fullest extent it should encompass recreation as well as tourism and all aspects of tourism both domestic and international. In part it is the outcome of a tourism industry which has maintained an effective lobby for government support for tourism and particularly international tourism.

The final concentration on international promotion, and the meagre resources is a product of a hostile administration.

Despite all the efforts, the end result was not radically different from that which went before.

Local and regional tourist organizations

At the local level the regional or local authority has a role similar to that of the central government and in many ways a more comprehensive and important one. Indeed, in the early days of mass travel stimulated by the growth of the railway network, public sector intervention in tourism was solely at the local level. There were no national tourism organizations.

The growth of large resorts, pioneered in Britain at the main seaside centres, encouraged the development of local tourism administrations to carry out the responsibilities of the host destination.

Much of the early work in resort development was led by commercial interests, which were very creative in their approach and had an instinctive appreciation of the art of marketing, even if the word had not been invented at the time. The poster and brochure, for example, still marketing aids of first importance, were invented by the resort and railways, shipping companies and their agents.

Mass expansion, growth of large companies and the trend towards more sophisticated entertainments and attractions, required much substantial investment in facilities and amenities, and the organization of festivals, fairs and other special events. The demand encouraged the local authority to undertake an interventionist and more entrepreneurial role in the major European centres. The local authority leadership continued over the years and now involves substantial investment in infrastructure and promotion. More recently, for example, large conference, exhibition and cultural centres have been built throughout Europe and in many other successful tourism countries, principally by municipal enterprise.

This intervention role required some specialization in the administrative organization since the tourism task has unique features, not least the partnership role of the public and private sectors in providing the wide range of services and attractions required. Furthermore resorts had to provide a level of services far greater than needed by residents alone, as the population increased substantially during the season, affecting the supply of public provision, for example in health, safety, transport and access (roads and parking), environmental enhancement including waste disposal, etc. This involves costs over and above the entrepreneurial task in attractions, information and promotion. Budgets have been, and can be substantial, often as large or greater than the national tourist organization funding. But the municipalities are usually at least to some extent traders and may enjoy substantial trading income related to visitor spending.

It can be easier for the resort local government and their electors to understand the benefits to the locality from visitor revenues. There is a degree of local patriotism and the desire to beat the competition at least in the region. Benefits to the town's traders are visible. The provision of transport facilities and attractions at a level and standard far higher than could be sustained by local demand can usually be appreciated, as well as the contribution to employment and general prosperity.

In recent years, however, this support has not always been forthcoming, either because the volume of traffic has become excessive at peak times or environmental damage is feared. In addition, with changes in movement and road congestion, links between the resident and visiting population may be more difficult to maintain on a basis of mutual respect and courtesy.

As with the central authority, forms of organization may vary; local tourist offices may be a department of local government. While this is still the preferred structure, there has been an increase in devolving operations, especially marketing, to specialist agencies operating with industry support. This is evidently easier in the larger centres where there is a larger trading base for such support. In France the Syndicat d'Iniative operates as cooperatives at the local level, but the regional and central tourism authorities are part of government.

In Britain the central function, as already explained, is a government responsibility although devolved in part to a variety of state agencies (the BTA, ETB, STB, WTB, arts, sports, training and regional development agencies, etc.) and is not well coordinated. There is in addition a regional structure of tourist boards (London, South, East, Southern, West Country, etc.) supported by local authorities and traders but independent of the central government or the national tourist office. Their work is linked at least loosely with a considerable number of local authority (counties, cities and towns) tourism departments, in turn supported in some case by devolved marketing cooperatives, supervised by the municipality.

Although as the OECD observed there is no single ideal form of tourism organization, there are some common principles or guidelines. There are two important requirements. First, the organization must fit the regional or local administrative boundaries, and second, there must be good coordination and cooperation at all levels of the public administration concerned and good working relationships with neighbours, especially if they constitute a visitor destination with a clear identity. Just as a branded product has a special goodwill value, so the same will be true of a resort area. Such cooperation is not always easy to achieve in a competitive situation. Marketing should be hived off to an operating agency or at least carried out in close cooperation with the producers or suppliers of the local services and attractions.

International organizations

There are a number of international bodies, both government and non-government, with tourism interests. Government bodies reflect the national government's interest in, and political will regarding, tourism intervention. In the industrialized countries, the tourism priority tends to be low. Because of the wide range of tourism activity the number of organizations with some concern or responsibility is great, but coordination and often cooperation as at the national level is weak. Furthermore, consultation with industry and operating sectors is often inadequate, as the sector's voice is weak. The main sector industry bodies inevitably present the case of their own trade, sometimes as in modes of transport in a competitive situation. Thus the collective tourism approach is hard to organize and sustain, even when cooperation at the operating level is effective.

The intergovernmental bodies and agencies are established in relation to administrative boundaries where governments have agreed to work together, both on a worldwide and on a regional basis.

United Nations

At the world level the United Nations Organization and its agencies are active from time to time in the tourism field, but their intervention is relatively limited to such matters as health and safety and, on a modest scale, in aid to developing countries and in environmental action. Governments are more active at regional or multilateral and bilateral level in a range of administrative and regulatory action covering security, including passports and visas, customs control and conditions of trade, safeguarding the national interest. Aviation is still subject to state regulation with limits on free competition. Exchange controls and the levy of taxes are areas for further international agreement in the work of removing constraints to free movement of travellers worldwide.

The following UN agencies have tourism interests to a greater or lesser degree:

1 The Economic and Social Council.
2 The UN Conference of Trade and Development (UNCTAD), mainly for developing countries.
3 The World Health Organization (WHO).
4 The International Labour Office (ILO).
5 The International Civil Aviation Organization (ICAO).
6 The International Maritime Organization (IMO).
7 The United Nations Development Programme.

The World Bank (International Bank for Reconstruction and Development) has been active from time to time in assisting tourism in developing countries. The United Nations Statistical Commission has helped to establish international definitions and recommended practices to improve information on the fast-growing international passenger movement.

World Tourism Organization

The World Tourism Organization (WTO), an intergovernmental body recognized by the UN as an official agency with a consultative status, has taken the lead in representing its member governments' collective view in tourism issues. Like its predecessor body, the International Union of Official Travel Organizations, it has developed useful technical programmes in statistics, research and the exchange of ideas and experience and in technical aid, particularly for poorer countries. The WTO has made efforts recently to strengthen its links with commercial and non-government partners through its system of affiliate membership which should help in the provision of practical guidance and as a basis for cooperative action.

However, the work of governmental bodies is inevitably limited by the low priority accorded to the industry by most governments and the lack of strong collective support from the operating sectors. Achievements at international level remain modest and experimental in scale, with limited success in representing tourism as the world's leading industry.

Non-governmental international organizations

As the work of the intergovernmental bodies expanded, trade sectors and professional bodies found it necessary to organize both at the world and regional international level, first to respond or react to government interventions, and second, where practical, to seek a more positive relationship in cooperative and collective tasks. The need for consultation at appropriate levels became more pressing and although clearly essential not always accepted by government bodies. Industry sectors have established their international associations or groups, such as:

1 Alliance International du Tourisme (AIT).
2 International Air Transport Association (IATA).
3 International Chamber of Commerce (ICC).
4 International Hotel Association (IHA).
5 International Road Transport Union (IRU).
6 International Union of Railways (UIL).
7 Universal Federation of Travel Agents Associations (UFTAA).

A considerable number of bodies have some interest in tourist matters from time to time, reflecting the wide-ranging nature of the trade. Unfortunately this has proved a major obstacle in attempts to establish a representative consultative forum. Recently the leaders of a number of major companies in travel and tourism, airline, hotel and tour operators set up the World Travel and Tourism Council (WTTC), with a brief to secure adequate recognition of tourism as the world's largest trade. This body of large commercial interests does not cover the public sector, which is a major operator in tourism, nor the professional sector bodies and trade associations whose task it is to represent their industries.

This division of interest is apparent at national level, where trade associations are well established but active tourism industry organizations are rare. They do exist in a number of countries, such as the Travel Industry Association of America, and similar bodies in Ireland, the UK, France, Denmark, Germany and Italy. For the most part they have few resources and limited influence on activity. But there are some exceptions. The need for such collectives increases as tourism grows, and governments in the industrialized countries withdraw from tourism intervention. As noted earlier in this chapter, Sweden and the USA abolished their National Tourist Offices, France has eliminated the post of Minister of Tourism and Italy has abolished the Ministry of Tourism.

International regional organizations

Both at UN and geographic regional level there are regional bodies concerned with their regional needs. So long as liaison is maintained, such regional action and support can be very effective in tourism. This is certainly the case in Europe, which is seen at world level as a destination entity with many common interests. The Council of Europe with Cultural Activities and the United Nations European Economic Commission are examples. The latter body, covering both East and West Europe, has been active in transport matters among others.

The European Union, the most powerful intergovernmental body in tourism, groups together 15 European countries. Aspects of the union's attitude to tourism were commented on earlier.

The Organization for Economic Cooperation and Development (OECD)

Established in 1961 the OECD aims
1 To achieve the highest sustainable economic growth and employment and a rising standard of living in member countries, while maintaining financial stability, and thus to contribute to the development of the world economy.
2 To contribute to sound economic expansion in member as well as non-member countries in the process of economic development.
3 To contribute to the expansion of world trade on a multilateral, non-discriminatory basis in accordance with international obligations.

Twenty-seven member countries represent the richer industrialized world, including Western Europe, Canada, the USA, Australia, New Zealand and Japan. Its Tourism Committee publishes a valuable annual report on Tourism Trends and Government Policies, and has had a long and successful history of action in removing restrictions on the free movement of travellers, largely but not entirely achieved in the members' territory. There has, however, been a regrettable trend by government to increase taxation of individual travellers, a practice previously condemned by the OECD.

Non-governmental regional organizations

At the regional level there are groups of state tourist offices concerned with regional promotion, such as the European Travel Commission (ETC), the Pacific Area Travel Association (PATA), the Caribbean Tourist Organization (CTO) and regional trade and professional bodies such as:

1 Association of European Airlines (AEA).
2 European Tourism Operators Association.
3 Eurochambres (Chambers of Commerce).
4 European Community Shipowners Association.
5 Confederation of the National Hotel and Restaurant Associations in the European Community.
6 European Community Federation of Travel Agents Associations (ECTAA).

There is a Federation of Tourism Sector Interests in the European Tourism Action Group (ETAG), to which 23 European and international tourism organizations belong, with representatives of the main interest, both public and private sector, serving the traveller. This body was originally formed through the sponsorship of the ETC, which remains a founder member. ETAG's continued activity as a liaison group and a voice of the tourism industry in Europe is due to a recognition that a forum for cooperation with governmental bodies, and the EU in particular, was necessary for both the trade and government.

Summary

Tourism, representing a large and growing mobile population, is much more than a major world industry. It is a phenomenon with great social as well as economic implications. For success there must be a public–private sector partnership. The destination public authority has obligations as well as benefits, a duty to act as host if paying guests are invited. Governments are major beneficiaries from high tax revenues derived from visitor expenditure.

Equally, as tourism becomes a mass movement there are social and economic impacts which cannot be left to market forces alone. In both the developed and the developing world there is a key role for the state and local government. The role is apparent, but the organization for action is not always understood and government policies can be inconsistent and inadequate. The range of interests involved makes the necessary cooperative and collective action difficult to achieve in a fully competitive market-oriented trade.

This is an area of substantial weakness for tourism and deserves more study and attention.

References

Burkart, A. J. and Medlik, S. (1981) *Tourism: Past, Present and Future*, Heinemann, London

British Tourist Authority (1990) *Annual Report*, March, BTA, London

Department of Employment (UK) (1985) *Action for Jobs in Tourism*, DoE, London

Economist Intelligence Unit (1990) *International Tourism Report*, No. 4, EIU, London

Lickorish, L. J., Jefferson, A., Bodlender, J. and Jenkins, C. L. (1991) *Developing Tourism Destinations*, Longman, Harlow, Essex, UK

OECD (1986) *Tourism Development and Economic Growth*, OECD, Paris

OECD, *Tourism Policy and International Tourism* (annual reports), OECD, Paris

Pearce, D. (1992) *Tourist Organisations*, Longman, Harlow, Essex, UK

WTO (1992) *Marketing Plans and Strategies of National Tourism Administrations*, WTO, Madrid

WTTC (1992) *Travel and Tourism*, WTCC, Brussels

Further reading

British Tourist Authority (1989) *Strategy for Growth*, BTA, London

Commission of the European Communities (1995) *The Role of the Union in the Field of Tourism*, Green Paper, Brussels

OECD (1996) *Tourism Policy and International Tourism in Member Countries*, OECD, Paris (annual reports)

Pearce, D. (1992) *Tourist Organizations*, Longman, Harlow, UK

WTTC, *Travel and Tourism* (annual reports), WTCC, Brussels

12 Tourism in developing countries

Introduction

For many of the poorer countries in the world tourism has become a major input to their development process. Although development is a concept which has many meanings, for most countries it is seen as being essentially a measure of economic progress. As such, most development indicators centre on changes in the gross domestic product (GDP), gross national income (GNP) or per capita incomes. It is recognized that these concepts are difficult to quantify, particularly in the developing world as statistical data is scarce and usually unreliable. Gross domestic product is a measurement of what is produced within the economy of a country. The concept of GDP per capita is simply the division of the GDP figure by the estimated population. The World Bank (1995), for example, classifies the relative stages of development of countries according to a range of per capita GDPs. The World Bank uses various bands of GNP per capita to classify countries (Table 12.1). However, it should be noted that as statistical data are usually unreliable in the developing countries, and often at best only an estimate of population figures is available, then the resulting GDP per capita is open to a degree of scepticism. Despite these problems it is still used as the major means of making relative assessments of levels of development between countries.

Economic development and economic growth

Despite the statistical difficulties mentioned, the less developed areas of the world are easily identified by using the classification set out in Table 12.2.

Table 12.1 Classification of countries by GNP per capita

Country classification	GNP per capita ($)
Low income	695 or less
Lower–middle income	696–2785
Upper–middle income	2786–8625
High income	8626 or more

Source: World Bank, *World Tables*, p. 763, 1995, Washington, D.C.

Table 12.2 Classification of countries by GNP per capita levels and by region

Income levels	Number of countries in regions				
	Sub-Saharan Africa	East Asia and Pacific	South Asia	Eastern Europe and Central Asia	America
Low	35	6	7	5	4
Lower–middle	5	14	1	18	17
Upper–middle	6	6	–	4	17
Total	46	26	8	27	38

Source: World Bank, *World Tables*, 1995, Washington, D.C.

It is important to make a distinction between economic development and economic growth. Economic growth is a quantitative measurement of increases in GNP and/or GNP per capita. It is a relative and comparative figure and tells us nothing about how the GNP is distributed within the country. It is a statistical measurement of economic change. Economic development, on the other hand, has a much wider interpretation. It attempts to see how economic growth has actually been used to improve the general living standards and well-being of the people of a country. One would expect economic growth, if used for economic development for example, to facilitate improvements in the provision of health services, education, infrastructure and the like. In order to separate both concepts, the United Nations Development Programme has developed a human development index which is published each year. This has a range of indicators such as number of doctors per 100 000 population, car ownership, access to education, levels of literacy, etc., which gives some indication of how a country is developing. The obvious point is that without economic growth, development can only take place in the presence of aid or other external donor contributions.

Developing countries: definition and characteristics

As a broad generalization, most of the developed countries in the world are those with membership of the OECD. Most developing countries are to be found in Africa, Asia, Latin America, Pacific and the Caribbean regions. Within this very broad group there are many different relative levels of development. For example, within Asia countries like Taiwan, Singapore and South Korea have rapidly developed and are some of the countries with the highest rates of economic growth in the world. However, in Asia there are also very poor countries such as India, Bangladesh and Nepal. In each of the regions of the world, there are relative levels of development which makes the concept of 'developing countries' a very broad one.

Developing economies are given different titles, e.g. less developed countries, developing countries, Third World countries. The latter expression is one which has gained much currency over the years. It is interesting to note how the term is derived.

Before the break-up of the former Soviet Union, the world was categorized into three major groups. First, were the developed, market economies, such as those who are members of the OECD. These are the most developed countries in the world which have a market economy as the major feature of their development. The second group of countries were members politically or economically of the old Comecom system, based very much on economic and political links with the Soviet Union. These countries tended to be characterized by economic planning based on centralized principles. The third group of countries were those in the developing world; some, e.g. Kenya and Barbados, followed free-market principles of development, whereas others, e.g. Sri Lanka, the Seychelles and Syria, were countries which tended towards more centrally planned economies. It was this third group which were collectively described as the Third World. With the break-up of the former Soviet Union, the term Third World is perhaps no longer appropriate as many of the former Comecom member countries are rapidly dismantling centralized planning and adapting to free-market economies. However, the term Third World is still used and as a broad generalization does describe a group of countries, some very large, e.g. India, Bangladesh and Indonesia, and other very small, e.g. Western Samoa, Fiji, St Vincent and Lesotho, which are facing different levels of development challenge.

There are perhaps six major features which are common to developing countries:

1 Most have narrow resource-based economies. They have limited manufacturing sectors and are heavily dependent on a range of agricultural exports to sustain their economies. There may be potential to expand the economies into minerals and mining, but often there is lack of resources both in capital and expertise to do so. Zaire and Namibia are two African countries which have considerable mineral wealth which is yet to be exploited.

2 Many are highly dependent on the export of primary products. In some cases this can be very narrowly based, such as on the export of tropical fruit or sugar which have limited comparative advantages on the international market. Many of these exports are also faced with tariff and quota barriers in the main importing countries.

3 Most require a large volume of imports from the industrialized developed countries. This has the effect of them having to buy at international market prices over which they have no control, e.g. oil imports. Rising import prices can generate inflationary pressures, causing economic instability.

4 As many are major exporters of basic primary products, e.g. coffee, tea and sugar, they are subject to export prices which are determined by the international market and which can fall or rise on a year-to-year basis. In order to overcome the most severe fluctuations, there are international commodity agreements, such as coffee, cocoa and sugar, which attempt to

build a buffer stock to ease the worst fluctuations in international prices. But in many cases this has not helped to protect the export earnings of the countries. These economic problems are further exacerbated by other pressures.

5 Most have weak infrastructure, undeveloped manufacturing sectors, high unemployment levels and a chronic shortage of capital. These deficiencies combine to provide a very poor base for economic development and diversification.

6 Many have very high rates of growth of population which jeopardize economic growth. A rapidly rising population can absorb whatever economic gains have been made by having to utilize that gain, not for investment in productive capacity, but simply to feed more people.

Identifying these six common characteristics presents a very simple analysis. One can find countries where certain factors would not necessarily apply and others where they do. However, as a generalization most of the developing countries are characterized by these problems.

The problems can be refined into three major areas. First, because of their low levels of development and because of their need for development capital, most developing countries have severe deficits on their balance of payments. This means that they import more than is covered by export earnings. This gap either leads to depreciating currency values and/or reliance on substantial foreign aid or loans. There is a further difficulty: in order to overcome the lack of development capital many countries have borrowed and are heavily indebted to foreign lenders. This in turn means that a large proportion of export earnings is often used to pay existing debts without being able to use these earnings for investment in new economic and social development. Many of the developing countries have recognized tourism as being able to provide an alternative source of foreign exchange earnings to service existing debt and to facilitate new investment.

Second, the lack of foreign exchange is a crucial constraint for many of these countries. Foreign exchange is required in order to conduct international trade and buy development goods, expertise and other skills which are part of the development process. Most, but not all, developing countries have currencies which are weak and often non-convertible. Tourism revenues provide an opportunity to relieve these constraints.

Third, in addition to these basic economic problems most developing countries, as noted above, are characterized by very rapid growth in population numbers and with the population being highly skewed to a high proportion of young people. These population pressures not only have economic consequences, but also political consequences on governments who must find work to absorb the growing numbers.

Tourism in development

It is against this economic and political background that most of the developing countries have seen tourism as a means of helping their development effort. As early as 1973, Erbes made the statement:

Everything seems to suggest that developing countries look upon tourism consumption as manna from heaven that can provide a solution to all their foreign settlement difficulties.

Although this is essentially a simplistic statement, it raises two questions. First, why should tourism be so regarded, and secondly, what is the role of tourism in economic development? In examining the first of these questions, it may be surmised that there are seven reasons which underlie Erbes's assumption:

1 Tourism is historically a growth sector. In the immediate postwar period and certainly from 1950 onwards, tourism as an international activity has been dynamic. Although the international oil crisis in the early 1970s and also later recession into the early 1980s affected growth trends, tourism recovered quickly. As noted in Chapter 4, the reasons for the growth in tourism were favourable economic and social determinants of demand. For most developing countries tourism offered a growth prospect which most other exports did not.

2 The major generating countries for tourists are the developed countries of the world. In turn, the developed countries are those which have hard currency. The earning of hard currency is of particular importance for most developing countries because this is needed to buy development goods, expertise and skills to support their development efforts.

3 As an export activity, tourism has one great advantage over other forms of exports – it is not faced with tariff or quota barriers. Most countries of the developed world do not put barriers on where their residents travel to, how much money they take with them, and how much money is available to them in a particular year. In 1967 the UK did have a foreign currency travel restriction, as did France in 1982. However, most countries now would not attempt to limit the travel propensity of their citizens and their export of currency. This is a very unusual feature which obviously makes tourism relative to other exports an attractive option for many developing countries.

4 Tourism tends to be an employment-intensive activity. Although this generalization does not hold true in every country, because tourism is essentially a service activity it tends to create more jobs per unit of investment than other more capital-intensive activities. Job creation is one of the most important economic and political necessities in the developing world and many governments support tourism in order to create employment opportunities. There is also the consideration that at the initial entry level to the industry, skills and training requirements are limited and therefore the employment costs of creating jobs can be relatively low.

5 Many developing countries are located in tropical or semi-tropical zones and can attract tourists because of the quality of the natural infrastructure, e.g. climate, beaches, scenery. Using this natural advantage as an input to tourism often creates very low entry costs for many countries, although of course these costs will increase as tourism numbers increase.

6 It is sometimes claimed that because a country will attempt to reflect its own traditions and culture in tourism development, there is a possibility

to create a tourism industry which reflects local rather than international standards. So, for example, instead of a concrete hotel with a tile roof, in some countries the alternative might be a wooden structure with a thatched roof. Because of the relative availability and cheapness of labour, there is also the opportunity of substituting labour for capital in building projects.

7 There also appear to be underlying factors which will support long-haul tourism. As many of the developing countries are distant from the main generating countries, air transport developments have been critical in the growth of international tourism. The development of new and bigger aircraft has meant that tourists can now travel much longer distances in more comfortable aircraft with a reduction in flying times . Furthermore, over the past 20 years the real cost of air fares have reduced. A third factor is that many people can travel long haul on the basis of inclusive tours which offer relatively cheaper prices. All these trends are increasing and it appears that most developing countries can look forward to a growth in demand for international tourism.

In reviewing these factors influencing the growth of tourism in developing countries, it is important to be aware of potential disadvantages. For example:

1 Although tourism is historically a growth sector in the global economy, this does not apply to every country or every region. So, for example, at the regional level Africa has traditionally been a very low recipient of international tourist arrivals, currently receiving less than 2 per cent of total international movements. Within Asia, countries such as India and Thailand have enjoyed high levels of growth, whereas others such Bangladesh and Pakistan have not.

2 Although tourism undoubtedly brings hard currency into a country, it also has to be recognized that a proportion of this currency leaks out to support imports for the tourism sector. So the gross earnings of the tourism sector will be much higher than the net earnings.

3 Although there is a relative absence of tariff and quota barriers inhibiting tourism movements, it should be noted that tourism is probably among the most competitive of international activities and therefore the relevance of price, value for money, personal safety, etc., often determines the competitive advantage of particular countries.

4 Although tourism is generally employment intensive it is often criticized as being an absorber of low-skilled people. Initially this is true; however, part of development planning should be to facilitate an upwardly mobile employment force which can create the middle and senior managerial cadres of the industry.

5 The natural infrastructure is an important input to tourism development, but there are many examples where the use of beaches, forest and other areas have caused serious environmental, social and cultural problems.

6 The use of intermediate technology, particularly in buildings and perhaps in substituting labour for capital in supplying services, is an attractive aspect of tourism's development potential. However, it has to be recognized that tourists do not have to accept any level of service. They

are discriminating and will not accept services which by local standards are high but may be low compared to international norms. This was something commented on by Cohen almost 25 years ago when he spoke of the 'environmental bubble'. Again this is an issue which has to be considered in planning.

7 The underlying factors increasing demand for tourism are likely to continue. However, as noted above, more countries are becoming involved in international tourism. There is growing competition for tourists, particularly for long-haul tourists, and factors such as security, health, quality of the product, value for money are causing many countries to look critically at their performance in the international marketplace.

There has to be some balance between the perceived advantages and disadvantages of tourism. This balance needs to be determined by very careful development of policies and by the implementation of those policies through tourism development planning. However, it should be noted that international tourism demand for any country is external. This means that despite careful development planning there are externalities which a country cannot control. For example, the Gulf War in 1991 had a dramatic effect on international tourism, in particular on countries in the Middle East, such as Egypt and Jordan, which saw their international tourism industry collapse. In the UK, the visits of American tourists also virtually ceased. Many of the external factors which influence demand cannot·be controlled by the tourist-receiving countries. This has caused some commentators to observe that tourism is a fickle and dangerous industry in which to put resources. There is also concern that seasonality of demand does not provide a good return on the resources used in tourism.

Some countries have very limited development options. For example, in many of the Pacific and Caribbean islands tourism is the major economic activity because it provides a better comparative advantage than exports of traditional products, e.g. bananas, sugar, citrus fruits. Perhaps one of major factors benefiting tourism is that it tends to have a very limited cyclical trend. Even after the Gulf War, Middle East countries began to recover visitor traffic quickly in the following years. Tourism is seasonal and the problem for many developing countries is that if a major political disturbance or natural disaster occurs before the season starts or in the early season, then often the season cannot be rescued for that particular year. But there are precedents which indicate that tourism has a fairly rapid recovery rate.

Summary

Although in world terms the biggest proportion of visitors still travel within Europe and within the USA, Canada and Mexico, and between these two regions, there is a definite growth in long-haul travel. As people become culturally more curious, have greater levels of disposal income and with attendant developments in air transport, there is every reason to believe that this trend will increase. Faced with a growing demand for visits to their countries, the onus must be on the developing countries to plan for their tourism sectors, to ensure that the disadvantages are managed and minimized, and potential advantages are achieved.

References

Erbes, R. (1973) *International Tourism and the Economy of Developing Countries*, OECD, Paris

Cohen, E. (1972) Towards a sociology of international tourism. *Social Research*, **39**, 1

World Bank (1995) *World Tables*, Johns Hopkins University Press, Washington, D.C.

Further reading

Harrison, D. (ed.) (1992) *Tourism and the Less Developed Countries*, Belhaven, London

Lea, J. (1988) *Tourism and Development in the Third World*, Methuen, New York

Lickorish, L. J., Bodlender, J., Jefferson, A. and Jenkins, C. L. (1991) *Developing Tourism Destinations: Policies and Perspectives*, Longman, Harlow, UK

Richter, L. K. (1989) *The Policies of Tourism in Asia*, University of Hawaii Press, Honolulu

United Nations Develoment Programme, *Human Development Report* (annual), New York

13   Tourism by world region

Introduction

Chapter 14, outlining future trends and forecasts, refers briefly to the dramatic growth of international travel in the past half-century, an annual average growth rate of 7.3 per cent, from 25 million arrivals in 1950 to 567 million arrivals in 1995.

According to the World Tourism Organization (WTO, 1995) tourism receipts grew from US$7 bn in 1960 to US$372 bn in 1995. However, these figures are expressed in current prices and do not take into account the marked effect of inflation. Nevertheless the statistics speak for themselves, reflecting the major expansion of the total movement.

While the largest movement takes place between neighbouring countries and on an intra-regional basis, long-distance travel has grown faster than domestic and neighbouring countries' movement. The world is on the move, and increasingly seeks new, exotic or distant places.

Overall growth hides substantial changes in demand, greater sophistication of travellers, frequency of travel and an intense segmentation or specialization in purpose of visit. These aspects of demand, vitally important in the travel trade business and in marketing tourism are explained in Chapter 9.

In addition to demographic and social change, there has been a virtual revolution in the economics of the business, with great reductions in real costs and prices, resulting from new technology and other efficiencies. These and other factors are altering mainstream travel flows on a geographic basis. There are emerging regions, newly industrialized countries and changes in relative wealth in industrialized countries. Some countries have lost their share of generally growing prosperity. Travel follows change in wealth (GDP) and in personal disposable incomes. These main world developments are intensified in travel by a revolution in personal mobility and communication.

Many of the changes in world movements are still at an early stage. The international travel trade in most of the main originating countries remains national or domestic market based, concerned principally with outgoing movement by their own nationals. Yet this is a minority share of the total tourism spend in such countries, taking into account revenue from domestic movement and incoming foreign visitors. Tradition, although now weakening, is still to a surprising extent a powerful influence on leisure behaviour and destination choice. Other factors such as language, custom, cuisine and education, also support the concentration in national markets.

Although world tourist arrivals have expanded massively, share by region has been changing with the recent more rapid growth of the emerging markets at the expense of the traditional tourism regions such as Europe.

Volume figures of arrivals need careful examination if comparisons are to be made. They are not always compatible with national or regional figures, especially those based on surveys, as they are derived from control systems in the main, and frontier crossing in particular.

Demand trends in travel now change more rapidly than ever, due both to alterations in consumer preferences and in the broad demand determinants. There is growing prosperity in the recently industrialized areas of the world. Within industry a move towards globalization on a world scale, the creation of more multinational companies and new trading networks can lead to massive new investment and rapid development, especially in new resort areas. New techniques in distribution trades and services, with computer reservation services and information technology, can greatly stimulate certain forms of travel, particularly in the international field. But there are also declining resort areas and weaker traffic flows, making tourism operation at the same time not only a massive business but one with greater risks and volatility in a highly competitive world marketplace.

Major alterations in geographic movement have been well charted by the WTO. Some of the new flows show rapid growth and very considerable potential for major expansion. The WTO has forecast that international tourism will double for most of the less developed tourism regions within a decade, with a much higher rate of growth than in the traditional tourism regions of the past such as Europe. There cannot be a uniform rate. Some regions will continue to do better than others and, for some, growth can no longer be taken for granted. Thus risks will be much greater for certain types of operation, particularly for those with heavy fixed capital investment such as hotels locked into one destination, which unlike transport, e.g. airlines or tour operators, cannot switch assets and operations rapidly to alternative routes and resorts.

The following examination of main traffic flows indicates changes in patterns of movement and market shares in total movement. It must be emphasized that from an operational and marketing point of view, and in the business of destination management, the macro approach to total movement trends is inadequate. Detailed examination of segments and geographic markets is essential. There are often counter-currents. Senior citizen travel, for example, can be highly resilient to recession in many areas. Independent individual travel can and does increase even when package travel to similar destinations is in decline. Some market segments are highly profitable. Business travel can earn high revenue from low or modest volumes of travellers and is usually less seasonal than mass holiday travel sold at discounted rates. For some destinations, low-volume high-revenue traffic may be preferred.

The following examples of sustainable change in the hotel and airline industries demonstrate the importance of supplementary information on both the supply and demand sides by trade sector and market segment, to illustrate major trends which global statistics of tourist flows cannot indicate.

The hotel sector

The hotel and accommodation sector has a tradition of lumpy growth in capacity. There is a time lag before investment in new capacity catches up with demand. In the 1980s, hotel capacity worldwide increased by 14.5 per cent from 8.7 to 9.9 million rooms (Horwath and Horwath, 1988), with Asia and the Pacific taking the lead with a 61 per cent increase. Heavy investment in North America led to substantial overcapacity. The industry suffered a marked reduction in occupancy and yields in the recession and troubled years of the early 1990s. Expansion in Europe was in general more modest, reflecting the lower growth rate.

Demand for higher quality and value for money at all levels continued, but there was also pressure on budget accommodation, and some trading 'down' in business travel. There were signs of more rapid change in trends in certain market segments; interest in family rooms, better facilities for single women travellers, fast food and take-away service, and bed and breakfast type provision.

Airlines

The scheduled airline industry achieved an average annual growth rate in productivity of 5 per cent in the period 1982–92. At the same time, real input prices (wage rates, fuel costs, etc.) declined, so that airline passengers benefited substantially from lower fares (Lyle, 1993). In the early 1990s demand weakened because of recession and political instability. Competition increased as excess capacity emerged. The airlines consequently made heavy losses in the years 1990–92 of over US$10 bn. Demand improved from 1993, but there were new challenges in privatization, globalization and liberalization.

New burdens afflicted the industry in the form of increased taxation, notably through new taxes on individual international passengers (e.g. airport exit levies) and environmental constraints.

The conclusion must be that without new cost-cutting technology, substantial continuing fare reductions in real terms may not be possible. In spite of this, the airline industry is looking to a further increase in passenger traffic of 5 per cent, compared with the WTO forecast of world tourism growth of 3.8 per cent per annum in the period 1990–2000.

Europe

By 1994, tourist arrivals in Europe reached a total of 330 million and receipts of US$175 bn (according to the WTO). Average annual growth over the previous 10 years was 4.4 per cent for arrivals, one point below world average. The decline continued in 1995 to 2.3 per cent – 1.5 per cent points below world average.

Although this expansion represents half the world's growth in the 10-year period, Europe has been losing world market share substantially, from over 72 per cent in 1960 to under 60 per cent in 1994. In terms of receipts, shares fell below 50 per cent for the first time in 1993 after recording persistent declines since 1960.

The majority of European visits are in the form of short trips, with short length of stay. Revenues in general, per visit, are low compared with long-distance travel. The longer the journey the higher the spend at the destination, and the differences are very marked. Certain segments are much more lucrative than others. Business travel, for example, in some of the leading European countries such as the UK can account for 25 per cent or more of total tourism income from a relatively small travel volume. As much as 50 per cent of the occupancy of international standard hotels in the leading cities represents business travel expenditure. Many enterprises in internationally favoured cities and resorts may be dependent on such travellers for more than 50 per cent of their revenue.

Traffic flow estimates indicate the relative concentration of the major tourism movements. Although traffic has expanded massively, it is still limited to a small number of major markets, destinations and routes. There are signs that geographic flows are changing quite substantially, but as Chapter 14 indicates it is a slow process with the leaders likely to remain in place for the next two decades.

While Europe's market share as a tourist destination has been falling consistently for some time, the outward flow, especially on long-distance routes, has been growing fast at an increasing rate. Although the major part of European residents' foreign travels, with increased frequency of trip, takes the form of an intra-European flow to neighbouring countries, the longer journeys show a much higher rate of expansion. Indeed, domestic travel in some countries is in decline.

The major tourist flows into the European countries are: intraregional, Americas to Europe, and East Asia and the Pacific to Europe, greatly influenced by Japan. The intra-European movements are by far the most important, accounting for a very high proportion of the total at 84 per cent, or nearly 250 million arrivals – in 1993 – with an annual average growth rate of 3.2 per cent since 1980.

Tourist arrivals from the Americas account for 7.5 per cent of the total and since 1980 have increased on average by 2.4 per cent per year, a relatively modest rate and far below most measures of market potential. Peak years were in the mid-1980s, exceeding 26 million arrivals (at frontiers), declining due to recession, political instability and other factors to 22 million in 1993. These WTO statistics record arrivals at frontiers at each individual country, not by individual trip to Europe.

Tourist arrivals from East Asia and the Pacific showed a high growth rate. Traffic almost doubled in the period 1980–90, but has declined modestly since to just over 8 million arrivals. However, further expansion from the area is likely and most long-distance travel movement to Europe has showed signs of improvement since 1993.

The WTO publishes tables showing the top destinations and top earning countries in the world (Tables 13.1 and 13.2). Seven of the top destinations are in Europe. The top five destinations accounted for 40 per cent of world

Table 13.1   World's top destinations

Rank	Destination	Tourist arrivals 1993* (million)
1	France	61
2	United States	46
3	Spain	41
4	Italy	26
5	Hungary	23
6	United Kingdom	19
7	Austria	18
8	China	18
9	Mexico	17
10	Germany	15

* Excluding same-day visitors.
Source: *World Tourism Organization.*

Table 13.2   World's top earners from tourism

Rank	Destination	Tourist receipts, 1993* (US$bn)
1	United States	56
2	France	24
3	Spain	21
4	Italy	20
5	Austria	15
6	United Kingdom	12
7	Germany	11
8	Hong Kong	8
9	Switzerland	8
10	Mexico	6

* Excluding international transport.
Source: *World Tourism Organization.*

arrivals. France was the top destination country, but 72 per cent of arrivals there came from only five nearby countries – Germany, the UK, Italy, Belgium and the Netherlands.

The *European Travel Monitor* (1995) provides much more detailed information about socio-demographic characteristics and country destination analysed by segment and over a period, based on substantial and continuing surveys in European countries. The trend information is becoming increasingly important. For example, although overall holiday trips showed a 2 per cent increase in volume in 1994, there were some marked differences by type of segment. Short holidays (1–3 nights) declined by 11 per cent, whereas long holidays (4+ nights) increased by 4 per cent. It is a feature of recession that more people economize on short trips to preserve the one longer annual holiday. Inclusive holidays increased by 6 per cent, a good recovery performance in the Mediterranean resort areas, but winter sports trips declined by 15 per cent. Fewer trips were taken to visit friends and relatives and on business travel.

Europe has the largest 'mass' international market, but increasing segmentation and specialization affects traffic flows . These are capable of moving in different directions, with varying rates of growth or decline and with changes in destination and seasonality over relatively short periods.

According to the *European Travel Monitor* (1995), outbound trips by Europeans (East and West) totalled 214 million in 1994. Of this total, 193 million were by West Europeans. This compares with a figure of 205 million in 1990. The *Monitor* suggests a marked effect of recession, but there were other longer term trends. Business travel has declined continually from 1990 at 34.7 million trips to 29.3 million in 1994. Travel by West Europeans to East Europe has continued to increase. Length of trip has been decreasing in recent years. The *Monitor* reports the average in 1994 not much different from the previous two years, at 9.9 nights. This, however, is much affected by the strong growth in short holidays of 1–3 nights average. Length of stay for the longer trips (4+ nights) was 12.3. However, expenditure has increased at a rate higher than inflation.

In a largely flat or weak market travel overseas on longer distance trips continued to increase at above-average rates: 20 million or 9 per cent of total in 1994, a rise of 2 per cent when the overall figures showed a slight decline. Travel overseas is now established as a longer term growth trend and is reflected in the figures showing Europe's loss of market share

The Americas

WTO records show that in recent years the Americas (North and South) have greatly increased their incoming movement and their share of world tourism. At the same time the importance of the USA, the chief originating travel market in North America, has declined. In the 10 years 1983–93, tourist arrivals in the Americas have risen by 46 million and receipts by US $63 bn, representing 31 per cent of world growth in tourism revenues. The average annual growth of arrivals over the 10 years was 5.9 per cent, a little above the world average. North America enjoys the highest share of the region's tourism at 74 per cent, with the USA as the leading destination followed by Mexico, Canada, Argentina and Puerto Rico.

The majority of the visitors to the countries of the Americas, 73 per cent in 1993, came from within the region. Europe at 14 million accounts for 14 per cent, with half that number coming from just three European countries, the UK, Germany and France. The WTO has forecast that inter-regional traffic will increase faster than long-haul movement in the future. The region is expected to maintain growth and hold its place as the second world tourist reception area, with perhaps a small increase in world market share.

Although the transatlantic traffic represents the largest long-distance route in terms of passengers, growth in outward travel from North America in recent years has been slow or negative due to a variety of factors (exchange rate variation, price, security, competition). US travel to Europe peaked in 1990 at 7 million visitors and did not exceed this record flow again until 1994. Traffic has resumed modest growth. This is in contrast to the rapid expansion of European residents' movement westbound, reaching a total exceeding the American eastbound traffic. Mexico, Canada and the Caribbean are the main foreign destinations for US visitors.

Middle East

Due in part to political instability, growth in the Middle East's tourism has been disappointing in the past 10 years. Annual average increase in arrivals at 2.3 per cent was less than half the world rate. The region's share of world travel has been less than 2 per cent since the beginning of the 1990s, amounting to just over 7 million arrivals in 1993, with receipts in that year at US $5 bn, both figures lower than the year before.

Egypt is the leading country, with nearly 30 per cent of total visits, followed by Bahrain at 20 per cent, Saudi Arabia and Syria at 10 per cent and Jordan at 9 per cent. These countries, with the exception of Bahrain, are the top earners. Intraregional movement, normally the major part of each region's traffic, was the second lowest after South Asia of all the world's regions at 43 per cent. Europe is the main market, with 2 million arrivals (over one-third of the total). However, the volume of intra-regional traffic has doubled in recent years to nearly 8 million.

There is a substantial outward movement, but as is normally the case, mainly to neighbouring countries; nearly 1 million from Saudi Arabia and over 1 million from Egypt. A feature of travel in many developing areas is a substantial outbound travel movement, including long-distance and high-spending travel from the educated and richer minority, whereas the vast majority do not have sufficient income to participate in tourism.

South Asia

South Asia has the lowest share in world tourism, 0.7 per cent. It has a low growth rate of 3.3 per cent in the past 10 years up to 1993, 2 per cent points below the world average. Arrivals in 1993 totalled 3.4 million and receipts US $2 bn. India accounted for 50 per cent of total arrivals, with 70 per cent of total receipts.

Intraregional travel flows represented some one-third of all arrivals, the lowest proportion of all regions, reflecting the low average incomes in many parts of the area and thus a low propensity to travel. Europe provided nearly half of all visits in 1993 (44 per cent). The WTO expect travel to double in the next decade, with a much greater increase in intraregional movement.

As already observed, the poor regions of the world continue to provide substantial outbound movement. India, which has well-developed sections of its vast economy and a large professional and middle class, sustains a flourishing outward flow, estimated by the WTO at over 1 million in 1993. One-fifth of visits were made within the region. There is a substantial traffic flow to Europe, especially to the UK, in spite of currency restrictions and other constraints. In this, as in other developing and poorer regions of the world, tourism flows are not always easy to assess or measure as there are pilgrimage, migration and other movements varying according to season or annual conditions. Part of such travel would not conform to the accepted tourism definitions and can be poorly recorded.

East Asia and the Pacific

Tourist arrivals in East Asia and the Pacific have increased faster in the period 1983–93 than in any other region of the world. Annual growth has averaged nearly 11 per cent, more than double the world figure. Receipts have grown by 17 per cent per year. China was the leading international destination in 1993, followed by Hong Kong, Malaysia, Singapore and Thailand. Top countries in terms of tourist receipts were Hong Kong, Singapore, Thailand, China and Australia. However, Oceania, including Australia, accounted for only 9 per cent of arrivals.

As already noted above, comparisons in terms of major flows need careful study to distinguish the different segments making up total movement. Socioeconomic characteristics and behaviour patterns, such as purpose of visit and length of stay, may vary considerably. As the above figures indicate, while Australia may have low volume it enjoys a sophisticated and high-spending travel movement. Other countries may have a variety of travellers, including high-volume low-spend traffic, as in ethnic or pilgrimage movement.

Intra-regional travel has grown more than long-distance travel in the region during the past decade, accounting for 77 per cent of the total 53 million arrivals in 1993. There were more than 9 million Japanese visits or 17 per cent of the regional movement. This area enjoys an increasingly well-developed international tourism trade.

Europe provided 8 million arrivals, with an average increase of 8.7 per cent per year, 1980–93. This compares with visits from North America at 5 million, with an average annual increase since 1980 of 6.5 per cent. The WTO forecasts the highest growth rate of all world regions for the next decade. Traffic should double between 1990 and 2000 to over 100 million arrivals, and double again by 2010.

East Asia and the Pacific is not only the top region for growth in incoming movement but is also becoming a major force in the world market as a generator of outbound movement, especially in long-distance travel, with a relatively high proportion of total outward movement, higher than in many developed regions including some countries in Europe. Over 45 per cent of Japanese tourist trips overseas were made to destinations outside the region; USA was the leading receiving country with 3.54 million visits and Europe in second place with 1 600 000 (ETC, 1994).

Africa

During the 10 years 1983–93, international tourist arrivals in Africa have grown on average by 8.2 per cent per year, but still accounted for only 2 per cent of world growth in the period due to the very low level of movement. Receipts have grown correspondingly by 9.2 per cent on average per year.

Table 13.3 Top five destinations in Africa, 1993

Rank	Country	Tourist arrivals (thousands)	% Change-over, 1992	Market share of total Africa (%)
1	Morocco	4 027	−8.3	22.5
2	Tunisia	3 656	3.3	20.5
3	South Africa	3 343	15.6	18.7
4	Algeria	1 132	1.1	6.3
5	Kenya	783	12.0	4.4
Sub-total (1–5)		12 941	2.4	72.4

Source: *World Tourism Organization.*

Arrivals totalled 17.9 million in 1993 and receipts rose to US$6.4 bn. Northern Africa has the highest share of traffic at 49 per cent, followed by Southern Africa with 34 per cent. Morocco was the leading destination in 1993, followed by Tunisia, South Africa, Algeria and Kenya. Fifty-one per cent of all visits came from within the region, mainly from neighbouring countries. This movement has shown a relatively strong growth rate of 13.5 per cent, 1980–93. Europe provides 5 million visits, one-third of total arrivals in the region, with France and Germany accounting for half.

Variation in traffic between the continent's subregions indicates some important trend changes, with North Africa losing share and South Africa gaining traffic quite rapidly (Table 13.3). There is a substantial outward flow, although incomes on average are low, limiting foreign travel. Nevertheless, there is a substantial worldwide movement, especially to Europe which enjoys the major share of the longer journeys. Tourists from South Africa alone are estimated at 2.3 million in 1983, with the UK the main destination.

Summary

Changing trends are very evident in the past decade. This was a period of unparalleled cultural, economic and structural change, with marked political effects.

Technological advance speeds up change. The greater ability for large-scale investment and rapid development helped to meet the greater volatility in demand trends.

Competitive pressures exert powerful market forces on a global scale, affecting regions and destinations in new and differing ways. There are and will be winners and losers in the world trade of tourism, which is as yet poorly served through governments' lack of understanding of the phenomenon. This leads to inadequate investment in human resources such as training and the provision of an effective research and database to monitor change.

References

ETC (1994) *Annual Report*, European Travel Commission, Paris

European Travel Monitor (1995) IPK, Munich

Horwath and Horwath (1988) *London Tourism: A Portrait*, Horwath and Horwath UK, London

Lyle, C. (1993) *Future Trends in Civil Aviation*, World Tourism Organization, Madrid

World Tourism Organization (1995) *International Tourism Overview*, WTO, Madrid

Further reading

OECD (annual) *International Tourism and Tourism Policy in Member Countries*, OECD, Paris

Waters Somerset, R. (1994) *Travel Industry Yearbook*, Child and Waters, New York

World Tourism Organization (1994) *Global Tourism Forecasts to the Year 2000 and Beyond*, WTO, Madrid

World Tourism Organization (1994) *Tourism Market Trends (by World Region)*, WTO, Madrid

World Tourism Organization (1994) *Tourism Trends to the Year 2000 and Beyond*, WTO, Madrid

14 Future trends

There are several ways of studying future trends. First it is important to examine the immediate past history, then the present position and how it has arisen, and lastly the outlook projected from the present.

Another exercise is the comparison of a variety of forecasts of traffic, by destination, by route and by sector. Most forecasts are usually at least in part a projection of past trends, with quantitative (econometric) models or qualitative modification.

Whatever methods are chosen, a detailed study of the main agents for change is essential. These are:

1 Demand determinants.
2 Supply-side response through industry development, taking into account external and general economic factors.
3 Political philosophies and the role of government.

Projecting from the past and present

Past experience is a good guide in studying trends, but in the present state of massive economic development and high technology this task has never been more difficult, particularly because of the vast scale of operation in world trade and commerce and the speed of change as a result of progress in technology. Tourism is no exception. Indeed, as it is a totally market-oriented activity in a highly competitive worldwide trade, consumer preferences leading to demand changes have a major influence on tourism movement.

Although tourism is a service industry, and sometimes in terms of foreign trade is referred to as an 'invisible export', in reality as the world's largest trade, its influence on economic development, especially in tourism destinations, is enormous. Tourism requires massive investment in infrastructure, which is a fixed long-term capital commitment. In particular, it is totally dependent for survival on transport infrastructure. The tourism trades' professional representative associations in Europe (ETAG, 1990) have warned the EU that growth forecasts indicating tourism will double by the year 2010 are quite unrealistic unless such investment takes place. Unfortunately governments, transport and tourism ministries do not always talk or plan together in tourism terms.

The large scale of operation in tourism, its great economic and social impacts, and vast potential for future development, make forecasting and forward planning more essential than ever. There must be a partnership by public and private sectors, embracing a range of trade sector activity and coordination between the services. Transport growth must match demand, but to realize the potential, destination or resort services must expand in a coordinated way. In practice, this rarely happens. However, modern techniques enable trades to expand quickly and catch up.

The scale and speed of resort development, especially for the mass markets in North America and Europe, demonstrate this. But tourism growth can never be taken for granted. History warns that even in periods when experts confidently predict long-term expansion, not all destination areas, nor all tourism and transport businesses succeed. The penalty for failure can be very great, even when massive tourism flows continue to increase. Forecasting and studying demand changes become more than ever necessary, but the tools for such work need much improvement.

Increasing volatility in tourism demand is a major difficulty. Travel and holiday taking even half a century ago, albeit on a much smaller scale, followed traditional forms. They could be predicted with some certainty. Many holidaymakers went to the same resort, and even to the same lodgings year after year. Familiarity with the destination and holiday companions was a popular attraction. Now there is increasing volatility in travellers' choice, fiercer competition with effectively the whole world to choose from, and powerful influences of external factors, some of which in the short term can have sudden and major consequences. Unstable currencies, for example, affect exchange rates and therefore prices. Recession, health and security challenges are all liable to affect current travel movement with little warning and to a major extent. As mentioned earlier, both the Libyan crisis in 1986 and the Gulf War in 1991 virtually halted the tourism movement from the USA to Europe, with the loss of several million visits and several billion dollars revenue.

However, tourism has so far proved resilient to recession and the turbulence of special security or health situations. Traffic has usually recovered quickly and continued at anticipated or even higher rates of expansion. But losses have been sustained, and in an uncertain world the risk continues. Each recession or pause in growth has taken longer in recovery. There can be some more permanent effects needing remedial action. The Chairman of the International Federation of Tour Operators (IFTO) pointed out that a Mediterranean resort at the end of the last decade gained an unfortunate reputation for inadequate standards and pollution which led to an early reaction from the market, in a very short time. Action to repair damage physically and in marketing terms was essential, but expensive in time and money. Environmental awareness is growing and likely to play a more determining role.

It is the longer term factors, often more difficult to predict, that can have massive impacts; for example, in technology especially in transport, in information and marketing, in economic and political changes. Furthermore, shifts in consumer preferences tend now to be longer rather than short term in their incidence.

Since the advent of wide-bodied jet aircraft in the 1970s, for example, air fares have been lowered substantially in real terms as technical efficiency reduces real costs. But this powerful influence in market expansion may be coming to an end. Revolutionary changes in air and indeed other forms of tourism transport cannot be expected on the same scale in the future. Indeed there may be counter-currents, through costly regulation, environmental controls and taxes. The World Travel and Tourism Council (WTTC, 1995a) forecast a 30 per cent rise in tourism taxation in the next decade.

Changes in purchasing power due to structural changes can either reduce or create new markets, as richer countries become poorer and developing countries become richer. The effect of recession or cyclical economic variation, normally shorter term, can clearly be seen. In the 1991 recession many major travel flows were reduced, some substantially, e.g. US to Europe, intra-European, and to the Mediterranean. In the case of Britain alone, package travel, mostly to the Mediterranean, decreased by over 20 per cent or by 3 million packages between 1990 and 1993. Changes of this size can have massive economic impacts on destinations, if prolonged.

But there are counter-currents. In the UK, total outward movement continued to increase in these years due to the strength of individual travel, and the total reached new record levels. At the same time, countries with expanding economies create new and substantial travel flows. Outward movement from Japan is a leading example. The newly enriched countries of Asia and the Far East also show signs of substantial outward travel. In Europe, while traffic from the north to the warmer south has reduced in growth and in certain areas in absolute terms, movement from the south to the north has expanded rapidly, especially from Spain and Italy.

Long-distance travel by European residents travelling overseas was one of the fastest growing market segments. In the 1990s, movement to and from Eastern European countries escalated as political barriers were removed. Traffic at first was much greater to the West as capacity of good-quality services was very limited in the Eastern countries.

The WTO (1992) recorded an 18-fold increase in world tourism flows in the four decades between 1950 and 1990. This enormous expansion, creating mass tourism on a large scale for the first time, was fuelled by rising incomes and leisure time, as the revolution in technology got under way in the industrialized countries. Greater efficiencies in operation, management and marketing led to substantial reductions in real costs and prices. But continuing cost reductions of this kind cannot be taken for granted.

There was almost continuous growth until the modest recession in 1981 and the much greater setback in 1991, partly the effect of the Gulf War, but also the longer term influence of a much more serious cyclical recession and the speed-up in structural change responding to new technologies. This has led to a marked increase in long-term unemployment and volatility in currencies and exchange rates. These uncertainties may cast a shadow over the older industrialized countries, especially in Europe, for some time to come.

The past massive growth, with little interruption, was heavily influenced by large flows of holiday traffic from cold northern industrial areas to south sunny beaches in both Europe and North America. Towards the end of the period, new emerging markets, notably Japan, South East Asia and the Pacific, began to add to growth movements.

Demand trends are changing. Increased segmentation by purpose of trip, greater specialization and choices in destinations, including many new areas throughout the world, increase competition. Some of the older and well-known resort areas are in decline at a time of the greatest expansion in travel ever known.

Between 1960 and 1990, Europe and the Americas maintained their position as the two leading tourism regions, in both reception and originating travel. Europe, for example, continued as the world's largest region in terms of movement, but suffered a major loss of world market share.

Agents of change

Demand determinants

The WTO continue to forecast annual average growth rates to the year 2010 of 3.77 per cent. Forecasters find it difficult to come to terms with some massive changes in travel movement. New demand trends have not developed to their full extent. Their powerful impacts are just beginning to make their long-term effect.

One of the most significant is the intense segmentation of the mass market. There is no longer one mass market for leisure time, but a number of 'discrete mass markets' and increasing specialization, resulting in a variety of distinct traffic flows, often moving in different directions. During the recession of the early 1990s when packaged travel fell substantially and US travel to Europe suffered catastrophic decline, total movement in many areas and many resorts did not diminish. Package travel was replaced by individual travel. New tourism flows replaced the absent American visitors.

Determinants of demand are the fundamental factors governing the market and together represent the market forces which control destinations and industry services. They are made up of demographic, economic and social influences. These shape consumer preferences, which govern the demand for travel attractions, and the special satisfactions at the destination – the true tourist product. On the supply side, industry responds through product development and price.

Planning for the future on a longer term basis, essential for development investment plans, must take into account major external factors which influence market forces. Principal influences of this kind are outlined in the following pages.

Demographic trends

The major world tourism markets in the older industrialized countries, Europe and North America, are affected by major changes, principally the increase in the proportion of older people in the population and a corresponding reduction in children, younger people, and in the active population making up the labour force. Such changes have both good and bad effects on tourism flows. The situation may well alter in the future, but demographic influences by their nature are longer term in their impacts.

Economic influences

New emerging industrialized countries benefit from new technology which represents a second industrial revolution. They can and do become rich very quickly; for example, Japan has a massive balance of payments and export surplus, whereas the USA and Britain have had large deficits. In recent years a number of European countries have greatly increased wealth and standard of living, e.g. Germany, but also Spain, Portugal and Ireland. Again Britain has lost out, falling behind in relative position. There has been a correlation in the past between GDP and tourism expenditure which in industrialized countries may rise at twice the GDP rate of increase. This may no longer be true in all cases, as structural change weakens the propensity to consume rather than save.

These changes are very substantial and affect consumer preferences and behaviour. In tourism terms, Germany is now close to the US as the chief tourism-originating country. Germans are the principal travellers in the international movement in Europe. But the formerly poorer countries, Spain and Italy for example, are now the source of a rapidly expanding outward movement.

Economic and trade effects can have major and sometimes volatile impacts on tourism flows, as inflation and variations in exchange rates influence travel movement to a major extent. These influences and instabilities are likely to be a feature of future expansion.

Social and life style changes

In the principal tourism markets the population, and especially the 'travelling population', have increased their personal disposable income very considerably in recent years. They are more mobile, take more frequent trips and travel farther away from home. A growing and substantial number are sophisticated travellers. New aspirations or objectives in travel, leading to intense segmentation and specialization, has altered seasonal patterns and type of services demanded, notably an increasing insistence on quality. Substantial benefits for the industry follow major improvements in seasonal flow and such improvements can continue as marketing expertise improves. But destinations in demand have altered. For some, the tide is going out, presenting great difficulties for the local trades and infrastructure.

According to Dr Eduardo Fayos-Sola of the University of Valencia, also now WTO's Chief of Education, we are now moving from the 'Fordian Era' of assembly line tourism into the 'New Age' of tourism. He described the influences which contributed to changes in the past and are contributing to current changes in the tourism sector (Figure 14.1).

The ETC (1995) annually charts these demand trends. The following findings for 1995 indicate the new factors which the tourism operator concerned with the longer term has to take into account.

Megatrends of tourism in Europe, 1995–2000 (ETC, 1995). Taking into account reports presented at the annual meeting of the market research directors of 27 European national tourist organizations and at recent tourism industry

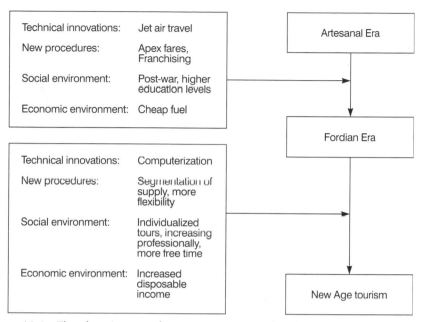

Figure 14.1 The changing era of tourism. (From Dr Eduardo Fayos-Sola, by permission)

meetings, the ETC has updated its statement of Megatrends for Tourism in Europe in 1995–2000 (ETC, 1996). This should be read in the light of the following comments:

(i) Europe continues to face fierce worldwide competition for tourism revenues and a continuing demand for higher quality and value for money.

(ii) Increased taxation and rising costs erode the continent's competitive edge. Price pressures have reduced yields which, if prolonged, could threaten investment and trained staff. Longer term structural changes in European economies, leading to high unemployment, poorer job security and lower economic growth, reduce growth in disposable income for travel.

(iii) Transport price reductions of past years are unlikely to continue. Diminishing government support and changes in distribution, putting pressure on small business, may adversely affect information and other services.

(iv) Tourism growth can no longer be taken for granted.

(v) On the positive side, the potential for travel spending, especially on international trips, is vast. Present levels of traffic are far below market capacity.

The following specific trends identified in past reports can be confirmed:

(i) Global travel spending, particularly transport spending in, into and from Europe, will increase faster than other budget items due to more frequent, albeit shorter, holidays. However, although daily expenditure will generally be maintained owing to higher quality requirements, expenditure per trip may decrease due to shorter duration of holidays.

(ii)   Long-haul holidays to and from Europe will increase even faster than intra-European vacation holidays, to and from practically all the continents, notably America, Asia and Oceania.

(iii) Within Europe, city travel will develop faster than summer and beach vacation holidays, due to the increase of 'short breaks' (with cultural or pseudo-cultural motivations) and of all forms of travel (for meetings, incentives, conferences and exhibitions), in spite of a temporary decrease in individual business travel. However, greater insistence on cost-effective business travel may limit spend per trip.

(iv)   Winter sunshine holidays, cultural winter tours and cruises will increase faster than winter sports holidays.

(v)   'Seasonality' in the immediate future should be regarded as a marketing opportunity rather than a problem, but requiring greater public–private sector partnerships to introduce practical initiatives.

(vi)   South–north, east–west and west–east travel will increase relatively faster than traditional north–south holidays, although the corresponding figures are still much lower.

(vii) Traffic across intra-European borders will increase faster than domestic travel in most European countries.

(viii) Air traffic, both short and long haul, will still increase faster than other types of transportation due to various factors, including new direct connections. In Europe, crowded airspace and long waiting hours could be a deterrent until these problems are solved. Rail transport will, however, also show strong growth, in particular owing to new, convenient rail links for short distances.

(ix)   Given the current trend towards individualization, packages and special 'offers' for inclusive independent arrangements will become increasingly popular, partly at the expense of group travel.

(x)   Late reservations and travel flexibility will increase faster as CRS and information dissemination systems become more comprehensive, although at present these benefit the business traveller more than the ordinary tourist.

(xi)   Travel by two age groups will increase faster than others. Senior citizens (due *inter alia* to growing numbers and increased means of pensioners), and possibly to a lesser extent young people, a segment which had been declining in recent years, provided that new travel opportunities are offered and promoted to capitalize on improved education – in spite of negative demographic evolution in the short term and restricted financial resources.

(xii) As a consequence, both the demand for cultural visits and cultural holidays and for active summer/winter holidays will grow faster than for other forms of vacation.

(xiii) Groups, including families, will tend to be smaller and more flexible.

(xiv) Price/quality ratios will play an increasing role in the choice of destinations and accommodation. The quality of the environment will become a determining element in attracting visitors, especially in coastal and rural areas; these latter in particular are gaining appeal.

(xv) Market segmentation will become more intense, so that products will have to be tailored to the special needs of each segment, e.g. senior citizen travel. Marketing expertise, including destination marketing, will play a more decisive part in influencing travel flows and destinations. Special-interest travel (for hobbies, sport, cultural interests, etc.), although at present a minority market is expected to grow rapidly.

Table 14.1 International tourism: world and regional prospects, 1990–2010

	Tourist arrivals (millions)			Average annual growth rate (%) 1990–2010
	1990	2000	2010	
Europe	283	372	476	2.6
Americas	94	147	207	4.0
East Asia and the Pacific	53	101	190	6.6
Africa	15	24	36	4.5
Middle East	8	11	18	4.1
South Asia	3	6	10	6.2
World total	456	661	937	3.7

Source: *World Tourism Organization.*

The WTO has taken the lead in studying and debating world trends, based on projections of its careful recording over the years of international tourism flows. This work is the basis of their forecasts for world movement. Table 14.1 presents conclusions for the principal world tourism regions. It indicates, on the basis of projecting past results, some major changes affecting mass movement and major destinations substantially. The WTO would be the first to acknowledge that situations can alter quite dramatically with fast expanding modern technology. Accordingly they give details of major influences likely to govern future traffic flows, in the period up to 2010, when world movement has the potential to double or grow even faster. This implies massive influence on world trade and social impacts, since tourism is already the world's largest trade.

The WTO set out the major factors, likely to determine long-term prospects for world travel, under four basic aspects: social, technological, economic and political as shown below.

Social

1 Demographic changes
   (a) ageing of population of industrialized nations
   (b) more working women
   (c) later marriage and families
   (d) singles and childless couples.

2 Increased paid leave and more flexible working time.
3 Earlier retirement.
4 Increased awareness of travel possibilities.

Technology and the supply side

Generally the outlook is good.

The world's productive capacity has never been greater. Industry responds by increasing scale and a conformity in operation and mass-produced products. This helps to build world markets in tourism services and other trades. Change and related investment with massive impact can come quickly. Resorts can develop on an ever increasing scale in a short time – just a few years – where previously generations of work would be needed. Markets respond as quickly, driven by improved communications in marketing reservation and purchasing systems. Transport and production changes, especially air transport, have had a major effect in the past three decades, mainly in the major growth of long-distance travel. To some extent these revolutions in technical efficiencies and related price have been completed, but organization and marketing change can still provide new and better services, new satisfactions and through further efficiency in organization even more price advantages.

IATA continues to predict long-term growth in air travel much in excess of WTO tourism projections. With average annual increase in international scheduled passenger traffic exceeding 6 per cent to the year 2010 this will mean that passengers will double to 800 million by 2010. Such forecasts assume continuing growth in GDP (Table 14.2).

Industry changes, probably greater in the future than ever before, are more likely in organization, management and communication than in plant and machinery. As economic activity grows even larger, economies of scale are sought through globalization and concentration of trade in building up multinational companies. Privatization, leading to increased competition, and new management practices improving efficiencies offer hope for continuing price advantages.

Table 14.2 Estimated GDP to 2010 by region*

	Western Europe		Total Asia/Pacific		North America	
	(US$, billions)	Average annual rate (%)	(US$, billions)	Average annual rate (%)	(US$, billions)	Average annual rate (%)
1980	3542		1667		2949	
1985	3816	1.5	2161	5.3	3376	2.7
1993	4600	2.4	3304	5.4	4055	2.3
2000	5597	2.8	4482	4.5	4903	2.8
2010	7278	2.7	6868	4.4	6107	2.2

* GDP figures are in 1980 constant terms.

Source: *International Monetary Fund* (IMF), miscellaneous banks, IATA analysis, ATAG (1996) *European Traffic Forecasts, 1980–2010.*

Marketing practices are becoming more sophisticated, using new techniques and leading to new product development better related to market trends, and more innovative pricing and improvements in distribution through the use of new technology.

This is potentially the most powerful of the agents for change in industry, affecting communication and information radically. Influence on the distribution and sales process is already evident. Computer reservation systems, data processing, electronic networks such as the Internet and E-mail and the greater use of video material can alter the shape of the retail and wholesale trade in travel. Already credit cards are increasingly used for direct and distance selling including sales in the home. Making the product easy to buy is a key marketing quality. The trend to greater independent travel by millions of sophisticated travellers and tourists capable of organizing their own journey by direct sales has already been noted.

However, unlike the move towards vertical integration in the 1970s, large companies have become more focused, specializing in one trade such as hotel chains, leisure businesses, catering or transport. For example, airlines have, in many cases, withdrawn from hotel ownership. But tour operators as an exception have expanded into retail and airline (charter) operation. The interdependence of many travel services may well encourage more agreements for cooperative working as large units expand.

Demand and supply determinants, the more powerful agents of change, seem on balance to be favourable for continuing long-term tourism expansion, with the caveat that much will depend on the individual destination country or resort, and the individual market and enterprise.

Political philosophies and the role of government

Politically stable marketplaces and destinations are essential for continuing tourism growth. Government is a major partner in tourism, as it has the principal responsibility for the destination. It must act as host, whether at local or national level. The government role is primarily to create favourable conditions for trade and above all to guarantee security and freedom to travel and trade. The state is also in many ways a principal beneficiary in tourism revenues and through other contributions to the economy.

Political philosophies, which influence social behaviour, and especially the role of governments may not prove to be so positive as the other agents in their impact. New technology speeds up structural change. But this, together with the move towards privatization in market-oriented economies, leads to government withdrawal from intervention in trade, including tourism support and promotion.

The major role of the state in tourism as regulator, financier, promoter and operator can be overlooked. Tourism is very much a public and private sector partnership. Tourism development, if left to the mercies of market forces, may take a very different shape. Government withdrawal can have negative as well as positive results. The gap between richer and poorer regions may widen considerably. Unemployment has risen to new heights in the older industrialized countries. This not only presents political and social costs and problems, but can affect consumer preferences, encouraging saving rather than spending discretionary income. Recession years have shown the substantial negative impacts of reduced travel spending. Unemployment places a growing and potentially unsupportable burden on state finance due to the generous social security funding agreed in happier times gone by. As inflationary pressures must be avoided in a liberalized world trade situation, governments may be forced to impose conditions at times, in the form of high taxes and interest rates, removal of subsidies and devaluation, to ensure economic stability. Such measures in the short term reduce national prosperity. Travel spending can be directly affected, as past experience indicates a link between a rise in GDP and a corresponding expansion of travel.

As already indicated, this may no longer be true in all circumstances. Structural change, for example, needs a much longer time scale for recovery than is the case in the traditional cyclical recession.

Governments are expected to help create favourable conditions for trade and a degree of stability through their economic policies. However, increasing public concern about environmental, consumer and social issues tends to lead to more regulation and constraint for tourism. Furthermore, the state is losing some control in setting key economic conditions in a liberalized world, where powerful international trading forces can exert a major influence on an individual country's commerce, currency and financial standing. In Europe, much power has been transferred from national authorities to the EU. Recognizing future dangers, the union is attempting to introduce a single European currency, 'the Euro', which it believes will assist the members' international trade. But it is by no means certain that the basic economic requirements for the introduction of the new currency can be met by the end of the century. Other major world currencies, such as the US dollar and the yen, represent powerful trading forces stronger than many of the European countries' central banks, so that a degree of exchange rate instability and costs is likely to remain.

The effects of some reduction, willingly or unwillingly agreed in government control of trading conditions, may well increase the difference between individual countries in the creation of wealth, standards of living, employment and exchange rates rather than lead to a general setback in tourism growth. However, it reinforces the view that continuing expansion in tourism movement and spending in some major markets can no longer be taken for granted. New countries with emerging economies will play a more important role in world travel and some of the older destinations and markets will decline.

Individual governments' ability to create conditions for prosperity and successful trading is no longer guaranteed, and may not be possible. Their power to ensure peace and security at all times, at home as well as abroad, now appears to be limited.

The OECD has pointed out that the record of governmental understanding and support for tourism in recent years is not good. Tourism, as the world's largest business, has poor priority in government policies and programmes in developed countries. Europe is particularly ill-served. There is no tourism policy in the EU. Tourism is not recognized as a Union competence. As a result there is discrimination in taxation, constraints in international travel and no programme of consistent support and encouragement.

Governments have great powers to help or hinder in fiscal measures, in financial support and in intervention through regulation or control. In many of these areas the European experience in recent years has not been helpful for the trade and the traveller. Taxes have increased. Environmental action, for example, has sometimes taken the form of one-sided state action and constraint, rather than cooperation and incentive, the most likely way to secure the essential partnerships with supporting industry responsible for tourism services and resources.

Consumer protection, another popular political platform, can result in impractical measures leading to a reduction in consumer benefits. The ability of the trades to contribute in solving one of the current principal political and social requirements of new job creation can be undermined by unsuitable regulations, for example, in relation to part-time work and unsocial hours.

Economic aspects

The World Travel and Tourism Council (WTTC), representing a number of the larger companies in international tourism (especially airlines, international hotel groups and travel agents and tour operators), has carried out in-depth economic studies on a world basis. Its research claims to demonstrate the lack of government appreciation of the size and importance of the tourist industry and even more significant its enormous potential for growth. The forecasts for growth far exceed those for any other major trade.

However, the WTTC has warned of the challenges as well as the opportunities and the need for government appreciation and action if these forecasts are to be achieved. Like good signposts, they can only point the way ahead. They do not take one step towards reaching the goal.

Generally most forecasts predict long-term growth in GDP and thus discretionary incomes (see Table 14.2). Leisure time, education and other demand determinants are already favourable in the world's developed countries. New emerging markets in Asia and the Far East are growing fast. However, there are uncertainties about future growth. Social and environmental fears could impede expansion in certain travel flows. There are new influences causing instability and a much more volatile market for many now essential travel services and tourist trips.

Creating wealth

Travel and tourism in the EU is estimated to produce more than ECU 966 bn (US $1.2 trillion) of gross output in 1996 (WTTC, 1996). This includes:

1 ECU 532 bn (US $639 bn) of personal travel and tourism consumption (13.4 per cent of total) within the EC by residents.
2 ECU 197 bn (US $236 bn) of capital investment.
3 ECU 100 bn (US $120 bn) of government expenditures to provide services to the EU travel and tourism industry.
4 ECU 9 bn (US $11 bn) of foreign trade surplus earned from international visitor spending.

This output makes the EU the largest regional producer of travel and tourism in the world, followed by the combined US/Canadian (i.e. Northern American) market. EU travel and tourism is expected to grow at a real compound rate of 2.7 per cent per year until 2006, to ECU 1.7 trillion (US$2.0 trillion) in gross output.

Adding value

In 1996, EU travel and tourism is estimated to produce 12.6 per cent of GDP. This compares with a world GDP level of 10.7 per cent.

The WTTC claims that GDP is a much better indicator of travel and tourism's net worth to the EU economy than usual measures like visitor counts, bed nights or even visitor receipts, since GDP is an economic fact which can be compared to the other sectors of the EU economy. Input/output measures certainly enable the tourism industry's contribution to the economy to be properly measured by government.

Creating value

Travel and tourism will generate an estimated 19.4 million jobs in 1996 in the EU, across a broad spectrum of economic activities. The industry accounts for 13.1 per cent of the workforce, providing one in every eight EU jobs.

Globally, travel and tourism is expected to yield 212 million jobs in 1995 – 10.7 per cent of world employment, or one in every nine jobs.

EU travel and tourism is expected to create 2.5 million new jobs over the next 10 years. This includes jobs in hotels, restaurants, airlines and car hire companies, as well as indirect jobs in hotel construction, aircraft manufacturing, auto servicing and government travel and tourism agencies.

Jobs generated by travel and tourism pay wages 2.6 per cent higher than the average EU industry. In 1996, per capita wages and salaries for EU travel and tourism are expected to total ECU 23 568 (US$28 312).

WTTC comments that as the industry which invented computerized global distribution systems and which manufactures and operates the most sophisticated transportation equipment ever built, travel and tourism is a high-tech employer.

In addition, travel and tourism also produces a large number of the low-tech, entry-level service jobs which are so important in addressing structural unemployment, particularly in city centres and rural areas where these problems are often most severe.

These overviews by the WTO and the WTTC are useful and practical. However, in a competitive and fast-changing world they need to be complemented by projections from each trade sector, and the public sector operating at local, national and international levels. Both the trades and the local authorities deal with the grass roots problems of operating and developing resources and services in a period of expected continuing high-level growth. These local and sector trends studies are needed as a basis for strategic plans. Chapter 9 illustrates the practical nature of such work, which is an essential basis for the marketing plan.

The International Hotel Association (1996) published a White Paper on the Global Hospitality Industry, 'Into the New Millenium', based on intensive research by Professor Michael Olsen of the Virginia Technical Institute and State University.

The research identified five events shaping the future of the lodging industry:

1 Capacity control
2 Safety and security
3 Assets and capital
4 Technology
5 New management.

These factors are likely to affect the whole of the tourism activity, as lodging is such a fundamental part of the whole.

'Capacity control' relates to the development of global reservation systems, so that the individual business can lose control of the sale of its own inventory – rooms, seats in restaurants or on transport, tickets to attractions, etc. New partnerships and alliances are beginning to develop on a worldwide basis.

The study suggests a likely shortage of both private and government capital, with corresponding competitive pressures on performance and yield.

New management will be tested, as technology will require new skills. The most important challenge will be the ability to handle 'the speed of change'.

Summary

The history of tourism is one of lumpy expansion, periods of massive growth interrupted by periods of recessions and stagnation. Equally dangerous at least in the shorter term is the common situation of lack of coordination and harmony in development programmes, especially the gap between transport improvement and accommodation levels. In the period of earlier revolutionary growth in air transport, with the introduction of the wide-bodied jets, the hotel stock in many European countries had been largely provided for a period of passenger ships and railways.

The problem was made easier to solve by great technical advances in building, development and operating practices. In developing countries it can be the case that accommodation expansion increases faster than transport. The rapid growth of tourism in China was greatly hampered by the lack of good transport within China itself. The same was true for a time in India, where the domestic airlines were greatly restricted in capacity.

Each separate trading sector must take into account the international situation, the national position and the situation of the sectors themselves, which together provide the necessary total supply of services for the visitor. They are in fact partners, independent of each other but at the same time interdependent. Even in a fully competitive market-oriented economy there is an essential place in tourism for a collective as well as a competitive role by both public and private operating sectors. But the machinery for coordination is poor.

This is necessary at the horizontal level, for example cooperation between government departments responsible for important aspects of tourism activity in the future. Similarly, tourism authorities when making their projections for massive future growth must take into account considerations of infrastructure, especially transport infrastructure.

Currently in Europe, transport infrastructure in roads and aviation is a major issue, with inadequate preparation for traffic to double in the next decade.

Most forecasts assume that these essential tasks of the public sector will be carried out effectively and that conditions for successful operation by industry will as far as possible be created by the state. The immense world potential for continuing substantial growth in tourism, especially international tourism, seems to be well established. The main determinants of demand are largely favourable. On the supply side, the trading sectors through increasing technology and operating efficiencies are able to reduce prices in real terms, and make it 'easier to buy', to meet market requirements and contribute to traffic growth.

But as always there are problem areas and challenges which threaten growth. Forecasts are at best measures of potential demand. Economic, technological and social pressures are not only expanding at a rate never known in the world before, but this expansion has given rise to a volatility in demand. Traditional behaviour patterns can no longer be relied upon. The as yet unknown effects of economic structural change on a grand scale could alter the outcome very considerably. Consumer preferences, the attitude to spending as opposed to saving, or to living on credit, can alter rapidly with major impact on an open market-oriented economy.

Government have shown in recent years a tendency to withdraw from tourism intervention, leaving too much development to market forces. Future growth is indeed a challenging prospect. This will require a high degree of planning and management skills in the public as well as the private sector, and major development of marketing distribution and reception services.

Coordination of the wide range of interests in government as well as in the operating sectors, especially in strategies, will be essential if the outcome for profitable sustainable tourism with its immense advantages is to be favourable. The crucial factor will be the recognition by governments in the developed world that their largest trade and employer deserves a priority in policies commensurate with the great potential benefits offered. The operators – the industry – also have a key task to create an effective voice for tourism and systems for collective as well as competitive action in preparing for the future.

References

ETAG (1990) *A Tourism Policy for Europe in the 1990s*, European Tourism Action Group, Brussels

ETC (1995) *Megatrends*, European Travel Commission, Paris

International Hotel Association (1996) *'Into the New Millennium'*, a White Paper on the Global Hospital Industry, IHA, Paris

World Tourism Organization (1992) *Tourism Trends Worldwide, 1950–1991*, WTO, Madrid

WTTC (1995a) *Travel and Tourism, Progress and Priorities*, World Travel and Tourism Council, Brussels

WTTC (1995b) *European Union, Travel and Tourism*, World Travel and Tourism Council, Brussels

Further reading

Air Transport Action Group (1996) *European Traffic Forecasts 1980–2010*, ATAG, Geneva

Jefferson, A. and Lickorish, L. J. (1991) *Marketing Tourism*, Longman, Harlow, Essex, UK

Middleton, V. C. T. (1991) *Marketing in Travel and Tourism*, Butterworth-Heinemann, Oxford

World Tourism Organization (1990) *Tourism to the Year 2000, Qualitative Aspects Affecting Global Growth*, WTO, Madrid

World Tourism Organization (1993) *Tourism Trends Worldwide 1980–92*, WTO, Madrid

World Tourism Organization (1994) *Global Tourism Forecasts to the Year 2000 and Beyond*, WTO, Madrid

World Tourism Organization (1994) *Tourism to the Year 2000 and Beyond*, WTO, Madrid

Index